MANI
Travels in the Southern Peloponnese

The Mani is the remotest, the wildest and the most isolated region of Greece. Cut off from the rest of the country by the towering range of the Taygettus and hemmed in by the Aegean and Ionian seas, this rocky central prong of the Peloponnese is the southernmost point of Mediterranean Europe. Between Cape Matapan, the ancient Taenarus, and the coasts of Africa, only a scattering of islands intervenes. Close to this ultimate point lies the cave which the classics say leads to Hades.

Local tradition has it that these mountains were the refuge of the Maniots' ancestors, the Spartans, after their fall. Certainly it is a precipitous, desolate and intractable region, and in being cut off from centuries of contemporary life elsewhere the Mani is rich in survivals and exceptions.

'This traveller understands Greece and the Greeks, their language, dialects, their humour, and self-laughter, their generosity and their vitality' *Daily Express*

'Quite outside the range of normal accounts of travel' *Daily Telegraph*

WINNER OF THE DUFF COOPER MEMORIAL PRIZE

Patrick Leigh Fermor, 1915–2011, was born of English and Irish descent. After his stormy schooldays, followed by the walk across Europe to Constantinople that features in *A Time of Gifts* (1977) and *Between the Woods and the Water* (1986), he lived and travelled in the Balkans and the Greek Archipelago. His books *Mani* (1958) and *Roumeli* (1966) attest to his deep interest in languages and remote places.

In the Second World War he joined the Irish Guards, became a liaison officer in Albania, and fought in Greece and Crete. He was awarded the DSO and OBE.

He lived partly in Greece in the house he designed with his wife Joan in an olive grove in the Mani, and partly in Worcestershire. He was knighted in 2004 for his services to literature and to British–Greek relations.

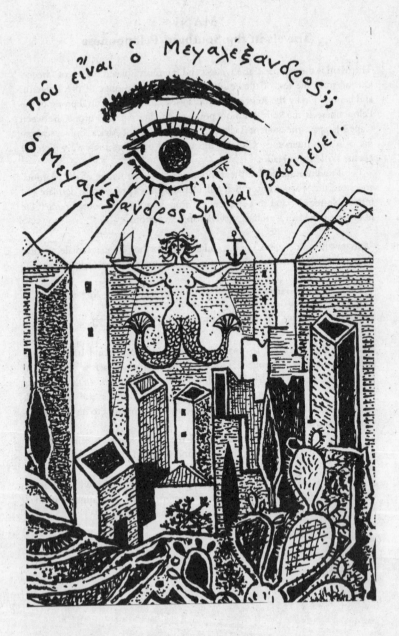

MANI

Travels in the Southern Peloponnese

PATRICK LEIGH FERMOR

JOHN MURRAY

Also by Patrick Leigh Fermor

The Traveller's Tree (1950)
The Violins of St-Jacques (1953)
A Time to Keep Silence (1957)
Roumeli (1966)
A Time of Gifts (1977)
Between the Woods and the Water (1986)
Three Letters from the Andes (1991)
Word of Mercury (2003) *edited by Artemis Cooper*
In Tearing Haste: Letters between Deborah Devonshire and Patrick Leigh Fermor (2008)
The Broken Road (2013)

Translated and edited
The Cretan Runner *by George Psychoundakis*

First published in Great Britain in 1958 by John Murray (Publishers)
An Hachette UK Company

This paperback edition 2004

27

Frontispiece and title page designed by John Craxton
Map drawn by John Woodcock

A CIP catalogue record for this title is available from the British Library

ISBN 978-0-7195-6691-2
Ebook ISBN 978-1-84854-543-4

Printed and bound in Great Britain by Clays Ltd, Elcograf S.p.A.

John Murray policy is to use papers that are natural, renewable and recyclable
products and made from wood grown in sustainable forests. The logging and
manufacturing processes are expected to conform to the environmental
regulations of the country of origin.

John Murray (Publishers)
338 Euston Road
London NW1 3BH

www.johnmurray.co.uk

WITH LOVE TO JOAN

Contents

CONTENTS

Preface

I HAD meant *Mani*, before I began writing it, to be a single chapter among many, each of them describing the stages and halts, the encounters, the background and the conclusions of a leisurely journey—a kind of recapitulation of many former journeys—through continental Greece and the islands. I accordingly made this journey, setting out from Constantinople, which seemed to be the logical point of departure historically, if not politically, for a study of the modern Greek world and then moved westwards through Thrace and Macedonia, south through the Pindus mountains, branching west into Epirus and east into Thessaly; south to all the rocky provinces that lie along the northern shore of the Gulf of Corinth, then eastwards through Bœotia and Attica to Athens. Next came the Peloponnese, the multiplicity of solitary islands and the archipelagos which are scattered over the Greek seas, the eastern outpost of Cyprus and the southernmost giant of Crete. I undertook this journey in order to pull together the unco-ordinated strands of many previous travels and sojourns in all parts of Greece, for I had begun wandering about this country and living in various parts of it a few years before the war. The war did not interrupt these travels though for the time being it altered their scope and their purpose; and since then they have continued intermittently until this very minute of an early morning on a white terrace on the island of Hydra.

This long and fascinating journey, like those which preceded and followed it, was a matter of countless bus-rides and long stretches on horseback and by mule and on foot and on inter-island steamers and caiques and very rarely, for a sybaritic couple of weeks or so, on a yacht. When I became static at the end of it the number of dog-eared and closely written notebooks I had filled up on the way was a forbidding sight. To reduce all this material to a single volume was plainly out of the question. The chief problem, if the results were to be kept within manageable bounds, became one of exclusion.

All of Greece is absorbing and rewarding. There is hardly a rock or a stream without a battle or a myth, a miracle or a peasant anecdote or a superstition; and talk and incident, nearly all of it odd or memorable, thicken round the traveller's path at every step. It seemed better, therefore, in writing, to abandon the logical sequence of the journey; to avoid a thin spreading of the gathered material over the whole rugged surface of Greece; to attack the country, rather, at certain chosen points and penetrate, as far as my abilities went, in depth. Thus I could allow myself the luxury of long digressions, and, by attempting to involve the reader in them, aspire to sharing with him a far wider area of Greek lands, both in space and time, than the brisker chronicle of a precise itinerary would have allowed. It absolved me from perfunctorily treading many well-beaten tracks which only a guilty and dutiful anxiety to be complete would have made me retrace in print; there was now no need to furnish this free elbow-room with anything which had not filled me with interest, curiosity, pleasure or excitement. To transmit these things to the reader is one of the two aims of this book.

The second aim, both of this and other books to follow, is to situate and describe present-day Greeks of the mountains and the islands in relationship to their habitat and their history; to seek them out in those regions where bad communications and remoteness have left this ancient relationship, comparatively speaking, undisturbed. In the towns and the more accessible plains many sides of life which had remained intact for centuries are being destroyed apace—indeed, a great deal has vanished since my own first visits to Greece. Ancient and celebrated sites are carefully preserved, but, between the butt of a Coca-cola bottle and the

Iron Curtain, much that is precious and venerable, many living mementoes of Greece's past are being hammered to powder. It seems worth while to observe and record some of these less famous aspects before the process is complete.

These private invasions of Greece, then, are directed at the least frequented regions, often the hardest of access and the least inviting to most travellers, for it is here that what I am in search of is to be found. This is in a way the opposite of a guide book, for many of the best-known parts of ancient Greece, many of the world's marvels, will be, perforce and most unwillingly—unless their link with some aspect of modern Greek life is especially compelling—left out. There are two thoughts which make this exclusion seem less unjust. Firstly, the famous shrines and temples of antiquity usually occupy so much space in books on Greece that all subsequent history is ignored; and, secondly, hundreds of deft pens are forever at work on them, while in this century, scarcely a word has been written on the remote and barren but astonishing region of the Mani.* Even with this thinning of the material it was impossible to prevent the theme from ballooning from a chapter into a fair-sized book; and there are many omissions. The most noticeable of these is the belief in vampires, their various nature and their origins, to which many pages should have been devoted. I left them out because so much space is already used up on Maniot superstitions. But fortunately, or unfortunately, vampires exist in other regions, though they are less prevalent than in the Mani; so I will be able to drag them in elsewhere as a red herring.

It only remains to thank the enormous number of Greek friends and acquaintances whose hospitality and kindness over many years has been of such help to me. I would like especially to thank Amy and Walter Smart for their kind hospitality in Normandy, and Niko and Tiggie Hadjikyriakou-Ghika for lending me the beautiful house in Hydra where most of this book was written.

HYDRA, 1958   P. M. L. F.

* A notable exception to this is the admirable chapter (*Maina*) in Mr. Robert Liddell's excellent book *The Morea* (Cape) which has recently appeared.

Kalamata

Anavryti

Kardamyli and Kampos

Sparta

Leuktra · Milia

BARDOUNIA

C.Trakhila

TAYGETUS

Githion

Arfingia

Fort
Passava

Ayeranos

Liméni · Vitylo

Areopolis
(Tzimóva)

P.Skutari

GULF

OF

Pyrgos

MESSENIA

Charouda

Phlomochori

Kotrónas

Kolokythia
Gulf

MTS.

10 Miles

P.Mezapo

Tigani rock

Mina

Kipula Pt.

Nomia

MT. KAKOVOUNI

Kechriánika

Kitta

Kyprianó

Salonica

KAKOVOUNIA

C.Grosso

Yerolimena

Layia

50 Miles

Alika

Kyparissós

Yanina

Volo

Marmari   Porto
Bay   Cayo

Cape Matapan (Taenarus)

AEGEAN

SEA

CRETAN

Patras

Athens

PELOPONNESE

SEA

Nauplia

Tripoli

IONIAN SEA

Mistra · Sparta

Kalamata

Monemvasia

C.Matapan

GULF OF LACONIA

CHAPTER I

South from Sparta

'YOU had better look out if you are going up to Anavryti,' said the young barber ominously as he snapped his scissors. He plunged them into another handful of dust-clogged hair. There was a crunch of amputation and another tuft joined the ring of colourless débris on the floor. The reflected head, emerging from a shroud in the looking-glass opposite, seemed to be shrinking visibly. It already felt pounds lighter. 'They are a queer lot.'

'Why must I look out?' The nature of the threat sounded ambiguous. The reflected Spartan faces along the back of the shop were bisected with happy grins of anticipation.

'Why?' The policeman leant forward. 'They'll have the coat off your back!'

An old Arcadian in a kilt went even further. 'They'll skin you alive, my child,' he said. A child, beaming at the barber's elbow said, 'They'll eat you!'

Their tone made it impossible to treat their warnings with too much concern. I asked why they were so much to be feared.

'Because they are Jews,' the policeman said.

'So they say,' one of the Spartans added.

'Of course they're Jews,' the Arcadian cried, turning on him. 'All the villagers in Anavryti and Trypi are Jews. Always have been.' By now the reflected men were rolling about with unrestrained laughter at the idea of these two semitic villages on top of the Taygetus mountains.

It was an outstanding bit of information. I had never heard of Jews in the Peloponnese. The only Jews in Greece, as far as I knew, were the Sephardim in the north—Salonika and a few mainland towns such as Yanina, Naoussa, Preveza and Arta and in a few of the islands—talking fifteenth-century Spanish and Ladino. Their story is well known. Expelled from Spain in 1492 by Ferdinand and Isabella, the Sultan had offered them hospitality in the areas of Constantinople and Salonika, just as the Medici had allowed them to take root and multiply in Grosseto and Leghorn. There is no anti-semitic feeling among the Greeks: Greek business men like to think they can outwit any Jew, or any Armenian for that matter; and, in the Karaghiozi shadow-play the Jewish puppets are amiably absurd figures in caftans and spiked beards called Yacob and Moïse, humorously whining broken Greek to each other in nasal squeaks. Their numbers have been cruelly reduced by the German occupation.

I asked if the villagers of Anavryti spoke Spanish. A priest's reflection leant forward clicking his tongue in the negative: he was the hairiest man I've ever seen. (What's he doing in here, I wondered. Orthodox clergy are forbidden to shave or cut their hair.) Two dark eyes seemed to be peering into the looking-glass through a hole in a black hayrick.

'No,' he said, 'they speak Greek like the rest of us. When Holy St. Nikon the Penitent, the apostle of the Laconians, converted our ancestors to Christianity, these people were living in the plain. They took refuge up in the goat-rocks, and have lived there ever since. They go to church, they take the sacraments. They are good people but they are Jews all right.'

'Of course they are,' the old Arcadian repeated. Shaven and shorn now, and brushed clear of the wreckage, I prepared to go. The old man leant from the window into roasting Sparta and, waving his crook, shouted through grinning gums equipped with a solitary grey fang, a repetition of his warning that they would skin us alive.

* * * *

The man who led the way to the mosaics—the only antiquity surviving inside the modern town of Sparta and a Graeco-

Roman one at that—had the same tale to tell. They were a strange lot; and Jews. . . . We followed him down some steps under an improvised roof. With a tilt of his wrist, he emptied a pitcher on a grey blur of dusty floor. The water fell in a great black star, and, as it expanded to the edges, shapes defined themselves, colours came to life and delightful scenes emerged. Orpheus in a Phrygian-cap fingered his lyre in the heart of a spellbound menagerie of rabbits, lions, leopards, stags, serpents and tortoises. Then, as effeminate and as soft as Antinous, Achilles swam to the surface among the women of Scyros. Next door another splash spread further enchantments: Europa—lovely, Canova-like, with cham-pagne-bottle shoulders and a wasp waist, heavy-thighed, callipy-gous and long-legged—sat side-saddle on the back of a fine bull breasting the foam to Crete.

'How pleased Zeus is to have her on his back,' the man observed. 'See, he's smiling to himself.'

When we left, the water was drying on the first mosaics, and the flowers and figures and beasts had almost faded back into invisibility. In the time of Pausanias the town's most treasured exhibit was a fragment of the shell of one of Leda's two eggs, the portentous double-yolker from which Helen was hatched. (The other one enclosed Clytemnestra, each of them sharing a shell with one of the heavenly twins.)

The fierceness of the blaze that had beaten on Sparta's main street all day had diminished. The Laconian plain grew cooler. A few miles beyond the roofs and a ruffling vista of trees, the Taygetus mountains shot into the sky in a palisade which looked as sheer and unscalable as the Himalayas. Up the flank of this great barrier a road climbed, searing it in mile-long sweeps and acute angles like a collapsible ruler; up, up, until it vanished among peaks whose paler rocks gave a half-convincing illusion of eternal snow. This was the road to Anavryti, the approach march to our private invasion of the Mani. A chance acquaintance from Mistra, who turned out to be the bank manager of sleepy Sparta, was waiting with his jeep as he had promised and, as we went spinning through the cool woods to the point where the great upward zigzag began, I repeated my questions about the inhabitants of Anavryti. 'Yes,' he said, hooting his way through a clinking herd of goats; their twisted horns surrounded us for a moment in a tangled spinney: 'they all say they are Jews but nobody knows why, or where they are from. It's probably rubbish.'

It was very puzzling. Perhaps he was right. And yet the Greek world, with all its absorptions and dispersals and its Odyssean ramifications, is an inexhaustible Pandora's box of eccentricities and exceptions to all conceivable rule. I thought of the abundance of strange communities: the scattered Bektashi and the Rufayan, the Mevlevi dervishes of the Tower of the Winds, the Liaps of Souli, the Pomaks of the Rhodope, the Kizilbashi near Kechro, the Fire-Walkers of Mavrolevki, the Lazi from the Pontic shores, the Linovamvaki—crypto-Christian Moslems of Cyprus—the Dönmehs—crypto-Jewish Moslems of Salonika and Smyrna—the Slavophones of Northern Macedonia, the Koutzo-Vlachs of Samarina and Metzovo, the Chams of Thesprotia, the scattered Souliots of Roumeli and the Heptanese, the Albanians of Argolis and Attica, the Kravarite mendicants of Aetolia, the wandering quacks of Eurytania, the phallus-wielding Bounariots of Tyrnavos, the Karamanlides of Cappadocia, the Tzakones of the Argolic gulf, the Ayassians of Lesbos, the Francolevantine Catholics of the Cyclades, the Turkophone Christians of Karamania, the dyers of Mt. Ossa, the Mangas of Piraeus, the Venetian nobles of the Ionian, the Old Calendrists of Keratea, the Jehovah's Witnesses of Thasos, the Nomad Sarakatzáns of the north, the Turks of Thrace, the Thessalonican Sephardim, the sponge-fishers of Calymnos and the Caribbean reefs, the Maniots of Corsica, Tuscany, Algeria and Florida, the dying Grecophones of Calabria and Otranto, the Greek-speaking Turks near Trebizond on the banks of the Of, the omnipresent Gypsies, the Chimarriots of Acroceraunia, the few Gagauzi of eastern Thrace, the Mardaïtes of the Lebanon, the half-Frankish Gazmouli of the Morea, the small diasporas of Armenians, the Bavarians of Attic Herakleion, the Cypriots of Islington and Soho, the Sahibs and Boxwallahs of Nicosia, the English remittance men of Kyrenia, the Basilian

Monks, both Idiorrhythmic and Cenobitic, the anchorites of Mt. Athos, the Chiots of Bayswater and the Guards' Club, the merchants of Marseilles, the cotton-brokers of Alexandria, the shipowners of Panama, the greengrocers of Brooklyn, the Amariots of Lourenço Marques, the Shqip-speaking Atticans of Sfax, the Cretan fellaheen of Luxor, the Elasites beyond the Iron Curtain, the brokers of Trieste, the Krim-Tartar-speaking Lazi of Marioupol, the Pontics of the Sea of Azov, the Caucasus and the Don, the Turcophone and Armenophone Lazi of southern Russia, the Greeks of the Danube Delta, Odessa and Taganrog, the *rentiers* in eternal *villaggiatura* by the lakes of Switzerland, the potters of Syphnos and Messenia, the exaggerators and the ghosts of Mykonos, the Karagounides of the Thessalian plain, the Nyklians and the Achamnómeri of the Mani, the little bootblacks of Megalopolis, the Franks of the Morea, the Byzantines of Mistra, the Venetians and Genoese and Pisans of the archipelago, the boys kidnapped for janissaries and the girls for harems, the Catalan bands, the Kondaritika-speaking lathmakers of the Zagarochoria, the Loubinistika-speakers of the brothels, the Anglo-Saxons of the Varangian Guard, ye olde Englisshe of the Levant company, the Klephts and the Armatoles, the Kroumides of Colchis, the Koniarides of Loxada, the smugglers of Aï-Vali, the lunatics of Cephalonia, the admirals of Hydra, the Phanariots of the Sublime Porte, the princes and boyars of Moldowallachia, the Ralli Brothers of India, the Whittals of Constantinople, the lepers of Spinalonga, the political prisoners of the Macronisos, the Hello-boys back from the States, the two pig-roasting Japanese ex-convicts of Crete, the solitary negro of Canea and a wandering Arab I saw years ago in Domoko, the Chinese teapedlar of Kolonaki, killed in Piraeus during the war by a bomb—if all these, to name a few, why not the crypto-Jews of the Taygetus?

We were gaining height at a vertiginous pace. As we turned the angle of each long slant, a new expanse of Laconia unfurled below. These foothills were already in shadow but the answering slopes of Mt. Parnon were immaterialized by soft light. Evening

sunbeams streamed obliquely through the mountain rifts, filling
with green and gold and gentle shades the swellings and the subsidences of hollow Lacedaemon. The sauntering loops of the
Eurotas had shrunk now to a thread whose track was marked
by oleanders opening cool green sheaves of spiked leaves and
pretty flowers of white and pink paper over little more than the
memory of water: a memory whose gleam, through the arid
months to come, would keep their bright petals from languishing.
Poplars, willows, aspens and plane trees fluttered along the banks
and olive groves speckled the mild slopes with silver-green, the
stem of each tree casting a longer shadow now. In a score of places
the slanting sunlight caught the discs of threshing floors, each as
smooth and as faultlessly circular as the base for a cylindrical
temple and shining now like coins. We climbed into a zone
where couples of eagles, patrician and aloof, circled and drifted
with a few furlongs of air between them through their last flight
of the day. Angular shadows were advancing over the plain
underneath putting out the flash of the threshing floors one by one.

Nothing in the grace and the enchantment of all this could
remind one of museless and unbookish Sparta. Time has erased
all suggestion of the hateful ways of that Potsdam of the Peloponnese and it is a message from long before, clear with the
indestructible truth of legend, that reaches the observer as he looks
down; an intimation as miraculous and consoling as the hand of
Argive Helen laid across his brow. He remembers that here stood
the palace of Menelaus, the gates where Telemachus and Peisis-
tratus reined in their chariot for news of Odysseus and stayed as
the guests of the red-haired king and his ageless queen and, lulled
by nepenthe, fell asleep. A few miles north-west lies the gorge
that led them back to Pylos. Reaching Kalamata* at sunset,
their wheels slowed down on the sands next day.

The bank manager set his jeep at the steepening slopes. It had
become a race with the sun. The shadow line was mounting the
sides of the Taygetus as inexorably as the tide, submerging us at
moments until a steep twist in the road, up which the jeep jolted

* Ancient Pharia.

headlong, lifted us buoyantly once more into a last precious radiance. But all at once, at a final sharp twist, we went under for good. The road turned inwards along a high green valley of trees and flocks fast filling up with twilight. As it grew darker, this high valley became stiller and more mysterious; the road dwindled to a winding track; at last the lights of Anavryti began to glimmer through the dark. Such is the force of suggestion that the first shepherd seemed to resemble, in the jeep's head-lamps, a light-skinned Yemenite. We expected, at any moment, to be surrounded by Shylocks and Fagins and Svengalis, like the wonderful caftaned populations, the forests of red and black beards, waxen faces, corkscrew side-whiskers and black beaver-hats (occasionally a rabbi's with a fox's brush coiled round the crown) that surround a newcomer in many of the villages of High Moldavia or Bukovina.

It was something of a disappointment to find ourselves, when we reached the centre of Anavryti, at the heart of an ordinary assembly of Laconian peasants. Here and there the will to believe would give an illusion of Hebraic characteristics, but when the stranger came nearer to the lights of the coffee-shop, the illusion would fade. The bank manager drove off into the night and, over wine after a meal of eggs and potatoes, we discussed ways of crossing the Taygetus into the Mani. 'The Mani!' everyone exclaimed. Why did we want to go there? They were a terrible lot: wild, treacherous people, knife-drawers—*machairovgáltes!*—and they shot at people from behind rocks. The dismay was general. Only one man spoke up for them—they were very good people indeed, he said; gentle as lambs to strangers.

Maps were unfolded and we twisted up the wick of the lamp. Most of the company recommended going westwards through the villages of Bergandéïka and Yannitza to the plains of Kala-mata, and then turning south along the west coast of the Mani. In the end, however, persuaded by a grave-looking middle-aged man called Yorgo, we decided on a route running south-west into the heart of the Peninsula. Although only the frailest of dotted lines crossed the multiplied contours of the map and the deepening

7

patches of purple and green along the Taygetus watershed, it looked shorter. As this was impassable to mules, formal bargainings for a beast were dropped and Yorgo agreed to shoulder most of our untidy impedimenta and guide us as far as the town of Kampos. Maps turn everyone into field-marshals, and forefingers were soon jostling each other across the painted paper landscape while a dozen mouths attempted to spell out the place names from the printed Latin characters, turning (naturally enough) the X's into CH, the P's into R's, the B's into V's, the H's into E's and spiritedly improvising sounds for the letters that had no similar symbols in the Greek alphabet; with strange results. Everyone had to put his finger on the little cluster of dots that pinpointed Anavryti. 'Na to!' they would say, clicking their tongues. 'There it is! Just fancy their knowing the whereabouts of our village, far away in London!' Their lamplit eye-sockets expanded with pleasure.

The village subsisted, they said, and prosperously too, on the tanning of hides—which arrived from the plains by mule and cart-load—with bark from the woods of the valley. They cut them up and sewed the pieces into boots and shoes. They also wove blankets and those thick rope mats that are used in the oil presses during the olive harvest. Little caravans of mules laden with their wares were always setting forth and their merchandise was peddled from house to house in the mountain villages and markets of Laconia and Messenia and Arcadia. These industrial and mercantile pursuits are unusual in a small highland community and, as several jugs of wine had been emptied, I at last risked the question which had been at the tip of my tongue all the evening: what was all this about the Jewish origins of their village and of Trypi? There was a cheerful outbreak of laughter.

'It's all nonsense,' one of them said. 'Those sleepy clodhoppers in the plains are jealous because we are cleverer and harder-working and above all,' he leant forward with a meaning smile, 'better bargainers than they are.'

'That's right,' another agreed. 'The Anavrytans are as bright as they make them. We can nail horseshoes on a louse.' He shut one of his eyes and a neat gesture with horny hands demonstrated this delicate smithery, the fingers of his left hand seeming to grasp a louse's hind leg, while those of his right plied an elfin hammer.

'We can fly,' another said.

'We could sell you the air,' a fourth added.

'We sleep with one eye open,' explained yet a fifth.

'The plains-people are jealous because our wits are quicker,' the first went on. 'They come up here to get wool and we send them off shorn!' Good humour was universal and more wine appeared.

'We're Christians just the same as they are and always have been.'

'Yes, but how long has this joke about Jewish descent been going on?'

'Always,' was the proud answer. 'For a century of centuries. . . .'

An elderly villager called Dimitri, who had adopted us for the night, led us home. Balconies almost as wide as the houses themselves, reached from outside by diagonal boxed-in staircases on wooden stilts, jutted above the lanes. On one of these Dimitri's wife spread scarlet blankets and quilts against the mountain air. Dimitri, smoking a last cigarette as he leant on the balcony's edge, said he thought there might be some truth in the story of the Jews and the flight from St. Nikon. 'But who can tell? It's such a long time ago . . . ages and ages . . . over a hundred years, perhaps . . .'

There was a new moon. Who *were* the Anavrytans, then? Probably ordinary Greeks, like the rest of Laconia. After all, the Kravarites had said that the mulberry-trees of Perista were planted there centuries ago by Jews, and the Tzakonians of Ay. Andrea had referred to the inhabitants of nearby Karakovouni as 'Jews'— meaning, perhaps, nothing more than 'strangers' or people ignorant of the Tzakonian dialect—and the Chiots are nicknamed 'Jews' because of their commercial acumen. . . . And yet the pursuits of the Anavrytans . . . it was a conundrum. After the Slav invasion of the Peloponnese, these particular mountains were the haunt of a wild Bulgarian tribe, the Meligs. Could some of these, remaining unassimilated longer than the rest and, still heathen, have been dubbed 'Jews', the name sticking even after their conversion and assimilation? There are no records, and it is impossible to discover. Wine-heavy sleep soon smoothed out these wrinkles of perplexity.

*   *   *   *

It was only very much later that this perplexity came anywhere near solution. For there had, indeed, been Jews in the Peloponnese. Gemistus Plethon (the great humanist of the court of the Palaeologues at Mistra a few years before it was overrun by the Turks, whose body Sigismondo Malatesta recovered and buried at Rimini) maintained that the inhabitants of the Peloponnese were of the purest Hellenic descent. The late Byzantine satirist Mazaris ridicules these assertions, in an atrociously written libel in the style of Lucian called the *Sojourn of Mazaris in Hades*, by dividing up the people of the Morea into Greeks (Lacedaemonians and Peloponnesians), Italians (the remains of the Latin conquerors), Slavs (Sthlavinians), Illyrians (i.e. Albanians), Egyptians (Gypsies) and Jews. As this was written with the declared purpose of attacking Plethon, it is suspect; but history lends some colour to his statement. The two wandering Spanish rabbis of the twelfth century, Benjamin of Tudela and Abraham ibn Daoud, talk of scattered Jewish communities through the length and breadth of Greece and the Empire. The Synaxary (which chronicles the lives of Orthodox saints) mentions that St. Nikon was unwilling to save the Laconian town of Amykli from the ire of the Christians unless the Jews were expelled, 'as the Jews, like the Melig Slavs of the Mani, were a great hindrance to the spread of the truth of the Gospel'. The Greek academician, N. Bees, records that Trypi was known as 'a fore-town of Mistra, Jewish Trypi'. So why not Anavryti as well? How long had all these Jews been established in the Peloponnese?

It was with great surprise that I found, in Flavius Josephus and in the first book of Maccabees, mentions of ancient links between Sparta and the Jews; how Jonathan, the high priest in the reign of Demetrius Nicator (circ. 140 B.C.), sent ambassadors to the Spartans, reminding them of their ancient bonds in the time of

Onias the High Priest and of King Areus II of Sparta (who reigned from 264 to 257 B.C.). More surprising still is a letter from the King: 'Areus king of the Lacedaemonians to Onias the High Priest, greeting. It is found in writing that the Lacedaemonians and Jews are brethren, and that they are of the stock of Abraham: now, therefore, since this is come to our knowledge, ye shall do well to write unto us of your prosperity. We do write back again to you, that your cattle and goods are ours and ours are yours. . . .' *

Unburdened as yet by all these complications, I slept on peacefully.

* Macc. I 12. 21-24.

CHAPTER 2

The Abomination of Desolation

ON the map the southern part of the Peloponnese looks like a misshapen tooth fresh torn from its gum with three peninsulas jutting southward in jagged and carious roots. The central prong is formed by the Taygetus mountains, which, from their northern foothills in the heart of the Morea to their storm-beaten southern point, Cape Matapan, are roughly a hundred miles long. About half their length—seventy-five miles on their western and forty-five on their eastern flank and measuring fifty miles across—projects tapering into the sea. This is the Mani. As the Taygetus range towers to eight thousand feet at the centre, subsiding to north and south in chasm after chasm, these distances as the crow flies can with equanimity be trebled and quadrupled and sometimes, when reckoning overland, multiplied tenfold. Just as the inland Taygetus divides the Messenian from the Laconian plain, its continuation, the sea-washed Mani, divides the Aegean from the Ionian, and its wild cape, the ancient Taenarus and the entrance to Hades, is the southernmost point of continental Greece. Nothing but the blank Mediterranean, sinking below to enormous depths, lies between this spike of rock and the African sands and from this point the huge wall of the Taygetus, whose highest peaks bar the northern marches of the Mani, rears a bare and waterless inferno of rock.

But all this, as we toiled up the north-eastern side next morning, was still a matter of conjecture and hearsay. Yorgo, trudging far above, stooped Atlas-like under our gear. The shoulder-strings of the Cretan bag in which I had stuffed the minute overflow burnt into my shoulders. . . . The chestnut trees of Anavryti were far

12

below, and as we climbed the steep mountainside and the sun climbed the sky, vast extents of the Morea spread below us. The going grew quickly steeper and the path corkscrewed at last into a Grimm-like and Gothic forest of conifers where we were forever slipping backwards on loose stones and pine-needles. Emerging, we could look back over range after range of the Peloponnesian mountains—Parnon, Maenalus, even a few far away and dizzy crags of Killini and Erymanthus, and, here and there, between gaps of the Spartan and Arcadian sierras, blue far-away triangles of the Aegean and the gulf of Argos. But ahead we were faced by an unattractively Alpine wall of mineral: pale grey shale and scree made yet more hideous by a scattered plague of stunted Christmas trees. These torturing hours of ascent seemed as though they could never end. A vast slag heap soon shut out the kindly lower world; the sun trampled overhead through sizzling and windless air. Feet became cannon-balls, loads turned to lead, hearts pounded, hands slipped on the handles of sticks and rivers of sweat streamed over burning faces and trickled into our mouths like brine. Why, we kept wondering, though too short of breath for talk, does one ever embark on these furious wrestling matches, these rib-cracking clinches with the sublime? Felons on invisible treadmills, our labour continued through viewless infernos like the waste-shoots of lime-kilns. . . . Finally the toy German trees petered out and the terrible slope flattened into a smooth green lawn scattered with flowers and adorned by a single cistus clump with a flower like a sweet-smelling dog-rose. Yorgo was waiting in a last narrow cleft immediately above. It was the watershed of the Taygetus and so sharply defined that one could put a finger on a thin edge of rock and say, 'Here it is.' A last step, and we were over it into the Mani.

A wilderness of barren grey spikes shot precipitously from their winding ravines to heights that equalled or overtopped our own; tilted at insane angles, they fell so sheer that it was impossible to see what lay, a world below, at the bottom of our immediate canyon. Except where their cutting edges were blurred by landslides, the mountains looked as harsh as steel. It was a dead, planetary place, a habitat for dragons. All was motionless. There was not even a floating eagle, not a sound or a sign that human beings had ever trodden there, and immense palisades of rock seemed to bar all way of escape. The perpendicular and shadowless light reverberated from the stone with a metallic glare and the whole landscape had a slight continual shudder, trembling and wavering in the fierce blaze of noon. The only hint of salvation lay far away to the south-west. There, through a deep notch in the confining mountains, gleamed a pale and hazy vista of the Ionian with a ghost of the Messenian peninsula along its skyline. Everything, except this remote gleam, was the abomination of desolation.

On a narrow ledge that overhung this chaos we found a miraculous spring: a trickle of cold bright water husbanded in a hollow tree-trunk lined with brilliant green moss. A wild fig-tree gesticulated overhead. Here, after long draughts, we lay with our feet propped on boulders. While sweat dried in salty craters and our pulses gradually slowed down we watched the thin blue wreaths of cigarette smoke melt into the sky as speech came slowly back. These empty peaks, according to Homer, were the haunt of Artemis and of three goat-footed nymphs who would engage lonely travellers in a country dance and lead them unsuspectingly to the precipice where they tripped them up and sent them spinning down the gulf. . . . All at once a further wonder came to increase our well-being: a cool breath of wind. This is one of the seldom-failing blessings of midsummer in the Peloponnese. After long broiling mornings when the afternoon, one would think, can only bring fiercer refinements of torture, the static air, heated beyond endurance, rises all at once like a Mongolfier and the sudden threat of that vacuum which nature abhors, drawing cool drafts from the sea along the winding canyons, sets up a delicious atmospheric commotion: a steady cool breeze that revives the traveller at his last gasp.

A faint tinkle of bells from the abyss told that faraway goats were shaking off the mesmeric stupor of midday. Yorgo, meanwhile, was busy slicing onions and garlic and green paprika pods into a concavity of the rock. Snipping the end off a cucumber, he handed it to Joan, who, without a word, stuck it on her forehead. (This curious custom spreads a welcome coolness on the forehead. It is common, in summer, to see people sitting over their food, or even walking in the street, with these mysterious dark green excrescences growing from their heads like the incipient horn of a unicorn's foal.) Reaching into the hollow of the log, he extracted three *paximadia* from the spring and wrapped them in a cloth to draw the water out before they got too soggy. These dark brown pumices of twice-baked bread—the staple fare of Greek shepherds and of the medieval Basilian hermits—can be kept for months. Hard as fossils, they are excellent; especially with garlic, when soaked to the right consistency. (The baked oblongs are fluted with deep clefts for easier breaking, and the detached fragments look like nothing so much as the brown treeless islets scattered round the coasts of Greece; in fact, many a small archipelago—notably the crags jutting from the Libyan sea off the south of Crete—are called *Ta Paximadia*.) Unwrapping the cloth, he put them on a stone, sprinkled the onions and tomatoes and peppers and cucumber with rock-salt and poured oil over them. Then he picked a fig leaf on which he piled a handful of olives in a black pyramid and pulled out a small bottle of wine. We joined him, he crossed himself three times, and we all fell to. When we had finished, emptying the glass in turn and mopping up the last puddles of oil with lumps of *paximadia*, he produced some small green pears which were hard and sweet. While we leant back smoking against boulders, he scrupulously collected what remained of the *paximadia*, kissed it, and knotted it in a cloth. There is a superstitious veto against throwing away all but the smallest crumbs of bread and the kiss is a thanksgiving and a memento of the Last Supper. He was a fair-haired, friendly but rather silent man.

'You shouldn't go to sleep under a fig tree,' he said, observing our falling eyelids.

'Why not?'

'The shadow is heavy.'

I had heard this before, especially in Crete. There is never an explanation of this heaviness, except that it is alleged to bring on vertigo and bad dreams; it is as odd as the Caribbean superstition that sleeping under the bells of a datura tree in flower drives the sleeper mad. I shifted a few inches out of politeness, though I have never felt the ill effects. Yorgo lay with his head on a stone.

When we woke up half an hour later, two small figures were standing at gaze a little distance off and behind them half a dozen goats had materialized, their presence unheralded by the clash of bells. We called to them but they neither answered nor moved, and it was only by dint of long coaxings and assurances that we were neither robbers nor outlaws that they ventured closer. They were two barefoot, raggedly dressed and ikon-faced little girls of ten and twelve, both of them extremely beautiful. They were tanned to a gypsy darkness, their hair was inexpertly bobbed and their brown legs were criss-crossed with the scars of thorns and thistles. They sat side by side on stones with their hands clasped round their knees and drank us in with immense black luminous eyes strangely compounded by innocence and wisdom under brows like arched and sweeping penstrokes, which seemed to fill their entire faces. Delicate, fine-boned and solemn, they could have been nothing but Greek; not so much the Greeks of the pagan world as the spiritual etiolation that gazes from the walls of St. Sophia and Ravenna: the bewildering combination of aloofness and devouring intensity that radiates from the eye-sockets of eastern Madonnas and empresses. They were called Anastasia and Antiope. Too shy to talk, almost their only utterances were an occasional cry—accompanied by a flung stone or a menacing flourish of their crooks—directed at a goat straying too far from the flock. Then they would sink into their silent and wide-eyed scrutiny. We gave them our remaining pears, and they thanked us with a polite gravity, but kept them, they said, to eat later. The pears remained like votive offerings in their cupped brown hands. When we rose and said good-bye, they asked us, suddenly articulate, why we didn't stay on, and the eldest waved her hand round the rocky landscape as if to say that their house was at our disposal. But we hoisted our bundles and set off downhill.

'Go towards the Good,' one of them said, and the other, 'May you have the Good Hour!'

The immobile figures of these two little Byzantines dwindled as we zigzagged downhill. Even at a distance we could sense the wide effulgent gaze which those four eyes aimed from their ledge half-way to the sky. They waved when we were just about to dip out of sight. There are very few people in these surroundings, Yorgo observed. 'They are wild and shy and not accustomed to talk.' He pointed straight up into the air. The canyon was closing round us. 'They see nothing but God.'

*   *   *   *

The mountain-side descending into the chasm was an upturned harrow of spikes, the spaces between the spikes were choked with boulders and loose stones and so steep was the slope that every other step unloosed a private landslide. Labouring downhill in cataracts of falling stones whose clatter sent echoes volleying along the ravine, we got to the bottom at last.

The torrent bed, filled with bleached boulders, wound away nowhere between confining walls of rock. It was utterly desolate. Sometimes the dry bed would widen into a broad pebbly loop, only to close again to narrows which must turn the spate of winter waters into a swollen turmoil of foam and spray. Now there was not even a trickle; only the occasional loyal emblem of an oleander. But one of the turnings brought us on top of a shady and idyllic clump of plane trees growing round the entrance to a cave. It was built up with flat stones into a fold for flocks, and a group of men and women were squatting or lying under the leaves. Donkeys were tethered to the lower boughs, and goats, whose far-off bells we had heard from the mountain top, nibbled invisible vegetation among the rocks. Bronze cauldrons of whey bubbled over fires of thorns, dripping cloths full of wet cheese hung from the branches among bright haversacks and crooks and blankets and a couple of double-barrelled guns and a portable cradle like a Red Indian papoose which swung like a pendulum. Wooden saddles, to three of which we were promptly bidden—

side-saddle, they make comfortable chairs when standing on the ground—were scattered about. The men and women, lean and dark as Algonquins, wore plaited wicker hats with brims almost a yard in diameter: great discs over which the shadows of the plane-tree leaves flickered and revolved and slid when their heads moved. We were given wooden spoons and half-calabashes of warm milk sprinkled with salt and then grilled about politics in England, the chances of war, the Cyprus question, Middle East strategy and the nature of the British Constitution.

One of the shepherds, with a hand laid on our shoulders, said the great bond between Greece and England was that we both had kings and queens. It was the first time we came in contact with the unshakable royalism of the Mani. Minute, long-necked casseroles were pushed into the embers, and, after coffee and farewells as cordial as though we were leaving after a month's stay, we continued down the gorge. Our hands were filled with gifts of almonds and pears, our stuff was piled on a mule and driven off by a boy of sixteen called Chrysanthos. Yorgo's office being accomplished, he shook hands and sped clean up the mountain-side as though he were wearing seven-league boots. Soon he was a speck far above us. He planned, incredible as it seemed, to be back at Anavryti by daybreak. His last words were a whispered admonition about the inhabitants of the Mani. . . .

Further along the gorge, Chrysanthos pointed to some scattered bones. 'There you are,' he said, 'the remains of a rebel.' I know nothing of anatomy, but they looked very much like the fragments of a human pelvis, a tibia and a couple of ribs. Then we noticed an old boot and a bit of rotted webbing. A little further on he picked up an empty cartridge-case and whistled down it.

'These mountains were full of the cuckolds,' he went on, 'a real stronghold. It took a man like Papagos to do them in.' He described, with staccato gestures of aiming and trigger pressing and all the onomatopoeia of a battle—the whistle of bullets, the stutter of machine-guns and the bangs of mortar bombs exploding— how the rebel force had been outflanked and destroyed. . . . 'The mountains stank of dead Elasites for weeks afterwards and a good

18

riddance of bad rubbish. But they fought like dogs. Like dogs!'
He bared his teeth. 'Because, after all, they were Greeks and they
knew how to fight. . . .'

The gorge grew claustrophobically narrow and the whirling
stratification of each side tallied as accurately with its fellow as if
a knife stroke had sliced them apart. They almost joined overhead
—spanned at one point, high above, by an old semicircular bridge
—plunging the narrow rock-strewn bottom into the half darkness
of a cave. Eaves and ledges of damp rock overhung and dripped
with stalactites and a thicker and thicker mantling of creeper and
weed and stunted trees choked the converging walls. It was
gloomy and dank, the rocks shone with sweating seams and the
tracks of snails and the passage was festooned with spiders' webs.
At each step their silken meshes snapped and we brushed the tangle
from our hair and faces.

'Not many people come this way,' Chrysanthos observed,
slashing through films of this grey rigging and wiping the tatters
from his stick. 'It's a bad place.'

He rattled the stick across some boulders and a small party of
bats went hurtling up towards the ribbon of sky overhead.
Once he dislodged a little owl of Pallas Athene which flew noise-
lessly to the branch of a wild fig and watched us out of sight, its
body in profile and its head full-face in the precise posture of
vigilant alertness one knows from Greek coins.

At last the walls began to slant outwards and subside. The sky
expanded. Curling down from the east, an old road, paved with
slabs, carried us up again over a milder hillside while the river bed
and its diminishing canyon trailed away to the west. We followed
Chrysanthos on to a knoll, which he said had been the site of an
old temple of Artemis, and sure enough, guarding the corridor
which led back to the pass, great irregular blocks of Pelasgian
masonry jutted in a bastion, and on the top of the knoll, presumably on the emplacement of the vanished temple itself, stood a
handsome old church embedded in scaffolding. The interior was
a jungle of lashed beams and platforms of planks, and three
masons in those neat paper caps, of the kind worn by the Carpenter

in *Alice in Wonderland* (made, in this case, of folded sheets of the *Akropolis* and the *Ethnikos Kiryx*), were sitting smoking among a débris of fallen plaster. They were repairing it, they said, as it had been struck by lightning the year before. They led us up a ladder to the top of the narthex. Daylight showed through gaps, fragments of the rood-screen were broken off, and great fissures crossed the painted walls. These were populated with lively seventeenth-century frescoes bright with the elaborate gilding of haloes and splendid with splashes of blue and scarlet robes; all were dominated by the church's patron, St. Demetrius, on a prancing steed. A ray of sunlight fell on a menacing figure of Apollyon holding aloft a flaming sword. A mason stroked his gorgoned breastplate, and the two hideous faces embossed on his brazen greaves.

'Look at those two ugly devils!' He pointed to one on the left leg. 'That's Stalin,' he said, then at the right, 'and that's Gromyko.'

The mountains were behind us, and the gentle foothills waved softly seawards dotted with villages and sparkling with threshing floors. Beyond the last hills lay the mild expanse of the Messenian Gulf and the westernmost peninsula of the Peloponnese, where Methoni and Coroni lay. To the north a grey shoulder of the Taygetus concealed the innermost part of the gulf, where sizzled Kalamata. In Galtes, the first village, we stopped for a glass of wine under a trellis with the priest and some peasants in those great Maniot hats, and continued downhill. The road unwound in easy loops. The late afternoon sunset softened everything and, combined with the relief of escape from the confinement of the mountains, it charged the air with a feeling of well-being and holiday. As the hills subsided into a little plain, we fell in with a troop of mules, three of which were mounted by young men. One was a god-brother of Chrysanthos, so in a moment we were hoisting our tired limbs into the saddle.

'From Kalamata?' the god-brother asked.

'No, from Anavryti.'

'Where's that?'

'The other side of the Taygetus.'

He plainly didn't believe it, until Chrysanthos assured him it was true. His sympathy was immediate. 'And the lady—I'm sorry, I don't know your name——?'

'Ioanna.'

'And the Kyria Ioanna too? *Po, po, po!* You must be dead! Those goat-rocks are enough to kill anyone. They are desperate things, they drag the soul out of you.' His face grew serious. 'There's only one remedy when anyone's as tired as that.' He spoke with the earnestness of a diagnostician. 'A medium coffee carefully boiled. Then, after half an hour,' he closed and raised his fist and made a gesture of pouring towards his mouth with an extended thumb, 'wine. Good wine. And a great deal of it.' His knit brow became still graver and to avoid all ambiguity he decided to re-phrase it. 'When you get to Kampos,' he pointed to the little town ahead of us, whose bells had been clanking for the last few minutes, 'you must drink a great deal of wine.'

We were riding through a grove of olives growing out of red earth scattered with stones. The twisted branches were strident with cicadas. The mules trotted along at a spanking pace, and, infected by the excitement of nearing home, they broke into something approaching a gallop. The little cavalcade kicked up a cloud of dust that the last rays of the sun turned into a trans-figuring red-gold cloud. We drew rein at the outskirts of Kampos, as the mules were going on to Varousia to collect sacks for wheat which had been threshed during the day. The sun had gone down but the trees and the first houses of Kampos were still glowing with the sunlight they had been storing up since dawn. It seemed to be shining from inside them with the private, interior radiance of summer in Greece that lasts for about an hour after sundown so that the white walls and the tree trunks and the stones fade into the darkness at last like slowly expiring lamps.

'Don't forget my advice,' the muleteer said and with a rattle of hoofs his brisk score of mules went pricking away through the olive trees in their strange aureole of dust.

*　　*　　*　　*

21

His prescription was excellent. Sitting in the humble *plateia* of Kampos after dinner, fittingly drugged with wine, all the weariness of the long day's trudge had resolved itself into a pleasantly blurring torpor. Over the rooftops and leaves in the glimmer of starlight and of the thin ghost of a new moon, the bulk of the Taygetus mountains looked steeper and more impregnable than ever. It seemed impossible that it was only that morning we had set off from that far away pseudo-Judaea the other side. . . . Self-congratulation, however, deflated slightly at the thought of Yorgo striding across them at that very moment. . . . A tall form, wishing us good evening and then subsiding on a chair, broke the trend of our sleepy talk. It was a lean, quixotic-looking man with hollow cheeks and beetling eyebrows. He put an *ekatostáriko* of wine on the table and filled the glasses. We asked him about the town of Kampos.

'It's a miserable place,' he said, 'a suburb of Kalamata, really, although it's several hours away, and the inhabitants are a useless lot. They're Vlachs.'

'Vlachs? Surely not in the Peloponnese?'

'That's what we call them.'

I said I had never heard of any Vlachs south of the Gulf of Corinth, and never expected to find any in the Mani.*

'This isn't the real Mani,' he said, 'it's what they call the Exo Mani, the Outer Mani. You have to wait till you get to the Deep Mani, the Mesa Mani, south of Areopolis, before finding true Maniots. They are quite a different thing. Honourable, tall, good-looking, hospitable, patriotic, intelligent, modest——'

'So you don't come from Kampos?'

'May God forfend!'

'Where from, then?'

'From the Deep Mani.'

* See page 70.

CHAPTER 3

Kardamyli: Byzantium Restored

KAMPOS by daylight was a hot, characterless little town and we were glad to leave. While we waited for the bus in the market-place, the Deep Maniot with the sorrowful countenance came loping towards us under his giant Mambrino's helmet of straw. He produced a clean blue handkerchief in which some plums and greengages were knotted. Peeling them carefully with a jack-knife, he dropped them into glasses of retsina to cool and then offered them in turn impaled on a fork. There are times in Greece when you feel you could live with as little forethought about food as Elijah; meals appear as though laid at one's elbow by ravens. Our benefactor was in the throes of acute melancholia. He hated living in Kampos among all these half-baked Vlachs. He spoke once more of the Deep Mani as a longed-for and unobtainable Canaan. Why didn't he live there? 'Don't ask,' he said, and made that tired circular gesture with his open hand suggesting a piling up of complications on which it was too tedious and vexatious to embark. 'Troubles . . .' he said. It occurred to me that he was perhaps involved in one of the feuds for which the Mani is notorious and had fled to these alien lowlands for refuge.

'You ought to be there in the autumn,' he said, 'when the quails fly over in millions. We spread nets and set traps for them and roast them on spits. . . . If you gave me your address in London and if God grants me life till the autumn I could get my niece down there to fill up a great can with quails in oil for you to eat as a *mézé* in London. . . . We could seal it up at the top with a soldering iron. . . .'

The bus rattled us along a switchback road above the Messenian

Gulf. Twice everybody had to dismount and negotiate bad bits of road, until, after an hour, we came in sight of Kardamyli, a castellated hamlet on the edge of the sea. Several towers and a cupola and a belfry rose above the roofs and a ledge immediately above them formed a lovely cypress-covered platform. Above this the bare Taygetus piled up.

It was unlike any village I had seen in Greece. These houses, resembling small castles built of golden stone with medieval-looking pepper-pot turrets, were topped by a fine church. The mountains rushed down almost to the water's edge with, here and there among the whitewashed fishermen's houses near the sea, great rustling groves of calamus reed ten feet high and all swaying together in the slightest whisper of wind. There was sand underfoot and nets were looped from tree to tree. Whitewashed ribbed amphorae for oil or wine, almost the size of those dug up in the palace of Minos, stood by many a doorway. Once more I wondered how these immense vessels were made. They are obviously too big for any potter smaller than a titan with arms two yards long. As usual, theories abound. Some say a man gets inside the incipient jar like a robber in the Arabian Nights, and builds up the expanding and tapering walls as they rotate on a great wheel; some, that the halves are constructed separately and then put together; others that they are cast in huge moulds; yet others assert that they are built up from a rope of clay that is paid out in an expanding and then a contracting coil until the final circle of the rim is complete; which is made to account for the ribs and the fluting that gird them from top to bottom. . . . I had heard, all over Greece, that they came from Coroni in the Messenian peninsula, only the other side of the gulf. It was strange that, even here, there should be such a conflict of solutions. There were only four men in the little group I asked among the beached fishing boats. If there had been more, no doubt the total of solutions would have risen accordingly.*

* I have been to Coroni since, and I now own one of these stupendous vessels. 'We build them bit by bit from the bottom,' the potter said, 'just as a swallow builds its nest.'

For the first time,—in conversation, and over the very few shops,—I became aware of one of the typical Maniot name-endings, one which is found nowhere else in Greece: Koukéas, Phaliréas, Tavouларéas, and so on. The last of these was the name of the schoolmaster, a charming and erudite man, who told us of the vanished temple of the nereids built there to commemorate the time the sea-nymphs came ashore to gaze at Pyrrhus, the son of Achilles—or Neoptolemos as he is called in Homer—when he set off for his wedding with Andromache's rival, Hermione. The church, dedicated to the Falling Asleep of the Blessed Virgin, now occupies the site. There was a marble rosette in the centre of the floor under which a dowser, some years previously, had divined the presence of gold in large quantities a few metres down; perhaps gold ornaments in some pre-Christian tomb. Strangely, nobody had got busy with crowbars. . . . In a little room in the schoolhouse was a *rose antique* funerary slab with a beautifully incised epitaph in Hellenistic characters commemorating the great love and respect that all his contemporaries felt for the deceased, 'the Ephebe Sosicles the Lacedaemonian'. The inscription ended with a delicate curved loop of knotted and fluttering ribbon. Above the village, in the burning and cactus-covered hillside, he pointed out two rectangular troughs hacked out of the rock: the graves, after all their vicissitudes, of Castor and Pollux; or so it was thought . . . they looked far too short for the great boxer and his horse-breaking twin whose constellations shine in the sky alternately. Further on a dark cistern was hewn in the mountain-side surmounted by a roughly carved lion's head and, yet further, hard by the golden church lay the castellated remains of a fort with dungeons and barred windows and rough-hewn staircases. The little castle and the church, we were told, were built by one of the descendants of the Palaeologi who had sought refuge here from the Turks after the fall of Mistra in 1461.

A large bell, green with verdigris, embossed with an effigy of a Catholic bishop with mitre and crosier and the legend that it was the 'gift of the heirs of the de Bolis family', hung in the belfry, —a present, perhaps, from the Venetians when the Maniots were their allies against the Turks; or loot from a pirate-raid. The schoolmaster said that Kolokotronis, when he was here with his klephts before the outbreak of the Greek War of Independence (for it was here that he foregathered with Mavromichalis and the Maniot leaders before attacking the Turkish garrison in Kalamata: the first act of the war after the standard of revolt was raised at the Monastery of Kalavryta on the 25th March, 1821), would play games of human chess in this very courtyard. The flagstones were chalked out like a board and his pallikars took up their positions in squares—I hope in the cool of the evening—while Kolokotronis, in his kilt and his fabulous fireman's helmet, would stand on the wall and shout the moves, his opponent doing the same at the other end. The loser was condemned to take the victor for a ride on pick-a-back.

It was a varied morning's exploration.

* * * *

I was alerted and fascinated by the schoolmaster's mention of the Palaeologi, the reigning dynasty during the twilight of the Byzantine Empire. The last emperor—Constantine XI Palaeologus Vatatses—died fighting in the breach on the day the imperial city was captured by Mohammed II. In another book* I have told the story of the tomb of Ferdinando Palaeologus in Barbados, whose granddaughter, Godscall Palaeologue, vanishes from historic record as a little orphan girl in Stepney or Wapping, her father having died at Corunna in 1692. Her imperial descent is based on the supposition that the emperor was survived by a third brother, a shadowy figure called John, as well as by the historically verified Thomas and Demetrius, joint despots of Mistra. There is no point in retracing here the slender putative thread of his line through Italy, Holland, Cornwall, Barbados, Spain and the East End of London. If John existed, which is open to question, this little girl may have been the last imperial princess of the house of Palaeologue. Alas, at the end of the seventeenth century

* *The Traveller's Tree* (John Murray), pp. 145-9.

she disappeared forever into the mists and fogs of the London Docks.

It is the belief of the Maniots, the schoolmaster told me, that the Maniots descend in part from the ancient Spartans and in part from the Byzantines of the Peloponnese, both of them having sought refuge from their respective conquerors in these inexpugnable mountains; in the same way that many of the Byzantine families of Athens sought asylum in the isle of Aegina. (As we shall see later, there is a certain amount of colour to both these claims.) The founder of the church and the fortified building, I was told, was a member of the Mourtzinos family, who were reputed to be descendants of the Palaeologues. The Mourtzini were a prominent family, and one of them—Michael Troupakis Mourtzinos—was the Bey of the Mani (a virtually independent prince, that is) from 1779 until 1782, when he was beheaded by the Sultan.

*   *   *   *

Here I must anticipate a few weeks. Some days after this, in the Deep Mani, a young man gave me the name of his uncle, Mr. Dimitri Dimitrakos-Messisklis, the Athenian publisher, who, he said, had written a book about the Mani. Back in Athens, I sought him out above his bookshop, discovering him at last up a steep flight of stairs: a learned and delightful elderly gentleman in a long cavern of books overlooking Constitution Square. Over coffee we talked about the customs and the history of the Mani, and his discoveries corroborated, amended and increased the information I had by then accumulated about the towers and the blood-feuds and the dirges. How remote, as the traffic roared below us, that stony wilderness already seemed!

When I left, he presented me with a copy of his book.* It is a wonderfully complete account of the Mani, its history and legends and topography and folklore; a model for county-historians anywhere. Here, in the part devoted to the Beys of the Mani, he

* *Oi Nyklianoi.* D. Dimitrakos-Messisklis. This is invaluable to anyone who is interested in these regions and can read Greek.

sets down the traditional genealogy of the Troupakis-Mourtzinos family. The beginnings are far shakier than those of the Cornwall-Barbados-Wapping Palaeologi. The first one mentioned is a Michael Palaeologus in 1482, only twenty-nine years after the capture of the City, descendant of a branch, it seems, of the Palaeologi of Mistra, who had three sons: Panayioti, Dimitri and Tzanetto. The descendants of Panayioti were known by the surname of Troupaki, either, the book states, because they defended themselves from an ambush by taking up positions in a hole—*trypa*, or, in dialect, *troupa*—or because these shadowy Palaeologi, escaping from Mistra through the gorges of the Taygetus to the Mani, hid from the pursuing Turks in remote grottoes, where, like troglodytes, they lived for years. . . . Finally, when the coast was clear, they all settled in Kardamyli. The nickname stuck and the imperial surname fell into disuse. . . . The next of the family to be mentioned (perhaps the intervening names have been omitted as they are of little interest to the general reader) is the ruling Bey already mentioned: Michael, whose name of Troupakis is now augmented by Mourtzinos,* another nickname, the dialect diminu-

---

* There is nothing unusual in this. Many Greek names have changed over and over again, and the majority of them derive from *paratsoúklia*, or nicknames, as indeed have most names elsewhere in some degree. It may seem odd that these possible Palaeologi, all else being lost, should not have clung to the one imperial heirloom—their name—which still remained to them. But the same phenomenon occurs elsewhere in Greece. e.g. Byzantine names in Crete, like Skordyli and Kallergi (the followers of Nicephorus Phocas), or Venetian ones, like Morosini, Cornaro or Dandolo, survive in large numbers; but many of their bearers have allowed them to be replaced, even in recent generations, by nicknames which have stuck. There is the same random survival and erasure of great Frankish feudal names—i.e., of the Ghisi, the Giustiniani and the Sanudo, names which appear over shops—in the Cyclades. In Crete, nevertheless, in spite of these changes, their descendants have an unrationalized but very definite awareness of their august origins, and in one or two of the large mountain villages where traditions are strongest—Lakkoi in the White Mountains, for instance, and Anoyeia on the slopes of Mt. Ida—the mountaineers, though they may have only half a dozen goats to their name, possess a tribal pride and a knowledge of the part played by each family in Crete's innumerable rebellions against the Turks and a feeling of hierarchy and *Ebenbürtigkeit* among them-

tive of *mourgos*, a bulldog; the complete name now meaning,
roughly, Bullpup-in-the-Hole. The Bey's son, Panayioti Mourt-
zinos, was Kapetan, or guerrilla leader, of Androuvitza; *his* son,
Dionysios Mourtzinos, became war-minister of Greece in 1830.
George Mourtzinos, the last of the descendants of Michael the
Bey, died in 1848.

By normal standards, this is, to say the least, a shaky pedigree;
especially at the beginning: those three phantom Palaeologi. . . .
But, just supposing they were verifiable, the rest, even allowing
for the gap which seems to precede Michael the Bey, might be
authentic. Not only were there no genealogists under the Turkish
occupation, but no archives or records, not even a parish register
of births and deaths, till a very late date. It is only in the Ionian
islands, which were under the Venetians, and among the Phanariot
families that reigned in the Danubian Principalities, that Greek
family records were kept; and, in those unchronicled centuries
of oppression and turmoil and massacre and guerrilla warfare, oral
tradition was the only link with time past. Fallible as it is,
exposed to every rumour and misapprehension and *post-facto*
accommodation, this is not always as unreliable as it might be
supposed. There are many cases where, in the teeth of all likelihood and logical supposition, it has been proved right.

But I knew nothing about the Mourtzini at the time; nothing
beyond the tradition that the former inhabitants of the castellated
dwelling, the founders of the church, were popularly supposed
to have been direct descendants of the Palaeologi. . . .

*   *   *   *

The quiet charm of Kardamyli grew with each passing hour.

selves which is almost Proustian in its intensity. Every shepherd, though he may
be unable to read or write, carries a mountain Gotha in his head. I was fascinated, a few years ago, by the quantity of coats-of-arms above scrolls bearing
Cretan names which may be encountered by any sheepfold, on the walls,
among those of other distinguished alumni, of the University of Padua; placed
there when Padua, like Crete till 1669, was a part of the Venetian republic. In
Crete itself, these insignia have vanished without trace.

Most unexpectedly, we discovered a little hotel consisting of a few rooms over a grocer's shop owned by Socrates Phaliréas, the cousin, it turned out, of a distinguished sculptor-friend in Athens. Equally unexpectedly, it was, in its unflamboyant way, very comfortable. No planks were spread here with hair-shirt blankets for a stylite's penance, but springs and soft mattresses and a wicker chair or two waited for tired limbs in old and mellow rooms; and the kind, deep voice of the gigantic owner, a civilized and easy-going host, sitting down now and then for a chat, induced in all such a lack of hurry that the teeth of time and urgency and haste seemed all to have been drawn.

The same leisurely spell pervades the whole of this far-away little town. Cooled in summer by the breeze from the gulf, the great screen of the Taygetus shuts out intruding winds from the north and the east; no tramontana can reach it. It is like those Elysian confines of the world where Homer says that life is easiest for men; where no snow falls, no strong winds blow nor rain comes down, but the melodious west wind blows for ever from the sea to bring coolness to those who live there. I was very much tempted to become one of them, to settle in this small hotel for months with books and writing-paper; the thought has often recurred. The *Guide Bleu* only spares it half a line, mentioning little beyond the existence of its four hundred and ninety inhabitants. It is better so. It is too inaccessible and there is too little to do there, fortunately, for it ever to be seriously endangered by tourism. No wonder the nereids made it their home.

Returning from a long bathe beyond the forest of reeds, we saw a boy carrying a large silver fish by the tail: a *salpa*. (I haven't discovered its usual name.) I bought it, and, while it was being cooked, we sat under a mulberry tree, whose trunk was white-washed right up to the start of the branches, on a terrace outside one of the few taverns. Like us, a few fishermen under their great hats were watching the sun sinking over the Messenian mountains, on the other side of which, sixteen leagues away, lay Pylos. A miniature mole ran out, and, alongside it, gently rocking with each sigh of the green transparent water, caiques were tethered a few yards above their shadows on the pebbly bottom. Oleanders leaned over a flat layer of rock across which the sea flowed with just enough impetus to net the surface with a frail white reticulation of foam which slid softly away and dissolved while a new one formed. A small distance from the shore rocks jutted, one bearing a whitewashed church, the other a miniature ruined fort. The sea's surface was striped with gold which turned as the sun dipped into pale sulphur shot with lilac. Beyond it the unruffled gulf sailed unhindered to the darkening peninsula opposite.

Thinking of our grilling fish, our minds strayed back to Kalamata (now hidden at the gleaming gulf's end), several years before.

It was midsummer in that glaring white town, and the heat was explosive. Some public holiday was in progress—could it have been the feast of St. John the Baptist which marks the summer solstice?—and the waterfront was crowded with celebrating citizens in liquefaction. The excitement of a holiday and the madness of a heat wave hung in the air. The stone flags of the water's edge, where Joan and Xan Fielding and I sat down to dinner, flung back the heat like a casserole with the lid off. On a sudden, silent, decision we stepped down fully dressed into the sea carrying the iron table a few yards out and then our three chairs, on which, up to our waists in cool water, we sat round the neatly laid table-top, which now seemed by magic to be levitated three inches above the water. The waiter, arriving a moment later, gazed with surprise at the empty space on the quay; then, observing us with a quickly-masked flicker of pleasure, he stepped unhesitatingly into the sea, advanced waist deep with a butler's gravity, and, saying nothing more than 'Dinner-time', placed our meal before us—three beautifully grilled *kephali*, piping hot, and with their golden brown scales sparkling. To enjoy their marine flavour to the utmost, we dipped each by its tail for a second into the sea at our elbow . . . Diverted by this spectacle, the diners on the quay sent us can upon can of retsina till the table was crowded. A dozen boats soon gathered there, the craft radiating from the table's circumference like the petals of a marguerite. Leaning from their gently rocking boats, the fishermen helped us out with this sudden flux of wine, and by the time the moon and the Dog-Star rose over this odd symposium, a mandoline had appeared and *manga* songs in praise of hashish rose into the swooning night:

'When the hookah glows and bubbles,'
wailed the fishermen,
'Brothers, not a word! Take heed!
'Behold the *mangas* all around us
'Puffing at the eastern weed . . .'

*   *   *   *

I woke up thinking of the Mourtzini and the Palaeologi. It occurred to me, drinking mountain-tea in the street, that I had clean forgotten to ask when the Mourtzinos family had died out. 'But it hasn't,' Mr. Phaliréas said. 'Strati, the last of them, lives just down the road.'

Evstratios Mourtzinos was sitting in his doorway weaving, out of split cane and string, a huge globular fish-trap more complex than any compass design or abstract composition of geometrical wire. The reel of twine revolved on the floor, the thread unwinding between his big toe and its neighbour as the airy sphere turned and shifted in his skilful brown fingers with a dazzling interplay of symmetrical parabolas. The sunlight streamed through the rust-coloured loops and canopies of drying nets. A tang of salt, tar, seaweed and warm cork hung in the air. Cut reeds were stacked in sheaves, two canaries sung in a cage in the rafters, our host's wife was slicing onions into a copper saucepan. Mourtzinos shrugged his shoulders with a smile at my rather absurd questions and his shy and lean face, which brine and the sun's glare had cured to a deep russet, wore an expression of dubious amusement. 'That's what they say,' he said, 'but we don't know anything about it. They are just old stories. . . .' He poured out hospitable glasses of ouzo, and the conversation switched to the difficulties of finding a market for fish: there was so much competition. There is a special delight in this early-morning drinking in Greece.

Old stories, indeed. But supposing every link were verified, each shaky detail proved? Supposing this modest and distinguished looking fisherman were really heir of the Palaeologi, descendant of Constantine XI and of Michael VIII the Liberator, successor to Alexis Comnene and Basil the Bulgar-Slayer and Leo the Isaurian and Justinian and Theodosius and St. Constantine the Great? And, for that matter, to Diocletian and Heliogabalus and Marcus Aurelius, to the Antonines, the Flavians, the Claudians and the Julians, all the way back to the Throne of Augustus Caesar on the Palatine, where Romulus had laid the earliest foundations of Rome? . . . The generous strength of a second glass of ouzo accelerated these cogitations. It was just the face for a constitutional monarch, if only Byzantium were free. For the sheer luxury of credulity I lulled all scepticism to sleep and, parallel to an unexacting discourse of currents and baits and shoals, a kind of fairy-tale began assembling in my mind: 'Once upon a time, in a far-away land, a poor fisherman and his wife lived by the sea-shore. . . . One day a stranger from the city of Byzantium knocked on the door and begged for alms. The old couple laid meat and drink before him . . .' Here the mood and period painlessly changed into a hypothetic future and the stranger had a queer story to tell: the process of Westernization in Turkey, the study of European letters, of the classics and the humanities had borne such fruit that the Turks, in token of friendship and historical appropriateness, had decided to give the Byzantine Empire back to the Greeks and withdraw to the Central Asian steppes beyond the Volga from which they originally came, in order to plant their newly-won civilization in the Mongol wilderness. . . . The Greeks were streaming back into Constantinople and Asia Minor. Immense flotillas were dropping anchor off Smyrna and Adana and Halicarnassus and Alexandretta. The seaboard villages were coming back to life; joyful concourses of Greeks were streaming into Adrianople, Rhodosto, Broussa, Nicaea, Caesaraea,

Iconium, Antioch and Trebizond. The sound of rejoicing rang through eastern Thrace and banners with the Cross and the double-headed eagle and the Four Betas back-to-back were fluttering over Cappadocia and Karamania and Pontus and Bithynia and Paphlagonia and the Taurus mountains. . . .

But in the City itself, the throne of the Emperors was vacant. . . .

Stratis, our host, had put the fish-trap on the ground to pour out a third round of ouzo. Mrs. Mourtzinos chopped up an octopus-tentacle and arranged the cross-sections on a plate. Stratis, to illustrate his tale, was measuring off a distance by placing his right hand in the crook of his left elbow, 'a grey mullet that long,' he was saying, 'weighing five okas if it weighed a dram. . . .'

Then, in the rebuilt palace of Blachernae, the search for the heir had begun. What a crackling of parchment and chrysobuls, what clashing of seals and unfolding of scrolls! What furious wagging of beards and flourishes of scholarly forefingers! The Cantacuzeni, though the most authenticated of the claimants, were turned down; they were descendants only from the last emperor but four. . . . Dozens of doubtful Palaeologi were sent packing . . . the Stephanopoli de Comnene of Corsica, the Melissino-Comnenes of Athens were regretfully declined. Tactful letters had to be written to the Argyropoli; a polite firmness was needed, too, with the Courtney family of Powderham Castle in Devonshire, kinsmen of Pierre de Courtenai, who, in 1218, was Frankish Emperor of Constantinople; and a Lascaris maniac from Saragossa was constantly hanging about the gates. . . . Envoys returned empty-handed from Barbados and the London docks. . . . Some Russian families allied to Ivan the Terrible and the Palaeologue Princess Anastasia Tzarogorodskaia had to be considered. . . . Then all at once a new casket of documents came to light and a foreign emissary was despatched hot foot to the Peloponnese; over the Taygetus to the forgotten hamlet of Kardamyli. . . . By now all doubt had vanished. The Emperor Eustratius leant forward to refill the glasses with ouzo for the fifth time. The Basilissa shooed away a speckled hen which had wandered indoors after crumbs. On a sunny doorstep, stroking a marmalade cat, sat the small Diadoch and Despot of Mistra.

Our host heaved a sigh . . . 'The trouble with dyes made from pine-cones,' he went on—'the ordinary brown kind—is that the fish can see the nets a mile off. They swim away! But you have to use them or the twine rots in a week. Now, the new *white* dyes in Europe would solve all that! But you would hunt in vain for them in the ships' chandlers of Kalamata and Gytheion. . . .'

The recognition over, the rest seemed like a dream. The removal of the threadbare garments, the donning of the cloth-of-gold dalmatics, the diamond-studded girdles, the purple cloaks. All three were shod with purple buskins embroidered with bicephalous eagles, and when the sword and the sceptre had been proffered and the glittering diadem with its hanging pearls, the little party descended to a waiting ship. The fifth ouzo carried us, in a ruffle of white foam, across the Aegean archipelago and at every island a score of vessels joined the convoy. By the time we entered the Hellespont, it stretched from Troy to Sestos and Abydos . . . on we went, past the islands of the shining Propontis until, like a magical city hanging in mid-air, Constantinople appeared beyond our bows, its towers and bastions glittering, its countless domes and cupolas bubbling among pinnacles and dark sheaves of cypresses, all of them climbing to the single great dome topped with the flashing cross that Constantine had seen in a vision on the Milvian bridge. There, by the Golden Gate, in the heart of a mighty concourse, waited the lords of Byzantium: the lesser Caesars and Despots and Sebastocrators, the Grand Logothete in his globular headgear, the Counts of the Palace, the Sword Bearer, the Chartophylax, the Great Duke, the thalassocrats and polemarchs, the Strateges of the Cretan archers, of the hoplites and the peltasts and the cataphracts; the Silentiaries, the Count of the Excubitors, the governors of the Asian Themes, the Clissourarchs, the Grand Eunuch, and (for by now all Byzantine history had melted into a single anachronistic maelstrom) the Prefects of Sicily and Nubia and Ethiopia and Egypt and Armenia, the Exarchs of Ravenna and Carthage, the Nomarch of Tarentum,

the Catapan of Bari, the Abbot of Studium. As a reward for bringing good tidings, I had by this time assumed the Captaincy of the
Varangian Guard; and there they were, beyond the galleons and
the quinqueremes, in coruscating ranks of winged helmets,
clashing their battle-axes in homage; you could tell they were
Anglo-Saxons by their long thick plaits and their flaxen whiskers.
. . . Bells clanged. Semantra hammered and cannon thundered as
the Emperor stepped ashore; then, with a sudden reek of naphtha,
Greek fire roared saluting in a hundred blood-red parabolas from
the warships' brazen beaks. As he passed through the Golden
Gate a continual paean of cheering rose from the hordes which
darkened the battlement of the Theodosian Walls. Every window
and roof-top was a-bristle with citizens and as the great company
processed along the purple-carpeted street from the Arcadian to
the Amastrian Square, I saw that all the minarets had vanished. . . .
We crossed the Philadelphia and passed under the Statue of the
Winds. Now, instead of the minarets, statuary crowded the skyline. A population of ivory and marble gleamed overhead and,
among the fluttering of a thousand silken banners, above the
awnings and the crossed festoons of olive-leaves and bay, the sky
was bright with silver and gold and garlanded chryselephantine. . . . Each carpeted step seemed to carry us into a denser rose-
coloured rain of petals softly falling.

The heat had become stifling. In the packed square of Constantine, a Serbian furrier fell from a roof-top and broke his
neck; an astrologer from Ctesiphon, a Spanish coppersmith and a
money-lender from the Persian Gulf were trampled to death; a
Bactrian lancer fainted, and, as we proceeded round the Triple
Delphic Serpent of the Hippodrome, the voices of the Blues and
the Greens, for once in concord, lifted a long howl of applause.
The Imperial horses neighed in their stables, the hunting cheetahs
strained yelping at their silver chains. Mechanical gold lions
roared in the throne room, gold birds on the jewelled branches of
artificial trees set up a tinkling and a twitter. The general hysteria
penetrated the public jail: in dark cells, monophysites and bogomils
and iconoclasts rattled their fetters across the dungeon bars. High

36

in the glare on his Corinthian capital, a capering stylite, immobile for three decades, hammered his calabash with a wooden spoon. . . .

Mrs. Mourtzinos spooned a couple of onions and potatoes out of the pot, laid them before us and sprinkled them with a pinch of rock salt. 'When we were a couple of hours off Cerigo,' Stratis observed, splashing out the ouzo, 'the wind grew stronger—a real *meltemi*—a roaring *boucadoura*!—so we hauled the sails down, and made everything fast. . . .'

There, before the great bronze doors of St. Sophia, gigantic in his pontificalia, stood Athenagoras the Oecumenical Patriarch, whom I saw a few months before in the Phanar; surrounded now with all the Patriarchs and Archbishops of the East, the Holy Synod and all the pomp of Orthodoxy in brocade vestments of scarlet and purple and gold and lilac and sea blue and emerald green: a forest of gold pastoral staves topped with their twin coiling serpents, a hundred yard-long beards cascading beneath a hundred onion-mitres crusted with gems; and, as in the old Greek song about the City's fall, the great fane rang with sixty clanging bells and four hundred gongs, with a priest for every bell and a deacon for every priest. The procession advanced, and the coruscating penumbra, the flickering jungle of hanging lamps and the bright groves and the undergrowth of candles swallowed them. Marble and porphyry and lapis-lazuli soared on all sides, a myriad glimmering haloes indicated the entire mosaic hagiography of the Orient and, high above, suspended as though on a chain from heaven and ribbed to its summit like the concavity of an immense celestial umbrella, floated the golden dome. Through the prostrate swarm of his subjects and the fog of incense the imperial theocrat advanced to the iconostasis. The great basilica rang with the anthem of the Cherubim and as the Emperor stood on the right of the Katholikon and the Patriarch on the left, a voice as though from an archangel's mouth sounded from the dome, followed by the fanfare of scores of long shafted trumpets, while across Byzantium the heralds proclaimed the Emperor Eustratius, Servant of God, King of Kings, Most August Caesar and Basileus and Autocrator of Constantinople and New Rome. The whole

City was shaken by an unending, ear-splitting roar. Entwined in whorls of incense, the pillars turned in their sockets, and tears of felicity ran down the mosaic Virgin's and the cold ikons' cheeks. . . .

Leaning forward urgently, Strati crossed himself. '*Holy Virgin and all the Saints!*' he said. 'I was never in a worse situation! It was pitch dark and pouring with rain, the mast and the rudder were broken, the bung was lost, and the waves were the size of a house. There I was, on all fours in the bilge water, baling for life, in the Straits between the Elaphonisi and Cape Malea! . . .'

. . . the whole of Constantinople seemed to be rising on a dazzling golden cloud and the central dome began to revolve as the redoubled clamour of the Byzantines hoisted it aloft. Loud with bells and gongs, with cannon flashing from the walls and a cloud-borne fleet firing long crimson radii of Greek fire, the entire visionary city, turning in faster and faster spirals, sailed to a blinding and unconjecturable zenith. . . . The rain had turned to hail, the wind had risen to a scream; the boat had broken and sunk and, through the ink-black storm, Strati was swimming for life towards the thunderous rocks of Laconia. . . .

. . . The bottle was empty. . . .

The schoolmaster's shadow darkened the doorway. 'You'd better hurry,' he said, 'the caique for Areopolis is just leaving.' We all rose to our feet, upsetting, in our farewells, a basket of freshly cut bait and a couple of tridents which fell to the floor with a clatter. We stepped out into the sobering glare of noon.

CHAPTER 4

The City of Mars (Areopolis)

A BLUE cloud uneasy with electricity had swallowed the peaks of the Taygetus. The valleys rumbled with thunder and even a few phenomenal drops of rain pattered on the hot planks of the deck. But, as strangely as the cloud had spun itself out of nothing, it dwindled and shrank and finally, reduced to a static and solitary puff, vanished, exposing the western flanks of the Mani once more in all their devastating blankness. The Taygetus rolls in peak after peak to its southernmost tip, a huge pale grey bulk with nothing to interrupt its monotony. Nothing but a tangle of swirling incomprehensible creases of strata strangely upheaved. Every hour or so a dwarf township, queerly named, sprouted from the hot limestone at the water's edge: Stoupa, Selinitza, Trakhila, Khotasia, Arfingia. Little towers, with heavily barred windows and circular turrets at the corners, dominated a narrow shelf of whitewashed quay. Village elders (among which there is always the black cylinder of a priest's hat) sat over their coffee on the ramparts clicking their amber beads as they watched the pother of loading and unloading. Sacks of flour were piled among the capstans and lashed to the waiting mule teams which set off amid the shouts and whacks of their muleteers up labyrinthine torrent-beds for barren invisible hamlets in the hinterland.

Trakhila was backed by a blessed dark screen of cypresses. (It is strange how certain trees can civilize the wildest landscape in the same way that a single spruce or Christmas tree can barbarize the most amenable in a trice.) Then the blinding emptiness continued for mile on mile over our port bow. Now and then, shadowless in the blaze, built of the surrounding rock and only with difficulty discernible from the mountain, a lonely house would appear. Once, on a high ledge, an ashy village was outlined by a thin kindly smear of green and later a castellated house stood by the water in a sudden jungle of unlikely green which turned out, as I strained my eyes, to be all cactus and prickly pear —Frankish figs as the Greeks call them—flourishing there with the same deceptive air of freshness with which a cascade of mesembrianthemum will run wild over a hill of pumice.

This was all reflected in a sea which lay as flat as a looking-glass except for the ruffle of our wake. Yet among the wheat sacks the dolorous face of many a black-coiffed crone spelt sea-sickness. This is a peculiar convention: for land-lubbers, the sea equals seasickness, just as passing a church evokes a sign of the cross, a funeral, tears and torn hair, and the mention of war, a deep sigh. It is none the less genuine for that, and to exorcize this ritual nausea, the smell of a cut lemon is thought to be sovereign. Accordingly, they all held these golden pomanders to their nostrils. . . . At Trakhila a man got in who was so dark that, if he had been in the West Indies or Egypt one would have assumed that he had a strong dash of Negro blood in his veins. The Captain, at a suitable moment, whispered that the stranger came from the Deep Mani; many of them, he said, were like that, as the result of the old slave market of Vitylo, where the Berber and Algerian pirates, as well as the Venetians and the Maniots themselves, used to put up their captives for sale. Or rather, he cautiously appended, that is what they say.*

Soon we were rounding a cape and sailing at a slant across a broad inlet that penetrated a few miles into the mountains. At the further end lay Oetylus (Vitylo or Itylo) and a jag of rock smothered by the sprawling ruin of a great castle. It was the Fortress of

---

* I have been able to find no verification of this Mani slave-market though the Maniots used to be famous corsairs and were not infrequently mixed up in the trading of slaves. Once in a blue moon one comes across a villager in the Morea whose appearance is ascribed to an isolated rape, a hundred and thirty odd years ago, by the Sudanese cavalry of Ibrahim Pasha.

Kelepha, built here by the Turks as a temporary foothold on the edge of the Mani they had never managed to subdue. But we were heading for the southern shore of the gulf, the frontiers—at last! —of the Deep Mani itself. A derelict, shadowless little port and a group of empty houses bereft of life appeared at the bottom of steep olive-covered rocks. The engine fell silent, and, as we drew alongside, the roar of millions of cicadas burst on the ear. It came from the shore in rhythmic, grating, metallic waves like the engines of an immense factory in a frenzy—the electric rattle of innumerable high-powered dynamos whirling in aimless unison. There was not a breath of wind and on the quay when we left the caique's cool awning the sun came stampeding down to the attack. We plunged for shelter into a slovenly kapheneion awhirl with flies. Lulled by their buzz and by the ear-splitting clatter outside we lay on the sticky benches for an hour or two, till the sun should decline a little and declare a truce.

*　　*　　*　　*

The road to the upper world was a stony way ribbed with cut blades of rock to afford purchase for the feet of mules bearing cargoes up to Areopolis from the hot little port of Limeni. Each olive tree, motionless in the still air, was turned by the insects into a giant rattle, a whirling canister of iron filings. But as the stony angles of road levered us higher the clamour fell behind and the road, swept by a cool breeze, flattened across two miles of a bare plateau, dropping abruptly to the sea on the west and soaring eastwards once more in a continuation of the Taygetus; and there ahead of us, half castellated and with its roofs topped by a tower or two and the cupola and belfry of a little cathedral— lay the capital of the Deep Mani. The narrow streets of Areopolis were all round us.

It had the airy feeling of all plateau-towns and in the direction of the Messenian Gulf the lanes ended in the sky like springboards. Inland the impending amphitheatre was fainting from its afternoon starkness into a series of softly-shadowed mauve cones. In these solemn surroundings the little capital held an aura of solitude and remoteness. But the sloping cobbled lanes were full of gregarious life as if the Maniots had herded there in flight from the cactus-haunted emptiness outside. Except for the Cypriots, they were the darkest Greeks I have ever seen. But whereas the Cypriots have soft and rather shapeless faces, the Maniots are lean and hewn-looking with blue jowls and rebellious moustaches. Their jet and densely-planted hair grows low on the forehead; it narrows their temples; and fierce bars of brow are twisted in scowling flourishes over black and wary eyes as if the brains behind them were hissing with vindictive thoughts. It was this fell glance that distinguished them, it occurred to me, from the Cretan mountaineers they might otherwise resemble. The eyes of the latter are open and filled with humour and alacrity. But, black-avized as they looked under their great hats, this cast of sternness and caution must be the atavistic physical trace of centuries of wild life, for their manners were the reverse. As we descended the cobbled streets, a murmur of greeting rose from the café tables in a quiet chorus uttered with a friendliness and grace that made one feel welcome indeed. (This is not usual in towns; even in villages it is the convention for strangers to greet first.)

The names over the shops had all changed once more from the -eas ending of the Outer Mani to the -akos of the Deep: Kostakos, Khamodrakos, Bakakos, Xanthakos. At the bottom of the main street, a primitive cathedral, smaller than a small parish church in England, stood in a cluster of mulberry trees. It was entirely whitewashed and topped by a tiled Byzantine cupola supported on a drum of pilasters and arches and flanked by a snow-white tapering belfry. A course of moulding painted bright yellow girdled the ribbed apse. Studded with alternate pink rosettes and bright green leaves, it might have been the decoration of a Mayan Baroque church in the uplands of Guatemala. Higher on the walls mauve pilasters supported a shallow colonnade enclosing panels of apricot, and clumsy six-winged seraphim spread their feathers in bossed and lumpy relief. Two childish sun-discs were surrounded by spiked petals adorned with currant-like eyes and wide grins, and the signs of the Zodiac sported across

42

the whitewash in an uncouth and engaging menagerie. The decoration over the main door was a real puzzle: a large panel in the same lumpy relief was picked out in yellow and black and green. Tudor roses and leaves and rosettes and nursery-rhyme suns formed a background for two angels, one in fluted robes, the other in armour and buskins; and between them, supported by two small and primitive lions rampant, a double-headed eagle with wings displayed bore on its breast a complicated shield whose strange charges had so often been painted over that if was hard, even standing on a café chair, to make them out. The eagle's two heads were backed by haloes, and something like the vestigial memory of a closed crown rested on the top of the shield while above the bird's heads an imperial crown, like that of Austria-Hungary or the Russian Empire, spread its two mitre-like ribbons. A scroll underneath bore the date ot 1798.

The double-headed eagle, the emblem of Byzantium and, in a sense, of the Orthodox Church, is a frequently recurring symbol in ecclesiastical decoration; the formula of its representation on the walls and floors of churches has scarcely changed since the imperial eagle of Rome grew a second head when Constantine founded the Empire of the East in 330. But the heraldic elaboration of the plaster bird over the door bore no resemblance to it. For all its uncouthness, the design—the haloes, the arrangement of wings and claws and tail—echoed the sophistication and formalism of latter-day western heraldry. I wondered if it could have been copied, quite arbitrarily, from the arms on a Maria Theresa thaler as pure decoration; but except for the fesses (or stripes) in the dexter chief which faintly resemble part of the Hungarian arms there is no similarity. Could they be inspired by the arms of Russia? It was unlikely, because of the date, which was twenty years after Orloff's abortive campaign in the Peloponnese, which effectively discredited Russia as the protectress of Orthodoxy. The only important event in local history for 1798 is the accession of Panayioti Koumoundouros as fifth Bey of the Mani. But, great local potentates as were the Beys, I have never heard that they adopted the use of arms. These emblems, with that date attached, seemed (and still seem) as problematical as an Easter Island statue in the Hebrides. I attach a faithful copy of this half-obliterated shield in case anyone can identify it and perhaps unearth a lost chapter of Maniot history.

In the blue-green sky beyond the mulberry leaves a bright star was burning so close to the waxing crescent of the moon that it seemed to have invaded the dim perimeter, forming a celestial Turkish flag. Most unsuitably, when one remembers the Mani's history.

* * * *

Very little is known about this remote province in the rest of the country but the name of the Mani at once suggests four ideas to any Greek: the custom of the blood feud; dirges; Petrobey Mavromichalis, the leader of the Maniots in the Greek War of Independence; and the fact that the Mani, with the Sphakian mountains of Crete and, for a while, the crags of Souli in Epirus, was the only place in Greece which wrested its freedom from the Turks and maintained a precarious independence. This, too, was about the sum of my knowledge, amplified by the haze of rumours, which (as so few non-Maniot Greeks ever go to the Mani) riots unchecked beyond the Taygetus. This deviation from the main flow of Greek history has produced many divergent symptoms and, before going further into its remoter depths, it is worth looking at the things in the Mani's past which have contributed to this idiosyncrasy.

Its geographical seclusion, locked away beyond the mountains on the confines of Sparta, and the steepness and aridity of its mountains are the key to the whole thing. Its history was one with that of Sparta until the monarchy ended at the turn of the third and second centuries B.C., when the cruelty of the tyrant Nabis decided many of the Spartans to flee beyond the Taygetus and found, with the Laconian inhabitants already established in the peninsula, a shadowy Republic of the Laconians. This was the first of the many flights for asylum which helped to form the present Mani. Their liberties went unmolested after the Roman conquest, which happened a few years after. Later on, Augustus, out of gratitude for Laconian help in the defeat of Mark Antony at Actium, confirmed these rights, and their history was without event until the Republic of Free Laconians was dissolved by Diocletian in his reform of the provincial administration in A.D. 297. The uneventful, orderly life continued under Byzantium, except for a new contribution of Spartans in flight from the Visigoths of Alaric in 396. The invasions of Slavs and Bulgars in the centuries which followed sent fresh waves of refugees; worse still, a savage Slav tribe, the Meligs, established themselves in the peaks of the Taygetus.

They were a terrible lot: strangers, talking a foreign tongue, who lived by brigandage. It is impossible to say how many they were, or how much they were absorbed into the Laconian stock of the Maniots. According to the only available sources, very little. Constantine Porphyrogenetus (who reigned at Constantinople at the beginning of the tenth century) mentions them in the book—

a kind of geographical and diplomatic history and guide to the Empire—which he wrote for the instruction of his son Romanus. After describing them, he expressly states that the Maniots themselves are unpolluted descendants of the old pagan Greeks. St. Nikon the Penitent, who converted the area from paganism a few decades later, found these Meligs an appalling handful. Peak-wandering robbers who lived off loot, they were 'led by the devil, entering houses by night like wolves ... miserable and evil fiends, bloodthirsty murderers, whose feet were forever leading them into evil. ...' (The saint baffled them by enveloping them in snowy clouds, and once, when some had robbed a monastery, he discomfited them with two huge mastiffs. But he managed to convert them in the end.) This turbulent minority, often mentioned in the Chronicle of the Morea, with time quite lost their language and their tribal conscience and by the twelfth century they were, like the other Slavs, swallowed up without trace in the Greek Orthodox Christian world of the Peloponnese. Sealed off from outside influences by their mountains, the semi-troglo-dytic Maniots themselves were the last of the Greeks to be converted. They only abandoned the old religion of Greece towards the end of the ninth century. It is surprising to remember that this peninsula of rock, so near the heart of the Levant from which Christianity springs, should have been baptised three whole centuries after the arrival of St. Augustine in far-away Kent.

The Frankish conquest of the Morea in the thirteenth century, when the Mani became part of the feudal fief of the Ville-hardouins, brought another swarm of refugees from Byzantine Sparta across the mountains; the falls of Constantinople and Mistra and Trebizond, yet more. Meanwhile, the pacific nature of the old Maniots had been changing—a process which began, perhaps, after the Byzantine victory over the Franks at Pelagonia* in 1261, when Emmanuel Palaeologus reclaimed the south-eastern Peloponnese for the Empire. The Frankish conquest had been a walkover; but, when the final disaster of Turkish invasion came, the Mani put up a stiff resistance: contact with the warlike Franks,

* Monastir (Bitolj), now just across the Serbian border.

46

their military training, and the late Byzantine triumphs in the empire's twilight had turned these descendants of the Spartans, quiescent almost since Thermopylae, into implacable warriors.

Their exploits against the Turks became fabulous and their feats of arms under their Epirote leader, Korkodeilos Kladas—the first of many guerrilla heroes—are some of the most brilliant in Peloponnesian history. In fact, so formidable were the swords and guns and the rocks of the Mani that, apart from punitive inroads in strength and the construction of one or two massive fortresses in which garrisons were cooped for uncertain and dangerous sojourns, the Mani remained miraculously free. More contingents arrived in flight from other parts of the occupied Greek world; a few from Asia Minor, and, after the Turkish capture of Crete from the Venetians at the end of the long siege of Candia* in 1669, a heavy shower of Cretans, who founded villages with Cretan names and scattered the already complex Maniot dialect with Cretan words and constructions; so that, to the Maniot -eas and -akos surnames were now added many that ended with the Cretan -akis.† This steady influx of strangers and the struggle, among the rocks and cactuses, for lebensraum, launched the Maniots, old and new, on innumerable vendettas between rival villages and families and clans. A kind of tribal system grew up not unlike that of the Scottish Highlands before the '45.

Some of these vendettas grew into miniature local wars and kept the Mani smoking with turbulence and bloodshed for centuries. For centuries, in fact, the only thing that could reconcile them was a Turkish inroad, when, suddenly, for brief idyllic periods of internal harmony, their long guns would all point the same way. Parties would leave to fight as mercenaries in the armies of the Doge. The poverty of the peninsula turned the Maniots into pirates, and their little ships were the terror of the Turkish and Venetian galleys in southern Peloponnesian waters. Their expeditions were undertaken less in search of riches than for the sober domestic need to buy wood,—fuel for lime burning

---

* Herakleion.

† This ending is not always Cretan. The formation existed in the Mani.

for the building of tall towers in their treeless villages—and guns, with which to shoot at their neighbours through the loopholes when these were built. Many of their piratical exploits, like those of the klephts and armatoles in the mountains of the mainland, had a patriotic reason. The best known case is the destruction of part of the Ottoman fleet in Canea roads with Maniot fire-ships.

The hamlets of the Mani were scattered across the mountains like scores of hornets' nests permanently at odds with each other, a discord which, as we have seen, only the Turks could resolve; so the Turks wisely left them alone under the rule of a Maniot holding the title of Bey of the Mani and the powers of a reigning prince; something after the style of the hospodars of Wallachia and Moldavia, with a nominal yearly tribute. But it was seldom paid. Once, I was told, a farthing was derisively tossed to the Sultan's representative from the tip of a scimitar.

The first of these rulers, Liberakis Yerakaris, reigned in the middle of the seventeenth century. By the age of twenty he had served several years as an oarsman in the Venetian galleys and made himself the foremost pirate of the Mani. Captured by the Turks and condemned to death, he was reprieved by the Grand Vizier—the great Albanian Achmet Küprülü—on condition that he accepted the hegemony of the Mani. He undertook the office in order to avenge himself on the strong Maniot family of the Stephanopoli with which he was in feud. He at once besieged them in the fort of Vitylo and captured thirty-five of them whom he executed on the spot. For the next twenty years he used his power and his influence with the Sublime Porte to campaign all over the Peloponnese and central Greece at the head of formidable armies, siding now with the Turks, now with the Venetians, marrying the beautiful princess Anastasia, niece of a Voivode of Wallachia,* ending his life, after adventures comparable to anything in the annals of the Italian condottiere, as Turkish Prince of the Mani and Venetian Lord of the Roumeli and Knight of St. Mark.

The Turks did not repeat the experiment for a hundred years.

* A member of the Duca family.

48

After the Orloff revolt petered out in 1774, the Turks revived the rank of Bey of the Mani, thinking it was wiser to have one man responsible for the tranquillity of the district. So during the forty-five years from 1776 to 1821, when the War of Independence broke out, the Mani was ruled by eight successive Beys, all except one of whom played the dangerous game of maintaining the interests of the Mani and of eventual Greek freedom while trying to remain on the right side of the Turks.* Two were tricked on board Turkish men-of-war and executed in Constantinople: one for attempting to extend his beydom beyond the Eurotas, the other as the result of intrigues at the Sublime Porte. The third, the wealthy Zanetbey, a great tower-builder, was deposed for his collusion with the Klephts and the discovery of a secret and treasonable correspondence with Napoleon, to whom he looked as a possible deliverer of the Mani. (He had prudently sent one of his sons to serve in the French army, another in the Russian.) He contrived to save his life by flight, continued his negotiations with the French and even persuaded them to send him boatloads of arms and ammunition which he distributed among the klephts and the kapetans. His successor was deposed for failing to put a stop to these dangerous goings-on. The fifth had a quiet reign. He organized the internal economy of the Mani, built roads, and became a member of the Philiki Hetairia, the secret revolutionary society which had begun to penetrate the whole Greek world. He was deposed for suspected collusion with his turbulent and outlawed uncle, Zanetbey, and was succeeded by his detractor, Zervobey, the only quisling. He was attacked by the family of Zanet and he only saved his life by seeking refuge in the palace at Tripoli with his friend the tyrannous and depraved Veli, Pasha of the Morea and son of no less a person than the terrible Vizier of Yannina, Ali the Lion. The career of his successor is overshadowed by that of the eighth and

* They were Zanetos Koutipharis (3 years), Michaelbey Troupakis (3 years), Zanetbey Kapetanakis Grigorakis (14 years), Panayoti Koumoundouros (5 years), Antonbey Grigorakis (7 years), Zervobey (2 years), Thodorobey Zanetakis (5 years) and the Petrobey Mavromichalis (6 years).

last of the Beys, the greatest of them all and one of the leading figures of Greek nineteenth-century history, Petrobey Mavromichalis.

After the Frankish conquest of Greece the Mani was a stormy feudal oligarchy of powerful families. Of these by far the strongest, the richest and the most numerous was the Mavromichalis clan. Various origins have been ascribed to them. There is a tradition that they were originally a Thracian family called Gregorianos which arrived here in flight when the Turks first crossed the Hellespont in 1340. It is certain that they were established in the west of the Deep Mani by the sixteenth century. In chronicles of the following centuries, the name abounds. There is a deep-rooted legend that their great physical beauty springs from the marriage of a George Mavromichalis to a mermaid; in the same way that anyone of the name of Connolly, in Celtic folklore, descends from a seal.* Their courage and enterprise were equal to their beauty, and Skyloyanni Mavromichalis—John the Dog—was one of the great paladins against the Turks in the eighteenth century. His son Petro was head of this vast family at the turn of the eighteenth and nineteenth centuries when the Mavromichalis were at the acme of their prosperity and power, a position chiefly due to the strategic and mercantile importance of their hereditary stronghold in the natural fortress of Tsimova and its attendant port of Limeni. This commands the only pass leading through the Taygetus to Gytheion and the rest of Laconia; it is also the entrance to the Deep Mani. Long before he was created Bey, his territorial influence and authority far exceeded that of his predecessors and when the beydom devolved upon him in 1808 it was the ratification of power which was already

* Nereids—the word used in the account of this legend—in modern Greek superstition are beautiful pale wraiths who haunt inland streams and springs. But this one is expressly stated to have been a salt-water dweller. The nereid, as opposed to the salt-water 'gorgon', is shaped like a human. The latter, the *Gorgona* that haunts the stormier parts of the Mediterranean, ends in two scaly and coiling tails. A Maniot grocer told me that the Mavromichalis nereid was possibly a deaf and dumb Venetian princess of the House of Morosini found sitting on a rock by the seashore.

absolute. His fine looks and dignity and gracious manners were the outward signs of an upright and honourable nature, high intelligence, diplomatic skill, generosity, patriotism, unshakable courage and strength of will: qualities suitably leavened by ambition and family pride and occasionally marred by cruelty. He too negotiated with Napoleon (to no great purpose, however, as the latter was too occupied elsewhere) and reconciled the warring clans. He imposed a truce to the feuds and conciliated the Troupakis and Grigorakis clans. These, egged on by the Turks in the hope that internal strife might soften up the Mani for invasion or at least neutralize it in the coming struggle for the liberation of Greece, were rival aspirants to the rank of Bey.

It was from the Mani that the first blow was struck. Petrobey and three thousand Maniots with Kolokotronis and a number of the great Morean klephts advanced on the Turkish garrison of Kalamata. After its surrender he issued a declaration of the Greek aspirations to the courts of Europe signed 'Petrobey Mavromichalis, Prince and Commander in Chief'. The banners of freedom were going up all over Greece, and the whole peninsula burst into those flames which, after four centuries of slavery, demolished the Turkish power in the country for ever and gave rebirth to the shining phoenix of modern Greece. Petrobey, at the head of his Maniots, fought battle after battle in these ferocious years; he takes his place as one of the giants in the struggle. He soars far beyond the rocky limitations of these pages into those of modern European history. No less than forty-nine of his family were killed during this contest and his capital of Tsimova was renamed Areopolis in his honour: the town of the war-god Ares. In the tangle of conflicting ideologies which followed the liberation Mavromichalis fell out with the new leader of the State, Capodistria. When he was imprisoned in the new capital at Nauplia, the Mani rose in revolt and Petrobey escaped and fled; but he was recaptured and re-imprisoned and two of his turbulent nephews, enraged at this insult, waylaid Capodistria and assassinated him. Mavromichalis achieved high honours during the reign of King Otto and died, surrounded with glory, in 1848. His descendants have played a prominent part in governments and war cabinets ever since, though none of them—how could they in the Athenian world of party-politics?—have equalled the stature of their great ancestor.

The name still rings unchallenged through the Mani and at that very moment the narrow streets of Areopolis were plastered with election posters displaying photographs of Petro Mavro-michalis, a great-great grandson and the present head of the family, a political figure of some prominence in the Royalist interest. His urbane, well nourished and patrician face, a monocle glinting in one eye socket, issuing from a stiff collar with a care-fully knotted tie and well tailored shoulders, looked out over the broad Maniot hat-brims with a nice combination of ministerial poise and the affability of the bridge-table. It was hard to associate these polished lineaments with the shaggy yataghan-wielding chieftains of the Deep Mani; with Black Michael and John the Dog. Still less with that beautiful mermaid floundering wide-eyed in a rock pool in the gulf of Kyparissia a few centuries ago.

CHAPTER 5

Lamentation

ALL Greece abounds with popular poetry. It is always sung, and there are different kinds for various occasions—birth, death, marriage, religious feasts, the welcoming of guests, drinking, the pasturing of sheep—and they vary from region to region: the klephtic ballads of Roumeli and the Morea, the oriental *amanés*, the improvised rhyming *mantinadas* of Crete which the *lyra* accompanies, the romantic Italianate *cantadas* of the Ionian isles, sung to the sound of guitars and mandolines—one could compile a long list. Nearly all of them, however, are written in the decapentesyllabic line, sometimes in rhyming couplets. The metre is slightly monotonous to read—it has something of the jaunty iteration of *Locksley Hall*—but sung, with their peculiar caesurae, repetitions of half lines, long drawn modulations and guttural ejaculations and apostrophes, they are full of life and variety. Many of them accompany Greek country dances.

Here again the Mani deviates. There is little dancing, and if one were writing a thesis to prove their descent, one might well adduce the absence of popular poetry among the Maniots as a heritage by default, a negative heirloom, of philistine Lacedaemon's enmity to the Muses. Naturally, this generalization is not quite true, for one form of popular poetry does exist in the Mani which has been largely extinct elsewhere since ancient times and this is so singular and remarkable, so representative of the sombre traditions of the peninsula, that it largely compensates for the dearth of all other kinds. The *miroloyia* ('words of destiny'), the metrical dirges of the Mani, are an isolated phenomenon.

Mourning and funeral rites have an importance in Greece that exceeds anything prevailing in western Europe, and the poorer and wilder the region—the fewer the tangible possessions there are to lose, and the less the possibilities of material consolations and anodynes—the more irreparable and sad seems loss by death. The expression of this distress is correspondingly more articulate. In these regions the thread of life is brittle. Survival seems something of a day-to-day miracle and life itself, in spite of the impetuousness with which it can be cut off, is doubly precious.

There is, in practice, little belief in a conventional after-life and the rewards and sanctions of Christian dogma. In spite of the orthodox formulae of the priest at the graveside it is not for a Christian eternity, for a paradise above the sky, that the dead are setting out, but the Underworld, the shadowy house of Hades and the dread regions of Charon; and Charon has been promoted from the rank of ferryman of the dead to that of Death himself, a dire equestrian sword-wielder. 'Charon took him,' a widow will sigh, contradictorily enmeshing her torso with a dozen signs of the cross. 'He left me for the Underworld . . . It was his destiny, it was written. He had eaten his bread and he had no days left. May God forgive all his sins and may the All Holy Virgin give me strength. . . .' When someone is ill, not only the doctor and the priest are summoned but the local witch with her incantations and charms, and when he dies, he is supplied with a coin for the ferryman; after his burial, the pagan funeral cakes are solemnly eaten and the men let their beards grow in sign of mourning. There is no clash in the Greek mind between these two allegiances, but a harmonious unchallenged syncretism comparable to the observances at many a Calabrian shrine. I once saw a Cretan priest exorcized by sorceress of a tiresome sciatica caused by the Evil Eye. For this relief he immediately lit a thanksgiving candle before the ikon of his patron saint.

The thread of life, then, is very brittle. In the remote mountains of Greece, on the bare rocks by day and by the glimmer of rushlights at night, the skull seems close to the surface and struggling to emerge. One sees it plainly beneath the hollow eye-sockets and cheeks and the jawbone's edge, and in old people, wasted by toil and poverty and fever and worry, it looms—the moment the bright glint of conversation fades to the dark and fatalistic lustre of thought—pathetically close.* Death is a near neighbour, slight ailments cause exaggerated anxiety among the most robust and more serious illnesses often induce the despair of a wild animal, an inability to fight against death which meets Charon half-way. Invalids often waste away without reason and their eyes reflect neither the impending joys of paradise nor the terrors of hell fire —the temporary rigours of Purgatory and the mists of Limbo have been omitted from Orthodox theology—but extinction, the loss of friends, the end of everything. The bright day is done and they are for the dark, and when the soul flutters away at last no one knows whither it is flying and a shrill and heartrending wail of bereavement goes up.

All over the Greek world—indeed, wherever the religion of Byzantium holds sway—village funerals are accompanied by outward signs of lamentation that come as a great surprise to those who have only witnessed the prim obsequies of north-western Europe. The mourning is the work of the women. It begins as a lyke-wake, a wailing and keening round the body by candleflame, and when the coffin is carried out into the daylight with the corpse rocking from side to side on the carrying shoulders, the mourning lifts to a crescendo that only fitfully subsides during the funeral service in church, to rise once more on the way to the cemetery, in the wild cries of the kinswomen: 'Oh my warrior! *Ah, to pallikari mou!* The arch and pillar of our house! Where are they

* The physical fact of death has no palliations or disguises. The sealed coffin of western Europe and the cosmetics and mummifications of North America are undreamed of. Every Greek child has heard again and again the agony of the death-rattle and seen the shrunken grey chaps, the fallen jaw and the closed eyelids of their elders. The coffin is left open until the last minute and only lowered into the grave when everyone has kissed the dead cheeks good-bye. The smell and touch of death are known to all, and dissolution too, for, three years after burial, the bones are ceremonially dug up to join those of the family. Even I have seen the bare skulls of two old friends; one in Crete, one in the Argolis.

taking him? Ah, my beautiful flower, my young cypress tree!'
This soars to a climax as they reach the grave, the mourner's
voice turns to an hysterical screeching howl, she staggers like an
intoxicated person, her coif falls off, her hair flies loose and
tangled over her face and she scarifies her cheeks with her finger-
nails till they are criss-crossed with red gashes and running with
tears and blood. The supreme moment comes when the coffin is
lowered into the shallow grave. Then,—in extreme cases,—uttering shrieks she has to be withheld by force from flinging herself
into the grave, a task in which her attendants are not always success-
ful. Dragged to the surface once more, the hysteria seems to
subside a little as the earth is thrown in, but all the way home,
shaken with sobs and outbursts of wailing at widening intervals,
she is supported and surrounded by a black-clad throng of women
who guide her staggering along the lanes. For days afterwards
during visits of condolence the same symptoms occur in a milder
form. The gravity of mourning loses ground before a sudden rush
of talk: he was the best of sons, a real warrior, such a good boy,
kind to his mother and father, so full of life, the best shot in the
village, he played the *lyra* so swiftly you couldn't see the bow, he
leapt higher than any of them at the dance, and flew like a bird!
What's the use of making sons with such pain and sorrow if
Charon steals them from us? Tears are soon flowing fast. The
mourner's face breaks and her voice sails up in the thin ritual
trance-like wail of the *miroloy*. She is at once surrounded, embraced
and gently scolded by her family who manage to quieten her bit
by bit. In a few weeks' time this dwindles and disappears. Gradually, backed by a host of comforting adages, the consolations of
fatalism assert themselves. The deep sighs and the black clothes
continue for life.

After the first reactions of awe and horror, the sight of the general ritual of misery is desperately moving and sad. The fact
that custom has evolved a formal framework for grief takes
nothing away from its authenticity or from the sting of pity it
evokes. There was a deep wisdom behind the orgiastic and
hysterical aspects of ancient religion; there is much to be said

in favour of this flinging open of the floodgates to grief. It might be argued that the decorous little services of the West, the hushed voices, the self-control, our brave smiles and calmness either stifle the emotion of sorrow completely, or drive it underground where it lodges and proliferates in a malign and dangerous growth that festers for a lifetime.

In these eastern funerals, it goes without saying that emotional and histrionically gifted women react in a more spectacular fashion than the rest. Tongues are sometimes clicked when funerals are discussed if a performance has been too obviously stagey, too shameless an exploitation of opportunity. Nearly everything in Greece has its balancing corrective. 'Poor old Sophia was piling it on a bit,' one sometimes hears people say, 'I couldn't look at her. . . .' The men of the family often appear uncomfortable while all this goes on; changing feet, turning their caps nervously round and round in their fingers, keeping their eyes glued to the ground with all the symptoms of male embarrassment at a purely feminine occasion. 'May God pardon all his sins,' the men say, 'May his memory be eternal,' and 'Let the earth rest upon him lightly;' and no more. For death and burial are one of the few occasions in Greek peasant life when women come into their own and take over. After long years of drudgery and silence and being told to shut up they are suddenly on top and there is no doubt that for some of them, famous *miroloyistrias*, wailers with a turn for acting and a gift of improvisation, these are moments secretly longed for. They will undertake immense journeys to bewail a distant kinsman, or even, in extreme cases, people they have never met. Some of them are in great demand. 'When I told old Phroso that Panayoti was dead and buried,' I once heard somebody observe with a wry smile, 'she didn't say, "May God pardon all his sins," but "What a shame I missed being there to wail for him. . . . Who did the *miroloy*? Old Kyriakoula? Po! po! po! She doesn't even know how to start. . . ."'

But the dirges of the Mani are a very different matter from these unco-ordinated cries. They are entire poems, long funeral hymns with a strict discipline of metre. Stranger still, the metre exists nowhere else in Greece. The universal fifteen-syllable line of all popular Greek poetry is replaced here by a line of sixteen syllables, and the extra foot entirely changes the sound and character of the verse.

> The klephts were sleeping by the brook and all the world was
> sleeping
> Only the youngest of them all lay with his eyelids open.

goes the ordinary Greek decapentesyllabic rhyming couplet. The sixteen-syllable line of a Maniot dirge goes like this:

> And when you reach the Underworld, greet all the Manis dead for
> me,
> Greet John the Dog and Michael Black, tell them we'll soon be
> meeting there. . . .*

They are sung extempore by the graveside, and it seems that the Maniot women, like the unlettered mountaineers in Crete in the invention of *mantinades*,† have this extraordinary knack of improvisation. There are, of course, certain conventional phrases that recur (like the epithets and the unchanging formulae that cement the *Odyssey*) which give time for planning the next two lines. But anyone who has heard the speed with which the Cretans can turn any incident on the spot into a faultless rhyming couplet and each time with an epigrammatic sting in the second line (here again the slow embroidered repetition of the first line by the company gives the singer a few seconds for thought), will not find this hard to believe. The similarity of these *miroloyia* with the themes of ancient Greek literature, most notably with the lament of Andromache over the body of Hector, coupled with the fact that this region remained pagan till six entire centuries after Constantine had made Christianity the official Greek religion, and with the fact that they only exist in the Mani, tempts one to think

* In printed anthologies these eight-foot verses are often split up into two lines, divided after the fourth foot.

† Improvised rhyming couplets in the ordinary fifteen-syllable metre of which each must be complete and epigrammatical, as they are sung antiphonally, or couplet after couplet, by each member of a company.

that here again is a direct descendant of Ancient Greece, a custom stretching back, perhaps, till before the Siege of Troy.

On the alert for dirges ever since arriving in the Mani, I had managed to collect a number of broken fragments people had remembered from past funerals, but nothing complete. It was rather a delicate thing and I felt ashamed to admit that I was hanging about like a vulture waiting for someone—anyone—to die and be buried and mourned over. I never saw a funeral there but I managed to find out a certain amount about how the dirges are sung. The chief woman mourner stands at the coffin's head and begins the *klama*, or weeping. It is her duty to welcome all the guests in the order of their importance, and, if possible, with a compliment for each and a word of thanks for their attendance. Then comes the *miroloy* proper, and it unfolds, in spite of the semi-ecstatic mode of delivery, in a logical sequence of proem, exegesis and epilogue. As the dirge continues, the knees stiffen, the hair falls in disorder, the headkerchief is stretched across the shoulders, an end held in each hand, which work up and down with a sawing motion in time to the slow beat of the metre. The breast is struck, the cheeks clawed, and very often the *miroloy* accelerates into a gabble and finally into wails and shrieks without meaning. If the dead man has been killed in a feud the dirge may finish with terrible curses and oaths of vengeance: the dirge-singer often tears her hair out in dishevelled handfuls and flings it in the open coffin; just, in fact, as Achilles and the Myrmidons cast their severed tresses on the bier of Patroclus. When she fades out, another woman 'takes' the *klama*; she begins with consoling words for the bereaved, continuing with compliments to the guests and an encomium of the dead. She in her turn dies down, another 'takes', and so the *klama* goes on. In the wailing over Hector, Andromache was succeeded by Hecuba and Hecuba by Helen. If the dead has left unprotected children, they are brought into the dirge like the fatherless Astyanax: who will look after them now? The tools of his profession are rhetorically invoked. If he were a shepherd, how will the ewes and the rams console themselves, what will become of his crook and his water-bottle? All, animate and inanimate, are shedding tears now for their lost master; if a mason, his bricks, mortar and trowel; if a soldier, his rifle and bayonet; a schoolmaster, his blackboard and chalk; a lawyer, his brief-case and rostrum and documents and red tape. At home, meanwhile, everything—tables and chairs, loom, handmill, olive press, saddles, the stones of the walls, the leaves of the olive trees, and the thorns of the prickly pear are all weeping together. What will become of them? Their sun and their moon have been taken away, the very breeze that ruffled the leaves. He was a lion, an eagle, but gentle as a lamb to his loved ones; but now he is in the dark world of shadows among his vanished kinsmen and ancestors, the dead warriors, the great-souled heroes of the Mani. . . . But it is not always an encomium. His faults are mentioned, and his deeds are assessed. Once, when an elderly village idiot with no relations was being buried, the women refused to sing a lament until at last, egged on by men who were shocked at this impiety, an old woman piped up: 'Ah, poor John, how you stank when you were alive! Why is it you don't stink now you are dead? . . .' Sometimes, in the inspired half-trance of the *miroloy*, the singer goes clean off the rails, drifting into personal reminiscence and old grievances, even into questions of politics, where, without any relevance, problems of taxation and economy, the fall of governments, the names of ministers and generals, the price of salt, the Bulgarian frontier, the need for roads or a new mole for the caiques to unload their flour—all in faultless sixteen-syllable couplets—weave themselves into the song, until the next mourner tactfully steers the *klama* back to its proper theme.

The singers are unable, except for a few disjointed fragments, to remember what they have sung. If the dirge has been in any way remarkable, it is pieced together afterwards by the bystanders. In this way many have passed into general circulation and women intone them for generations afterwards as they spin and weave and press the olives. Collections of *miroloyia*, many of them of high poetical value, have been made and new ones are constantly emerging.

I despaired of ever hearing a *miroloy*. But on our last day in Areopolis, drinking at a little tavern that sold excellent wine brought from Megara by the barrel, I fell into conversation with a flaxen-haired young man called George Chryssikakis. The talk was soon steered in the direction of my obsession. What, never heard a dirge? He would take me to see his cousin Eleni; she was one of the best *miroloyistrias* in the Deep Mani. He picked us up in the early evening and led us through a maze of lanes to a small white house on the edge of the precipice which sank to the Messenian Gulf. Here, surrounded by flowering herbs in white-washed petrol-tins, his old aunt and his cousin Eleni were knitting under a pomegranate tree. His cousin was a handsome, plump young woman with apple cheeks and bright disarming eyes, quite unlike the sombre crone I had expected. Coffee and spoonfuls of jam were soon produced, and when we were settled under the russet bombs that grew on the branches, George made her recite half a dozen *miroloya*, all very beautiful. But nothing, at first, would make her sing. She laughed self-consciously, and said that singing a dirge without a death was like trying to get *kefi*** without drinking wine. 'No, go on, Eleni,' George insisted. 'I promised them. Sing them the one about the English airman. They'll like that.'

'The English airman?'

'Yes, the poor fellow who was shot down at Limeni—just over there—during the war. We gave him a fine funeral and Eleni sang the *miroloy*: we were all very sorry for him.'

She gave a resigned sigh, laid the sock she was knitting in her lap and folded her arms. After collecting herself for a few seconds she began slowly singing in a high thin voice. It was a strange, unseizable tune in a minor key and unspeakably sad and beauti-ful. Whether it was the music or the words, I soon felt a tightening of the throat and pricking behind the eyes and that odd crawling sensation of the nape and scalp that writers must mean when they talk of the hair standing on end. When she finished, her eyes were full of tears. I begged her to sing it again. I transcribe it here, trans-lated word for word, so that nothing should be lost in the attempt to put it into verse:

* In this instance, *kefi* means well-being, high spirits. It has several senses.

He shone among thousands like the sun,
He was a moon among a hundred thousand,
He was the bravest of all the officers.
Such a bright star should never have fallen to the ground.
It was more fitting for him to dine at a king's table,
To eat and drink with a company of a hundred,
To be singled out from three hundred men,
And when he walked abroad for a thousand five hundred to follow
    him.
But it was his destiny to fall to earth here at Limeni
When our allies flew to fight the barbarian Germans.
The English pilot and his comrade fell into the sea here
And the world and the peoples are weeping his sad death.
One was washed ashore here, sorely wounded,
And the word ran from village to village:
'An Englishman is lying on the shore.'
The whole world ran with bandages and lint
To heal the captain's woe and save his life.
But the young man was dead.
So they joined his hands and closed his eyes
And now the whole wide world is weeping;
Weeping for his dew-sprinkled youth
Which was as clear as the cool waters of May.
Bravery was in his step, his motion was that of an eagle,
His face was that of an angel, his beauty like the Virgin Mary's.
His bravery lays us deep in his debt,
For it was for the honour of Greece that he came.
What will his mother and his sisters do without him?
We arrayed our fearless captain like a bridegroom
And men armed with guns bore him along the streets,
And all the world brought wreaths of laurel
So that this hero should be buried, as it was fitting,
Among the olive trees of Saint Saviour.
Let us pray the All-Mighty One and the All-Holy Virgin
That a bomb may fall into the camp of the Germans
And blow their fortress to broken pebbles.
But let us not be touched or harmed
And let the English fly safe home again.

CHAPTER 6

Into the Deep Mani

GEORGE had taken us under his wing. When we set out for the bus that was to carry us further south, there he was wrestling with us for our bags, insisting hotly that we were strangers and guests and that it would be a disgrace to him if we carried them even a step. 'It would bring dishonour on our town,' he said. Again there was the little flutter of salutation as we threaded the lanes of Areopolis. In the space by the bus stop an old man was sitting with his hands crossed over the crook of his stick enjoying the afterglow.

'See that old man?' our guide whispered. 'Guess how old he is.'

'Eighty? Eighty-five?'

'He's a hundred and twenty-seven.'

The old man confirmed this through toothless gums and followed his affirmation with a complacent chuckle. The departure of the bus cut off any further talk, and we rattled across the cobbles knee-deep in poultry on the front seats with bunches of basil and marjoram and rosemary on our laps which Eleni the dirge-singer had sent as a leaving-present. We shook free of the outskirts of the town, and the remains of daylight were fading fast over the gulf below us in a smoky trail of amber and blue-green. A hundred and twenty-seven! He was born two years before Byron died in Missolonghi. George IV, Charles X, and Alexander II were on their thrones, Wellington, Metternich and Talleyrand scarcely more than middle-aged. His earliest memories would include Petrobey at the head of his rough Maniot army, with each guerrilla a bristling porcupine of long-barrelled guns, scimitars, khanjars, yataghans and silver-bossed pistols, lugging bronze cannon across the cobbles of Tsimova ... The first thing he overheard must have been tales of burning towns and pyramids of severed heads, the slaughter of Ibrahim's negro cavalry, decapitations and impalements. Perhaps he heard, across the gulf and the mountains, the sudden roar of the guns from Navarino, and dimly realized, with the sudden clangour of bells, that Greece was free. . . . Speculation proliferated in the falling shadows. The decomposing bus travelled, bucking and rearing, deeper into the Deep Mani. Restless hens clucked underfoot, olive trees whizzed past in the dark. At one stop, outside a rural café, a woman lifted a small boy to the level of our window and told him to take a good look at the strangers. 'He's never seen any before,' she said, apologetically; then added, 'neither have I. . . .'

We pulled up at last at the furthest point the bus could manage on that battered road in the solitary tree-lined street of the village of Pyrgos and found quarters—palliasses stuffed with straw and laid on planks—in the khani. Like so many of them, it was half tavern, half grocer's shop, lit by a hurricane lamp on a table where old men were drinking. The khani-keeper and his wife were a kind, gentle couple, greatly distressed at luxurious Europeans putting up with their summary accommodation. After a supper of beans we were alone in the shop except for our hostess with a black clout tied round her head and her feverish son who lay beside her in the shadows under a pile of blankets. She was winding wool. A black and white cat slept on a sack of groceries. Joan wrote letters and I worked at my notes by the uncertain lamplight. The windows opened on to a moonlit waste of rock and stone, and a little distance off a tall thin tower, silvered by the moon along one of its rectangular flanks, rose into the boiling night. Our pens scratched industriously. Suddenly the innkeeper's wife broke silence.

'What are you writing?' she asked Joan.

'A letter to England.'

'Well, tell them in London that you're in the Mani, a very hot place where there's nothing but stones.'

'That's just what I'm saying.'

* * * *

64

The surrounding rocks appeared even bleaker by day than they had done by moonlight. The rough skyline of the Taygetus had sunk considerably, and the successive humps went leapfrogging southwards in diminishing bounds. The tall tower stood on the edge of the same seaward-sloping ledge as the village and here and there about the stony landscape similar solitary towers rose like pencils. A young policeman on leave offered to accompany us to the nearest and tallest, after which (as '*Pyrgos*' is the Greek for 'tower') the village, like a hundred others in Greece, is presumably named.

It stood there like a blank rectangular Italian campanile or a tall Early English belfry stripped of its gargoyles and finials. It looked doubly tall as there was no pointed doorway, no west window or church's roof-tree to break the line of the eye from base to summit. It was built of massive, well-squared stone. In appearance it was a relic of the Dark Ages and in western Europe it would have been adorned with battered scutcheons. But there was nothing except a clumsily hewn date over the doorway. Inside it was cold and dark. The sunlight filtered through grim slits at the end of diminishing angular funnels cut through walls a yard thick. It suggested a belfry so convincingly that one expected to see ropes disappearing through slots in the thick beam-borne planks overhead, their tallies waiting moth-soft and wine-coloured in mid-air for the grasp of bellringers. There was the familiar creak of the step-ladders, the danger of worm-eaten or missing boards, the same thrusting open of trap-doors as a new layer of cobwebbed emptiness met the eye from floor level; the childish feeling of adventure as storey after storey fell below (how long will it go on?). At last we reached the fifth and highest from which the lower world of olives and rocks and sea appeared in fore-shortened oblongs through apertures which louvres should have sliced into cross-sections. Our interruption had set the dust moving and a thin golden shaft of light falling aslant the dungeon-like gloom was alive with whirling motes. The policeman slapped the cold slabs affectionately.

'This tower belongs to the Sklavonákos family,' he said,

'relations of the Mavromichalis and formerly the great Nyklians of the area.'

I had heard this unfamiliar word *Nyklianos* several times lately and never anywhere else in Greece. What did it mean? It appeared from his answer that the Nyklians, in contrast to the *achamnómeri* or villeins, were a sort of military, landowning aristocracy, a rough-and-ready Maniot version of Japanese feudalism, of which the bey or the *bashkapetan* (above all, the head of the Mavromichalis family) was Shogun, and the greater and lesser Nyklians the daimyos and samurais, some of whom would wander abroad like mercenary rônins. I asked him what on earth the word came from; it means nothing in ordinary Greek. He didn't know, he admitted; then, lighting a cigarette with the engaging bashfulness of a patrician among the plebs, he told us that he himself belonged to the Nyklian family of Glezakos of Glezos. This queer feudalism, an odd deviation from the democratic world of post-Byzantine Greece, sounded so peculiar that I determined to find out more.

Vaults were hewn out of the limestone for the storing of powder kegs and a barrier of heavy boulders enclosed a wide expanse of solid, creased stones like unhewn marble all round the tower. It contained a couple of low stone sheds roofed with slabs and a minute whitewashed oratory. Cisterns drilled out of the hard matrix of rock were reached by a narrow well-shaft with no steyning. Illiterate and feudal, these early war-lords must have lived like tenth-century barons. There was no sign of the amenities anywhere, still less of the arts or of polite learning. We were conjecturing the date of its construction, allowing for every imaginable time lag: we wouldn't be far out, we decided, in the sixteenth century. The date over the door of the tower was, amazingly, 1812.

A tight-meshed network of walls covers this sloping country till the loose ends trail a little distance up the steep flank of the Taygetus and die away among the boulders. They are there for no purpose of delimitation. It is merely a tidy way of disposing of the stones that otherwise cumber the fields in order that, here

and there, an inch of two of dusty earth may afford enough purchase for wheat grains to germinate. A little crescent-shaped
bastion of flat stones shores up the precious soil round the roots
of each olive tree. Winding labyrinths of walled lanes meander
among the walls and trees as arbitrarily, it would seem, as the
walls themselves. The solid rock of the Mani breaks through the
sparse stubble fields in bleached shoulders and whales' backs and
tall leaning blades of mineral and all is as white as bone. Sometimes groups of these blades cluster so thick that they give the
illusion of whole villages; but when you reach them after clam-
bering a score of walls, there they are in all their bare senselessness:
fortuitous dolmens and cromlechs and menhirs. Once in a while,
however, the wreck of an almost prehistoric ghost-village does
appear: a sudden gathering of walls, the shells of half troglodytic
houses with broken slab-roofs and thresholds only to be entered
on all fours, the rough-hewn blocks pitched headlong by wild
olive and cactus with only a rough cross incised on a lintel or a
carved unidentifiable animal to indicate that they date from later
than the stone age. The only other buildings are innumerable
microscopic chapels, their shallow slab-roofed vaults jutting like
the backs of armadilloes; an occasional farmstead, and the abandoned peel-towers of the Nyklians. The pale marble world of
rock and gold stubble and thistle and silver-grey olive-leaves
shudders in the midday glare, and one feels prone to test the
rocks (like spitting on a flat-iron) before daring to lay a hand on
them or to lie down in an olive's fragmentary disc of shade.
The world holds its breath, and the noonday devil is at hand.

In summer, ghosts are said to roam the Mani in the hottest
hour of the day, in winter at the darkest hour of the night. If
their mortal predecessors have been killed by an enemy, they wail
for revenge. Summer ghosts haunt graveyards, ruined churches
and cross roads. A man's blood is supposed to shout out loud the
day before he dies and if he perishes by violence his blood remains wet on the spot until a wooden cross is driven into the
ground there; then it dries up or drains away. (The Maniots
have a death fixation which is almost Mexican; perhaps the

blazing light, the naked rock and the cactuses engender the same processes in either place.) The dead are turned into werewolves until forty days after their death and, stealing indoors at night, they eat the dough out of the kneading-troughs—any trough that is empty when it should be full is a werewolf's work. Witches are said to lead people in a trance up the mountain-side at dead of night to torture them there. Regular sleepwalkers, of which there seem to be a number, are known as the *string-loparméni*, the witch-taken ones. Then there is a terrible devil called Makrynas,* 'the faraway one', who invariably appears in deserted places in the haunted hour of noon. I have not been able to learn what he looks like or what harm he does, but he is usually encountered by women who run away shrieking in panic through the rocks and olives. Could he be Pan himself, up to his old game with the latterday descendants of Syrinx and Echo? The nereids, the oreads, the dryads, the hamadryads and the gorgons all survive transposed in the minds of country Greeks. The Faraway One may be the chief woodland god himself.

Belief in the prophetic importance of dreams, a pan-Hellenic superstition, is even stronger here than in the rest of Greece. In Greece, one 'sees' a dream, but the exegesis of what one sees varies from region to region. In the Mani, in unconscious con-formity with many modern theories, it goes by opposites. The dream-taste of sweetness or the sight of sweet things—cakes or a honeycomb, for instance—spell poison and bitterness; flowers mean sorrow, churches are law-courts and prison, a roofless house is a grave, eggs—the symbol of paschal concord—foretell high words and a quarrel; a prison is freedom and lice are money; and so on. There are some exceptions to this system. Dream-beards and -hair mean trouble, birds foretell damage, a pool of water lying in the road threatens difficulties; a gun presages the birth of a boy, a handkerchief that of a girl. To have meaning, a dream must be short—a sort of illuminating flash. Long dreams are attributed to indigestion and discounted. They can also be dis-

* It is also a local name for the Taygetus, so it might be a kind of spirit of the range.

regarded when the earth is open at the time of ploughing and sowing. If a dream seems totally irrelevant it may be the case of a wrong address, as they are sometimes delivered by mistake to people with the same name as the true destinatory. The dreamer must try and find out the real addressee and hand the dream over. If the explanation is not clear there are old men in each village with mantic powers. They cross-examine the dreamer like expert diagnosticians. 'So you saw some birds, eh? Flying low or high? From left or right? Were they big or small? Did they perch on branches or settle on the rocks?' They listen carefully to the answers and click their tongues concernedly, admitting they don't like the look of it, or pat the patient on the back, saying he has nothing whatever to worry about. In either case they prescribe a course of action. One is reminded of Hector and Polydamas before the attack on the Achaean ships.

There was not a single school in the Mani until the 1830's and it is without a doubt the most backward part of Greece. Hence the almost total absence of literature and culture. The sombre traditions of the region continued unhindered for centuries. There are other symptomatic observances of these traditions apart from the general concentration on death and revenge. There was always great rejoicing over the birth of a son——'another gun for the family!'—in fact the male children were referred to as 'guns'—and after the appearance of a first-born son, each visitor bringing a gift would fire off a shot before entering with the wish that the newcomer might live and open the way for others to follow. Figs and *raki* from Kalamata were offered to the guests in his honour. With girls it was the opposite. There were neither gifts nor rejoicing nor congratulations; they were only useful as gun-breeders and drudges and dirge-singers. There are no dowries; the groom's family provides the house and its gear and donkey-loads of grain. A sun is carved or painted on the cradle of a baby boy, a moon on that of a little girl.

There are no *panagyria* (those joyful rustic kermesses that celebrate saints' days in the rest of Greece), no singing or dancing. Like all south-eastern Europe, the gloomy passion for virginity reigns supreme, a prize reserved for a loveless match, and the usual bloodthirsty sanctions for infidelity prevail. Understandably, it seldom occurs. Only men are mourned at their death, but women wear black for even their remotest male relations. The women's life is one of constant toil—in the house or the fields, at the olive press or at neolithic handmills which are a sort of unwieldy pestle and mortar. They set off to reap far-away corn patches, sickle in hand, their wooden emblematic cradles slung papoose-like from their shoulders. When the cisterns dry up in summer, they trudge for miles with kegs on their backs to fill with brackish water near the sea at one of the half-dozen trickles of the Deep Mani. The maledictions of the Mani are supposed to be the bitterest and the most effective in Greece.

Life, in fact, is wretchedly poor and overcast with sadness. In the past it was entirely shadowed by the blood feud. The thing that kept the Maniots going was their fierce sense of liberty, their pride in living in one of the earliest places in Greece to have cast free of the Turks. It is very seldom that a Maniot enters domestic service. Maniot beggars are unknown. Cattle theft does not exist, and doors are never locked. It is part of their regional pride that prompts them to dismiss the inhabitants of the outside world as 'Vlachs'. At last I learnt the meaning of the word which had so puzzled me the day we arrived in the Mani! It has nothing to do with the nomads of the Pindus. A Vlach is a plain-dweller, a descendant of *rayahs*, a *vile bourgeois*, and Maniots who leave the peninsula to live like them are said, with accents of scorn, to have 'gone Vlach'.

It is a life of bitter hardship. One last superstition is very moving. If a woman has lost a male child (a 'gun'), she carries her next-born son out into the street in her apron shouting, 'A lamb for sale. Who'll buy a lamb?' 'I will,' says the first passer-by. He pays a small sum, stands godfather to him at the font, then hands the lamb back to its mother. It is a ruse to cheat Charon by confusing the familiar track with a false scent.

*   *   *   *

The Nyklian policeman rolled over and awoke under the olive tree, where we had talked ourselves into the blessed somnolence of a siesta, and led us in the cool of the evening along one of those stony lanes that wandered down the slope towards the sea to show us the old church of Michael the Taxiarch,* in the minute village of Charouda. The little place was surrounded by positive orchards of prickly pear, some of them growing over twenty feet high: vast branching tangles of green ping-pong bats and of malformed fleshy hands bristling with fierce needles, their rims equipped with half a dozen bulbous thumbs. The church was a little golden basilica standing among cypresses and topped with a brood of cupolas gathered round a central dome. The walls inside were beautifully frescoed, the usual saintly figures evolving across the plaster walls with an elegant and loose-limbed freedom. There are many of these engaging little churches in the Mani. They absorbed all the available grace and piety that existed in the stony breasts of the old Maniots. Occasionally they are Athonite and cruciform but usually basilican: the square centre of the katholikon is flanked by two short aisles, and ended by three apses. Massive stone beams spanned with golden diameters the four semi-circular arches that bore the pendentives from which the dome grew; similar horizontals enclosed the lesser arches and crossed the top of the iconostasis and all these beams, like the capitals that topped the pillars, were carved with a rough intricacy of bosses and crosslets and Byzantine motives of leaves and bunches of grapes and sunflowers. Over the door a complex skein of calligraphic Byzantine abbreviations, conjoined letters and ligatures unravelled itself into a dedicatory inscription and the information that the church was built by 'the humble Roman, Michael Kardianos'; *Romaiòs*, of course, meaning Byzantine, a Greek of the Roman Empire of the East. Why is it stated? What other nationality can have been there to make this worth mentioning? For once the Nyklian was at a loss. The date followed,

* *Taxiarch*, in the Greek army, is the rank of brigadier. In orthodox hagiography, it is the epithet of the Archangel Michael, the commander of the Heavenly Host.

always a conundrum in Byzantine churches, as the numbers are written in the tormenting old Greek way—which makes ancient mathematical computation a nightmare even to think of—with oddly arranged letters of the alphabet and appended apostrophes, and additional peculiar symbols arbitrarily inserted into the alphabetical system for 6, 90, 900 and 6000. Add to this that the Byzantine epigraphic script, like certain flowery Arabic inscriptions, is more an intricate means of decoration than a device for conveying information; add to this again that if it is painted, the paint is usually half defaced, and if carved, chipped into semi-illegibility; add finally that the dates are reckoned not from the birth of Christ but from 5508 B.C. (an oddly hard figure to remember), the Biblical date of the Creation—which must be subtracted from the date inscribed—and the reader will have some idea of the difficulties of deciphering the dates for someone as bad at any kind of figures as I am. I often get it wrong, even after ten minutes with pencil and paper, and I plainly did so in this case, as my notebook says the Taxiarch was founded in 1211, and a reference book says 1373; or rather, it was founded in 6881 as opposed to 6719; not ͵ϛφιθ' but ͵ϛωπα',* during the wars of John VI Cantacuzene and John V Palaeologue, in fact, as opposed to the short-lived Frankish empire of Byzantium to which I had assigned it. Nothing could be simpler. . . .

Perhaps, then, the founder's race was worth mentioning to show that he was an Orthodox Byzantine and not one of the Catholic Venetians who were by then established in the Messenian peninsula or one of the Frankish barons of the Peloponnese; a proud affirmation that the Empire was Greek—Romaic—once more, and the Mani part of the Orthodox Byzantine Despotate of the Morea.

The stony churchyard had several new graves. Burial is a problem here, as the earth is seldom more than a few inches deep and hacking trenches out of the rock with adzes must be a back-

---

* The strange first digit is the symbol for 6, not a terminal sigma. The preceding inverted apostrophe makes it 6000. It is also the Byzantine abbreviation for the combined letters *sigma* and *tau*. . . .

breaking task. I had been told that the dead in some parts of the Mani are buried in their shrouds, as wood is too scarce for coffins; they are borne to the churchyard on a ceremonial coffin or a bier; then, after the *miroloyia*, lifted off and laid in the shallow graves for their temporary sojourn. The same recesses must be used many times over. These new graves of Charouda were adorned at their heads with something I had never seen before; two rough thick sticks stuck in the ground at an angle of forty-five degrees, crossing in saltire with white rags twisted untidily round their upper ends, like so many uncouth St. Andrew's crosses. They were the staves, the Nyklian said, with which the pall-bearers had carried the coffins. Why were they planted in that position? Nobody knew. They had an oddly pagan aspect, like part of the gear of a voodoo tonnelle. Again, the late conversion of the Mani came to mind and the possibility that here again was a pagan survival; or some uncouth shamanistic practice the Meligs had brought with them from central Asia or the Great Balkan range and, before their absorption, bequeathed to these newly baptized mountains.

Catchments like swimming baths were squared out of the rock to drain off and husband in the wells every available drop of water. Sitting in an upper room in the house of a friend of the policeman, we watched the daughter of the house drawing water from a deep well leading to a cistern in the white rock. What a time it took till the half brackish, half sweet and slightly cloudy liquid appeared; it was as if the delay were caused by slow and tender decanting in some subterranean cave! She put the jug on the table in the darkening room and a plate of prickly pears, peeled of their thorny coating but full of pips; also a plate of lupin seeds, and a flask of *ouzo*. Poor Maniots! The policeman sighed and said that he sometimes woke up in the night, thinking of a glass of crystal spring water. Sometimes he dreamed of yoghourt and cakes—*baklavas*, *trigonas* and *kadaifs*. Trouble, poison and bitterness, in dream language, I thought, to go by his talk of the afternoon.

There is little enough in the Deep Mani. Pigs are the only

important livestock with, fortunately, abundant prickly pears to
feed them on as well as their masters. A few thin goats keep alive
on thistles. A little corn and oats are the only crops; beans, garlic,
artichokes and these lupin seeds the only garden produce; plenty
of olives, a few almond and fig and carob trees; otherwise nothing but cactus and thorns and stones. The bread used to be made
of maize, beans and vetch till wheat began to arrive at the beginning of the century, and there was more of everything since
they had built the road to Pyrgos. Two cheerful phenomenally
old men in cartwheel hats had joined us. They settled slowly with
joints cracking like cap-pistols, and the girl leant back against the
wall with her arms folded. Like many of the girls we had seen
in this queer region, she was extremely beautiful: a pale, clear
face both virginal and spiritual with an intensely aristocratic bone
structure, and large, dark, Shulamitish eyes. When she leant forward to pour the *ouzo* or tip out a new plateful of lupin seeds
she put her left hand across her breast to keep her long thick
plaits from sweeping across the table, leaning back again afterwards in attentive silence, her face alert and smiling. Her
few gestures were deft and distinguished and informed by a
patrician lack of fuss. It was a miracle that these waterless rocks,
alongside the cactuses and the thorns, could give birth to her as
well.

The shades of evening were obliterating those mountains.
Bit by bit the last rearguard of the cicadas had fallen silent.
Outside, the desolate spinney of gesticulating ping-pong bats was
hardening into silhouette and the sun was disappearing in a sad
elaborate pavane over the bare sea. Bare, because the Messenian
peninsula had been drawing away westwards to its ultimate
cape as we moved down the Mani and now had died away. Due
west of the window the sea ran unencumbered for hundreds of
miles in a straight line, until, just missing the southernmost rocks
of Sicily, it broke on the far-away Carthaginian coast. I watched
the conflagration die in a suitable mood of sunset melancholy,
that affliction of northern people in the Mediterranean. *Son-
nenuntergangstraurigkeit!* It was a sudden feeling of exile and

strangeness and of the limitlessness of history which left these Maniots untouched.

Their discourse of livestock reminded me all at once of the last injunctions of George Katzimbalis in the Plaka before leaving Athens, '... dirges, yes, wonderful dirges! And I believe they have extraordinary bullfights! *Des corps à corps!* They're all tremendously strong fellows with biceps like this,' his eyes became twin beads of urgency as he extended his thumb and fingers like gauging calipers agape to their utmost; 'they catch hold of them by the horns and wrestle with them for hours, tiring them out —the bulls are tremendous brutes—and then with a sudden twist of their arms,' George's fists, grasping ghost-horns, described two brisk semi-circles, 'they whirl the whole bull round in mid-air, yes, in mid-air—*crac!*—and bring it down flat on its back in a cloud of dust!'

I asked the Nyklian and the old men what they knew about wrestling with bulls in the Mani; about *tavromachia* . . .? There was a bewildered pause.

'Wrestling with bulls?' one of them said. 'I've never heard of it.'

'Never,' the other said.

'For one thing,' said the Nyklian, 'there are no bulls in the Mani.'

'No cows either,' said one of the old men.

'Not even a calf,' said the other.

'Or a tin of bully beef,' said the beautiful girl.

'In fact the only horned animals in the Mani, except the goats,' whispered the old man beside me (a bachelor, whom some years in the tin mines of Lavrion in the nineties had endued with a tang of obsolete urban sophistication), 'are the husbands.' With a thumb like a fossil, he indicated his neighbour whose ravaged gums parted to allow a thin wheeze of tickled laughter to escape,*

---

* Jokes like this, I have noticed, are only risked in regions where such a suspicion is unthinkable. In the feuds of the Mani, infidelity or questions of female honour are the rarest of all *casus belli*, in the same way that blasphemous oaths and profanity are always most prevalent in communities where religious belief and practice are unchallenged.

and everyone began to laugh. Quietly at first, and then the idea of the phantom bulls began to grow on us. 'Bulls indeed!' The dark room was soon ringing with hilarity. 'Bulls in the Mani!' One of the old men leant forward in a horn-grasping posture, 'The very idea . . .' The girl filled the glasses again, holding her plaits back and laughing happily. Tears of laughter had begun to flow by now. 'Plenty of pigs!' said one of the old men. 'Yes, we could wrestle with pigs,' said the other, mopping a rheumy eye. The Nyklian policeman lifted his glass and said:

'Here's to the bulls of the Mani, the best breed in Greece.'*

* In point of fact, George Katsimbalis may have been nearer the truth than my interlocutors. The association of the Mani and bullfighting was implanted in his mind by the brilliant short story 'Petrakas' by Spilio Passayanni, himself a Maniot, describing just such an encounter.

CHAPTER 7

Dark Towers

THE Deep Mani road still hobbled on for a few miles, the cratered and rock-strewn surface becoming more lunar in aspect with each advancing furlong. We got a lift along it next morning in a brittle-looking lorry full of water melons for the thirsty Maniots. The three young fruiterers, with *tango* moustaches and side-whiskers, plastic belts, bi-coloured shoes and coloured combs projecting from their hip pockets, seemed queerly townish after the rough-hewn peninsulars. A skittish little celluloid can-can dancer jerked to and fro on a string before the driver; the other two, buried to the waist in dark green footballs, clutched the sides to avoid being unhorsed, groaning a *mánga* song about the last tram rattling through the rainy streets of Athens. The road petered out into a stony foot-path. Half a dozen mules were waiting, and the three fruiterers unloaded their wares with the skill and speed of Rugby-forwards passing, then drove off waving towards the delights of Gytheion or Kalamata. A muleteer took our stuff, promising to leave it at a *kaphenion* in Yeroliména where we could collect it next day, and the cavalcade set off in a column of dust. The grooves of chariot wheels over these rocks are an indication that transport facilities have declined since ancient times. On the foothills of the Taygetus stood the villages of Vamvaka and Mina spiky with Nyklian towers, the latter dominated by one immense campanile. But we took a lane running seawards steeply down to the derelict village and the little bay of Mezapo.

This small combe whose rocky sides were asprawl with the cactus-choked shells of earthquake-shattered towers was deserted except for two half-naked men sifting gravel (who knocked off for a cigarette and a short chat about politics; both were eager Royalists) and a woman flinging coloured rugs onto the sea: floating parallelograms of lemon yellow, brick red and magenta, which, up to her thighs in water, she was thrashing with a heavy stake. A little boat lay beached and after a search through the ruins we discovered a haggard boatman sitting gazing at an enormous fish about a yard and a half long which was stretched before him on the pebbles. Great gashes showed where the head and the dorsal fin had been cut off. He said it was a *palamida*—a kind of tunny—but the head, which he said he had thrown away, had been severed so far back that the awful suspicion that it might have been a shark flitted through our minds. It was steely blue on the back, a colour which faded through paling gun-metal to a white belly. As he was off to Pyrgos to sell it that afternoon he told his daughter and son to row us across to the Tigani. The girl was twelve and the boy eight and both looked half-wild. We asked her about sharks. After a great deal of hesitation she told us, with her eyes protruding as she rested on her heavy scull, that a vast fish had been landed last year and when they opened it, a man's hand and an army boot were discovered inside. Asked if any had appeared since, she shut her eyes and flung back her head in a shocked negative.

The Tigani is a spit of rock like the handle of a frying pan (which is what the name means) stretching from the other side of the bay three miles from Mezapo and expanding at the end to a great high rock. This is covered with a ruin: the Castle of the Mani, the Maina, or in French, *le Magne*—from which the whole region takes its name. It was built by William II de Ville-hardouin, fourth Frankish prince of the Morea, in 1248, and was one of the three great fortresses defending his domain of the south-eastern Peloponnese; the other two were Mistra and Monemvasia. All three fell to the Byzantines after their crushing victory over the Frankish chivalry at Pelagonia and became bastions of the Byzantine Despotate of Mistra. The connecting pan-handle is a filament made of wicked cones and serrated jags of

rock pocked every few yards with salt pans. The rocks felt
as sharp as razor-blades through our rope soles. A shadowless,
desolate wilderness. In this pitiless glare, two tatterdemalion and
barefoot women, a mother and daughter in antique straw hats
as wide as umbrellas, their faces burnt black by the sun and
eyebrows and tangled hair caked white with dried brine, were
gathering rock-salt in broad wicker baskets. They worked here
all summer, they said, and sometimes in the winter too, sleeping
in the huge cave by the chapel of the Hodygytria (Our Lady of
Guidance), where there was a little spring of brackish water for
them to drink and dip their *paximadia*. It wasn't much of a life,
the mother said. How much could they sell the salt for? It was
the equivalent, in drachmae, of sixpence an oka. And how much
could they gather in a day? On good days, she said, a bit more
than an oka; on bad days, rather less. It all depended. Then she
threw back her head and let out a laugh of genuine amusement
in which there was not a trace of bitterness.

They led us nimbly on their bare feet from rock to rock until
we reached a shallow, stepped ramp for cavalry leading up the
bluff of stone to the sally-port of the castle. How horses can ever
have made their way across that jagged wilderness remains a
mystery. Most of the walls are down, scarcely an arch remains
and the maze of corridors and courtyards are now a vast chaos
of large limestone blocks chopped from the sides of the rock on
which the fortress stands. Countless wells sank to deep cisterns,
one for each day of the year, said the woman. The castle must
have been colossal. She told us that it had once been owned by a
beautiful young princess; but a powerful king came with many
ships and captured it after a long siege. The princess, rather than
fall into his hands, mounted a white horse, spurred it to a gallop
and leapt over the parapet, down into the sea below, where the
horse, breasting the waters of the bay, bore her to safety. . . .
With her forefinger, the woman outlined a round slot in the rock
which was dented there by one of the horse's hind hooves as he
leapt into the void.

Another legend, embodied in verse, tells of a mysterious

79

potentate, Mavroeidis, the Black-Shaped One, who brought a 'five-times' beautiful princess here against her will, to make her his wife. He fortified the castle with steel and iron from the country of the Franks, adorned it with crystal from Venice and with pearls and marble from Constantinople, filled the tanks with glittering goldfish and imprisoned the princess in a tower of bright glass. But Charon galloped up on his black horse and challenged the castellan. They fought in full armour on a steel threshing floor. The sinister duel went on for hours until at last the Black-Shaped One was down. Charon compelled him to bring the girl from her glass tower and pointed ominously along the coast to the last wave-beaten cape. There, he cried, lay the path; he was taking them to his cavern in the cliff side. It led to the Underworld and the land of Tartarus where the dead lived: a pitch-dark warren hung with cobwebs, all its branching caves softly padded with the tresses of beautiful maidens. They were never seen again.* (Taenarus, the ancient entrance to Hades, lies about fifteen miles from here as the crow flies.)

At the extremity of the peninsula the castle wall jutted above a sheer drop in a rampart cloudy with cystus and thyme and overhung with swags of elderflower that filled the air with a scent one might expect more readily at Bodiam or Pevensey than among the battlements of this Grecian headland. Lizards darted over the hot slabs and froze at gaze in stances of arrested action. It was odd to think of Frankish sentinels shouting the alarm here, at the sight of Byzantine or Saracenic galleys, in the patois of Normandy and Champagne; of the fair-haired garrison hauling mangonels to the battlements under the fluttering lion rampant of the Villehardouin. . . . To the north-west hung the phantoms of the Messenian Cape and to the north cape after cape of the Mani followed each other, each growing dimmer in a succession of uptilted table mountains. The sea blazed with gold from the horizon to the spiked base of the rock, where it was a purplish blue that turned green in the shallows. The rock blades were

* Much of the imagery of this poem suggests a kinship with Byzantine poems of the Akritic Cycle.

rimmed with white foam. I threw a stone which took several seconds on its trajectory. It fell back almost out of sight so that I had to crane forward like a gargoyle to see it strike the sea, its faint plop startling a cloud of gulls from their ledges; they circled mewing above the slowly expanding disc of white foam.

Back among the salt pans, the woman offered us a drink from their pitcher and a share of their *paximadia* and dried olives. This little store was hidden on a shadowy ledge along with their shoes. We refused and tried in vain to give them some money for showing us the castle. It was quite impossible. We left them there under their immense hats, growing smaller with each oar-stroke. I often think of them. They are probably scraping for salt among those infernal rocks at this very second.

* * * *

We got out of the boat on a lonely, crescent-shaped ledge of rock that almost surrounded a deep blue pool. The children rowed back to their ruined village and we dived out of the blaze of the noonday into the cool world below. It was a blue-green paradise of submarine canyons and grottoes and rock shelves with copses of dark green seaweed. But when, after lying comatose in the sun, we dressed and tried to strike inland again, the rock wall (which had looked so easy from the sea) was unscalable. It was only after wading and scrambling along the shore for half an hour that we could find a way up a slithering landslide that threatened to deposit us into the sea below at every step. At last, panting, thorn-riddled, caked with salt and dust and bitterly regretting the woman's pitcher of water, we levered ourselves onto the blank Mani again and stumbled up an endless lane of rolling pebbles and ankle-snapping boulders in the stagnant glare. The sun and the sea had unhinged our joints, turned our limbs to lead and our throats to limekilns. 'Tell them you're in a hot place called the Mani, where there is nothing but stones'; the words of the innkeeper's wife rattled around in our empty brain pans. There was not a tree to relieve the skull-like blankness. The miracle of the afternoon wind had failed; the balloon had not gone up. At last, turning a shoulder of rock, two broken towers came in sight in a clump of prickly pear. Our spirits revived at the thought of water. But, hard as we knocked on their doors, nobody opened; a thing which was all the more strange as a middle-aged man peered at us through the bars of an upper window. So we dragged ourselves from the doorstep and the harrowing trek continued. But at the top of the next switchback of lane the sight below made us wipe the sweat from our stinging eyes and gaze.

On the other side of a hot valley rose a long saddle of rock on either end of which a village was gathered and each village was a long solid sheaf of towers. There were scores of them climbing into the sky in a rustic metropolis, each tower seeming to vie with the others in attaining a more preposterous height: a vision as bewildering as the distant skyline of Manhattan or that first apparition of gaunt medieval skyscrapers that meets the eye of the traveller approaching San Giminiano across the Tuscan plain. But there were no bridges or ships here, no bastioned town wall or procession of cypresses to detract from the bare upward thrust of all these perpendiculars of sun-refracting facet and dark shadow. The tops were sawn off flat, the gun slits invisible. These two mad villages of Kitta and Nomia shot straight out of the rock in a grove of rectangular organ pipes, their sides facing in every direction so that some of the towers were flanked with a stripe of shade, some turned bare and two-dimensional towards the sun, others twisted in their sockets and seeming to present two visible and equal sides, one in light and one in shade, of symmetrical prisms. Nothing moved and in the trembling and fiery light they had the hallucinating improbability of a mirage.

We crossed the intervening ossuary of hillside and stepped inside the nearest town. The canyons of lane that twisted through the towers were empty and silent as though the inhabitants had fled an aeon ago or a plague had reaped them all in an afternoon. And yet there were signs of recent life: a dozen sacks of dried carob-pods in a courtyard, a child's cart made out of a box and fitted with castors of cotton-reels, a scythe leaning against an iron-studded door. A cat stretched sound asleep along the coping of a wall. Cobbles or slabs of stone alternated with the muffling dust underfoot and tower after tower soared on either hand. The town was empty or locked in catalepsy, paralysed in a spell of sleep which seemed unbreakable. The main square was scarcely larger than a room, and the steep ascending planes of masonry that elbowed it in on all sides lent it the aspect of the bottom of a dried-up well from whose floor sprang a few motionless mulberry trees. The heat and stagnation, the heavy breathlessness of the air and the warm smell of the dust cast a mantle of utter strangeness over this town. It seemed not Greece at all but a dead city of Algeria or Mauretania that a marauding desert tribe had depopulated and abandoned, vanishing into the Sahara or the Atlas mountains three lustres ago. An admonishing silence hung in the air enjoining the newcomer to walk on tiptoe and laying a finger across his lips.

We soon stopped our vain and sacrilegious tattoo on the shutters of the only shop and settled under a stone loggia in speechless exhaustion. The walls of the little square were white-washed in a dado several yards high and the worn ledge of a stone seat ran all the way round. Misspelt slogans in lurching black characters across the whitewash cried *Long Live the King!* Another said *long live eternal Greece*, and a third, *Death to all Traitors*. Even the cicadas in this necropolis were silent.

Our torpor was broken at length by the appearance of an old woman in black with a face like a flint. She clicked her tongue in commiseration and padded quickly away, returning with a pitcher and a glass and a plate of prickly pears, saying she had sent her great-granddaughter to rouse the shopkeeper. He arrived, tousled with sleep and repeating, as he unlocked the shutters, that it was a shame we had been made to wait. 'In Kitta, too!' he said waving his hand at the towers. 'I'm sure it wouldn't happen to me in London. . . .' I had a vision of his solitary and despairing figure in a mysteriously deserted Piccadilly, squatting with arms akimbo on the steps of Eros's statue in a heat wave . . .

He spread a table under a mulberry tree and loaded it with

fried eggs, chopped tomatoes, onions, garlic and some bitter wine and forked lumps of pickled pork dripping in oil out of a heavy jar. (This is called *Syglino*, and though very salt, it is excellent.) Our benefactress had been joined by one of her gossips, another fierce nonagenarian; they sat croaking together, leaning over their sticks on the stone seat under *Death to all Traitors*. There was something baleful about these two black-coiffed figures under the snarl of the slogan: they looked implacable and fate-spinning crones. I remembered that in the old days of the Deep Mani, when their toiling and gun-breeding days were past, the role of the old Maniot women resolved itself into the three functions of fostering the birth of more and more 'guns' among their descendants, instilling them with hatred of their enemies by egging them on to vengeance, and singing dirges for the dead. The *miroloy* being in a way their one means of self-expression, and skill in keening the only way to fame and consideration, the proliferation of guns and the fostering of feuds by exhortations to revenge and the ensuing bloodshed became matters of vital importance, a question of supply and demand; no guns and feuds, no dirges . . . I felt ashamed of this uncharitable fancy when the second old woman croaked an order to a small descendant and made him milk his goat into a glass, and bring us as a gift the warm and foaming contents. . . .

As the heat subsided, the *rouga*—for that is the name of these little squares in tower-villages (the one in Kitta is further distinguished by the nickname of the Nest)—began to fill with black headkerchiefs and circular hats. The men were the darkest Maniots I had so far encountered. By the time we left, the bench was crowded and the *rouga*, like a room at a party, was covered with standing and operatically interchanging groups, while the towers overhead echoed with the thick dialect of the region. Kitta fell behind us, the towers laying lath-like shadows across the hillside which were broken by boulders and buckled by the fall and upheaval of the ground. It is the ancient Messe 'famous for its doves', once mentioned by Homer as having sent a contingent to swell the host of Agamemnon before Troy. Dusk was gathering as we entered the great stook of towers called Nomia, and the gulfs between them were a-twitter with wheeling bats. A young man from Kitta had befriended us, taking us to dine at his uncle's in the nearby village of Kechriánika, which lay in the middle of a thick wood. Just before the trees swallowed us up, we looked back at the faintly discernible towers of Kitta and Nomia where lights were beginning to twinkle.

'Nyklianika meri!' he said in accents of wonder. 'Nyklian places!'

After a convivial supper we all lay down to sleep under the little oak trees on soft pallets of brightly-coloured blankets and pillows like stones of destiny. A little owl had settled somewhere near in the branches and its thin cry punctuated the long wail of a klephtic song from the village where someone was leaning back and sending up a scanned baying of the moon.

CHAPTER 8

A Warlike Aristocracy and
the Maniots of Corsica

THE time has come to sort out my gleanings about the
mysterious Nyklians and workings of the blood feud. The
former I owe almost entirely to the notes assembled by
Mr. Dimitrakos-Messisklis in his fine and little-known book,* as
nobody in the Mani seemed very clear about their origins. The
latter—about which they know everything—I owe to conversa-
tions with Maniots in a dozen different villages.

In 1295, during one of those civil wars that did much, between
the reigns of the Frankish emperors and the Turkish capture of
Constantinople, to weaken what was left of the restored Byzantine Empire, Andronicus II Palaeologue sacked Nykli in Arcadia.
This town, on the site of which Tripoli now stands, was originally
a colony of Spartans from Amoukli. When the Morea was conquered by the Franks, Nykli, owing to its position at a centre
of communications, became strategically important and the seat
of a powerful barony; and when the Frankish power began to
decline, it was largely inhabited by those strange hybrids of Greek
and Frankish blood known as 'gasmouli'. Sometimes the French
language and the Catholic religion prevailed, sometimes Greek
and the Orthodox, though the tendency to Hellenism and Orthodoxy increased with time. After the attack of Andronicus, not
one stone was left on another, and the Nyklians fled. A number of
them (according to my authority) took the steep but well-worn
tracks across the Taygetus to the south of the thinly populated

* See page 27.

86

Mani, settling in exactly the regions of which I have just been writing. Their headquarters, in fact, were at Kitta, and the name may have some kinship with the Frankish words *cité* or *città*.* From them, perhaps (for all here is nebulous), ideas of a feudal hierarchy, modified by the wild ways of the Mani, caught on. When the Mani filled up during the following centuries and struggles for local power were engaged between village and village and family and family, *Nyklian* was the word used to apply to those that came out on top. Before, life in the Mani had been semi-troglodytic, uncouth in the extreme, but fairly pacific. Now, families began to fortify themselves behind thick walls and under slab-roofs. Quarrels and feuds for the elbow room of families increased with the thickening population, and the chaos lasted from the fourteenth century until late in the nineteenth. Those that shook themselves out of the ruck, then, were the Nyklians; the subjugated ruck were the *achamnómeroi*, the hinds or villeins. There is something very strange about these centuries of struggle for local dominion over those barren stones; for the grazing rights on the rare blades of grass and possession of the ledges where corn could grow and olive trees take root and for salt-gathering rights along the awful shores. The Nyklians always established themselves on high ground and they alone had the right to roof their houses with slabs of marble. The villeins were forced to inhabit the lower parts of the villages, their thin roofs well within range of the Nyklian towers. These humble helots were forbidden to support their roofs with semi-circular arches like their betters and they were often referred to merely as 'the donkeys' by the Nyklians. They were subjected to every kind of contumely and scorn. They were, however, allowed to carry arms, and they would help their Nyklian overlords in inter-Nyklian strife and piratical expeditions. Some, endowed with an unusual share of valour or cunning, would raise themselves to Nyklian status, and be accepted as such; but, though it was considered no shame for a Nyklian to marry a villein girl, it was a disgrace for a Nyklian girl to marry a villein. It was, in a sense, an open aristocracy,

* *op. cit.*

though the sword was the only key. It goes without saying that when, about 1600, the first towers began to change the skyline of Mani villages, they were an exclusively Nyklian prerogative.

As time passed, the power of the Nyklians acquired the patina of continuity, and their pride of race grew. The boast of Spartan origins was stiffened in many cases by claims of imperial or noble Byzantine descent, and, in a few cases, of kinship with the great feudal families of the Franks. With the passage of generations and the branching of offshoot families, clans were formed, and into these, it seems, minor Nyklians and even villein families were welcomed. But, though no records were kept, there was always a consciousness of who were, or were not, kith and kin. Their boasts were again reinforced by feats of arms against the Turks; and, of course, against each other. As the population grew, several Nyklian families would often inhabit the same village, each of them determined to dominate the rest and grasp the kapetanship. To do this they had to be in a position to destroy their competitors' houses by bombarding them from above with boulders and smashing their marble roofs; so the towers began to grow, each in turn, during periods of truce, calling his neighbours' bluff with yet another storey, and so climbing further into the air until they were all perched at the top of fantastic pinnacles. Apart from tactical considerations, the standing of a family was assessed, as it was in San Giminiano and Tarquinia and Bologna, by the height of its towers, with the result that villages thickly populated with Nyklians jut from the limestone like bundles of petrified asparagus.

Something of the same feudal hierarchy prevailed in the Outer Mani, but everything went more smoothly there. Villages and districts accepted one family as their kapetan and usually this heredity went unchallenged. The head of the kapetans was the archikapetano or *bashkapetan* whereas in the Deep Mani, where there were several Nyklians competing in each village for the chieftainship, no permanent *status quo* existed and a family could only maintain its position by force. It was of overriding importance, for a family determined to remain on top, to breed more and more guns. In many cases the immediate struggle of day-to-day warfare was only a symptom of the year-to-year breeding-race; they were often neck-and-neck. Hence the double delight over the birth of a gun, the rejoicing that surrounded a sun-cradle, the sorrow over a moon; in a dozen years each of the guns would be able to grasp a match-lock. In this world of chronic anarchy it is obvious that anyone who hoped to rule over such a people must be strong in towers and guns and wealth and prestige: which conditions held true with all the Beys of the Mani—though the Deep Mani often refused to recognize this omnipotence—but especially true of Zanetbey Grigorakis and truest of all of Petrobey Mavromichalis, Deep Maniot of Deep Maniots, and Nyklian of Nyklians.

Wherever the blood feud reigns, some system of mitigation, some code of rules, is automatically evolved; or life, already a hazardous business, would become unlivable. The Corsicans obey certain unwritten laws. The Sicilians have their *omertà*, the Albanians and the Epirotes the *bessa* system and even the Cretans, who have less inhibitions than any about their *oikogeneiaka*—their 'family troubles'—admit a few vetoes and conventions. They have the same purpose as the laws of chivalry in the barbarism of the Dark Ages. The lack of any of these limitations, in spite of certain links with the comparative respectability of the *mafia*, is perhaps the most notable aspect of gang-warfare in large American towns.

Though the Maniots use the Italian word, the vendettas of the Mani were originally a matter of clan or family, not individual, warfare. They were rarely launched, as they are in Crete today, by a slight or an insult to the *philotimo*,* feminine honour, the forcible abduction of a bride by a party of braves, cattle-rustling or any momentary cause. The killing of one Deep Maniot would certainly have his family up in arms, determined to 'get the blood back', to avenge the dead kinsman by the death, not necessarily

* *Amour propre*, for the time being. I shall have to enlarge on this complicated word in a later book.

of the guilty man but of the pick of the offending family, which was deemed corporately responsible for the crime. But they were usually launched after family conclaves, with a definite object in view, which was no less than the total annihilation of an opposing Nyklian family, the number of whose guns and the height of whose towers offered a challenge to the village hegemony.

In these contests, the first blow was never struck without warning. War was formally declared by the challenging side. The church bells were rung: *We are enemies! Beware!* Then both sides would take to their towers, the war was on, and any means of destroying the other side was fair. The feud would often continue for years, during which it was impossible for either faction to leave their towers by daylight. Water, supplies, powder and shot were smuggled in at night and the gun slits bristled with long barrels which kept up a regular fusillade all day long. If they were in range and lower down, the enemies' roofs would be smashed with flung rocks and sleepers were shot at night by enemies creeping up and firing through chinks in the wall or through windows imprudently left unguarded. Marksmen were sent out on *khosia*, as it is called, to lie in wait for isolated enemies in lonely places—behind rocks, up dark lanes or in the branches of trees—to pick them off, cut them down with a sword or stab them to death. It was the aim of each side to destroy any member of the other, but it was a double success if they killed a prominent one. Sallies from the towers were sometimes made and gun-fights moved from street to street while the rest of the village remained prudently indoors. The rough jottings of a primitive Deep Maniot surgeon in the eighteenth century show, by the astonishing number of scimitar and yataghan and dagger wounds recorded in his practice, that hand-to-hand battles were very frequent. The same source also proves that women, as gun producers, were not exempt, and their casualties were heavy. A favourite stratagem was the neutralization of the fire-power of an enemy tower in order that a picked band, by a bold rush or by stealth, might pile wood and hay against the base of the tower, soak the fuel with oil and set fire to it in the hope of burning the defenders to death or cutting them down with bullets or yataghans as they ran for it. Sometimes the door itself was blown down with a powder-keg and combustibles and burning brands were pitched into the bottom chamber. In lucky cases the powder magazine would be touched off and the whole tower, with its defenders, blown to bits. A detail that sounds almost incredible but which evidence bears out, is that entire towers were built under fire: the walls facing the zone beaten by the enemy were reared by night, the remainder during the day, with the defenders firing from one side while the masons laid one great limestone cube on another until they had overtopped the enemy.

The discovery of gunpowder and of the burning of lime for tower building were deemed priceless godsends by the Maniots. A third inestimable boon was the importation of cannon. Heavy pieces* cast in Constantinople or Venice or Woolwich were joyfully lugged from the shore by men and mules and hoisted into the top chambers of the towers while teams of mules wound up the stony valleys under loads of powder-kegs and shot. They were now able to bombard enemy towers a quarter of a mile away or if, as it often happened, they were only across the street, to batter each other to bits at point-blank range. When two powerful Nyklians of the same village were at war, it must be remembered that each side owned a number of towers and the opposing sides were sometimes several hundreds strong. At the height of a feud these forests of towers were plumed with the flashes of cannon, the air was a criss-cross of the trajectories of flying balls; shot came sailing or bouncing along the lanes, every slit concealed a man with a gun, every wall a group from which the slightest enemy movement would draw a hail of musketry, singing and ricocheting and echoing through the labryinthine streets. There were, as we have seen, frequent mêlées at close quarters and all the approaches to the village were posted with the *khosia*-men of both sides lying in ambush and cancelling each other out. The neutral population, though allowed to move about the streets

* The barrels of the few I have seen lying about in Maniot villages are about two and a half yards long.

at their risk, wisely resumed the troglodytic existence of their forbears or moved to other villages till the two factions had fought it out.

The theatres of war were no larger than the area bounded by Piccadilly, St. James's Street, the east side of St. James's Square and Pall Mall; the equivalent, in distance, of the cannonading of Brooks's by White's, Chatham House by the London Library, Lyons Corner House by Swan and Edgar's, almost of the Athenaeum and the Reform by the Travellers'. Sometimes it lasted for years: a deadlock in which the only sounds were the boom of cannon, exploding powder, the collapse of masonry, the bang of gunfire and the wail of dirges.

On certain specific occasions, the vendetta code afforded a temporary relief to this lunatic state of affairs: a general truce known as the *tréva* (also a Venetian word) during the seasons of ploughing, sowing, harvesting and threshing and the winter gathering and pressing of the olives. The opposing sides, often in next-door fields, would ply their sickles or beat the olives from the branches with long goads in dead silence. The truce was also a chance to restock the towers with victuals and ammunition by night. At last on an appointed dawn, when the sacks of grain and the great oil jars were full, all would start up again hammer and tongs.

There was another curious means by which a single member of one of the feuding families could obtain a temporary private truce called *Xévgalma*, or Extraction. If a man had to cross no-man's land on an important errand like a baptism, a wedding, a funeral, the search for a surgeon or, in later times, to go and vote, he would take a *Xevgáltes*, an extractor, with him; a heavily armed neutral, that is,—if possible a Nyklian with whose family the other side would be loth to start trouble, a man whose presence momentarily extracted his companion from the feud. 'I've got a *Xevgáltes*!' one would shout from behind cover. 'Who is he?' the enemy Nyklian would ask from the tower. 'So and so.' 'Pass,' the Nyklian would shout back, and the two would advance into the open and go on their way unscathed. Any hostile gesture towards his protégé would automatically put the extractor's clan in feud with the offenders. Sometimes the answer, if the extracting clan was not sufficiently to be feared, would be, 'I don't accept your extractor.' In such a case, they would stay where they were. If when they had left the village a *khosia*-man refused to accept the extractor he would shoot the protégé down and his clan would have an additional war on their hands and a host of new guns would be added to the havoc.

There were several ways in which these affairs could end. The logical one was the destruction of one side by the other. What was left of the losing side would scatter to other villages leaving the winners in possession of their shattered towers, their olives, their stony corn-plots, their prickly pears and salt-pools: uncontested masters of the place until some rising Nyklian family should have assembled or procreated enough guns to challenge them. Over fifty Maniot villages owe their foundation to these sudden diasporas. But Maniot custom offered several other solutions. If the losing side wanted to avoid annihilation they could sue for a *psychiko*, a 'thing of the soul'. The whole family, their leaders in the van, unarmed, in humble garb, heads bowed and hats in hand and bearing themselves with the submission of Calais burghers, would approach the other side, who were seated, fully armed, in the *rouga*. They would kiss the hands of the parents whose children had been shot and petition for pardon. This would be graciously granted and the winners would dictate the terms of co-existence in the village of which they would now assume command.

In the case of the isolated killing of a member of one family by another, unrelated to any general policy on either side, if it was proved that it was a mistake or done in drunkenness or if the two families were linked by military alliance or by blood or god-relationship the ritual consequences could be avoided by an offer, on the part of the offending family, of *psychadelphosyne*, or soul-brotherhood. Then the offending side expressed sorrow and true penitence and the actual killer made himself the especial protector and benefactor of the wronged family. Unlike *psychiko*, this was equally honourable to both sides and often the beginning of an indissoluble bond. All these matters were settled by a local council of elders known as the *Gerontikí*, the only institution lower than the Bey or the *archikapetan* which maintained any semblance of order in the Mani. Their function was not unlike that of the Courts of Honour which, in pre-1914 Germany and Austria-Hungary, weighed the pros and cons of quarrels in the *Hochjunkertum*, enforced or discouraged a duel, appointed the weapons and the terms and decided when honour had been satisfied. Needless to say, when two powerful Nyklians were determined to fight it out, neither side paid any attention to it. But sometimes, when a village war had continued for years with a parity of casualties and destruction on both sides and no possible verdict in sight, they were content, *faute de mieux*, to accept the conciliation of the *Gerontikí*. Final peace—which was appropriately known as *agape*—was concluded at last by a meeting in the *rouga* of both sides. There in the middle of the ruins they would quite literally kiss and make it up; embracing, drinking to friendship from the same cup, and paying reciprocal visits of ceremony. The *agapes* were quite often lasting. The Turkish threat, again, would reconcile all parties, and sometimes supernatural intervention would call a cease-fire. The most famous case is the appearance of the Blessed Virgin to the Mavromichalis and Mourtzinos families in the middle of a battle with the warning that a Turkish host was approaching. They crossed themselves, embraced and advanced to meet the enemy side by side. The longest truce of all was the general *tréva* called by Mavromichalis on the eve of the War of Independence. Everyone, in these times, went heavily armed. They would sit talking in the *rouga* in the evening with their guns across their knees, and before celebrating Mass, priests would carefully lay their guns across the altar at a handy distance. In spite of the local piety there were several murders and fights in church during Mass.

At the victorious end of the War of Independence, the Mani, except for enlightened innovations like cannons and guns, was still living in the Dark Ages. No region in Greece was more awkward to fit into the modern European state which Greece's rulers were bent on constructing. The Maniots were pro-English, Capo-distria's party pro-Russian. They started badly with insurrections and the assassination of Capodistria and they were alienated by sorties from Kalamata to put down the inter-Nyklian wars. Who were these newly liberated Vlachs who had the effrontery to interfere with the habits of five hundred years? The Maniots had been free far longer, they maintained, and, what was more, had no doubts about how freedom should be used. Capodistria had stamped out piracy but the ordnance still flashed merrily in scores of villages. The old private music of gunfire and dirge continued just as it had in the good old days. The blood-feud flourished, Nyklian challenged Nyklian, the villeins knew their place, the towers multiplied, their summits climbing higher than ever before. The towers themselves, for Nyklians and Govern-ment alike, had become the symbols of Maniot nonconformity. King Otto's regency, diagnosing in them the root of all Maniot strife, determined, in order to bring the Mani into line with the rest of Greece, to smash them. The Maniots—the Nyklians, that is, for they were the only ones whose opinion mattered— became still more firmly resolved to cling to them. But there was worse to come. The old guerrilla days were over, the Regency was building up a modern conscript army and the Nyklians were outraged to learn that all had to begin at the bottom in a revolutionary competition of merit in which Nyklians might con-ceivably find themselves under the orders of promoted villeins. It was like trying to persuade the Malatesta and the Baglioni to go through the ranks commanded by the stable hands of Rimini and Perugia. They put their foot down, refusing not only to discuss the demolition of towers or limitations of height or number, but the very idea of a Maniot formation which was not auto-matically officered by Nyklians.

Out of patience, the Regent determined to act. The whole region, like the Highlands after the Battle of Culloden, must be reduced and pacified and a party of the 11th Bavarian regiment, imported by Otto's regency to back the new regime, marched into the Mani with orders to occupy and destroy the towers.

They moved accordingly into a number of towers in Tsimova which had not yet become Areopolis. The Deep Maniots rose and besieged them. Understanding their peril the Bavarians beat a hasty retreat but thirty-six of them were captured in a tower and sold back to the State by the Maniots at the ransom of a *zwan-ziger* a head. Four companies of Bavarians, who the locals termed 'the vinegar-baptized', were promptly despatched to Petrovouni, where the Maniots had fortified themselves, and in the ensuing battle against eight hundred Maniot villagers, they were badly beaten. In the retreat half of them were killed with bullets and slingstones. The Government in Nauplia was in despair. A force of six thousand, complete with artillery, was next despatched to besiege Petrovouni under a General Schmaltz,—and forced to retreat to Gytheion yet again. In the negotiations that followed, the Maniots, urged by a Mavromichalis and a Grigorakis (both descendants of Beys), surrendered Petrovouni; a few towers on the edge of the Outer Mani were bought by the State, a limitation of height was published but not observed and a general amnesty declared. It was really a victory for the Mani.

The Nyklians had their own way in the end, and their end was their undoing. An intelligent Bavarian officer called Max Feder, who spoke Greek and knew the Mani and who was indeed a personal friend of all the great Nyklians, travelled the peninsula and, at amicable gatherings in the village *rougas*, enrolled all the kapetans and his Nyklian friends as officers into a militia unit called the Maniot Phalanx, which he commanded successfully in the suppression of other disorders in the Morea. They slowly accustomed themselves to western military notions. The distance between Nyklian and villein decreased, and bit by bit they became partisans of the *status quo*. Kindness and tact succeeded where coercion had been powerless. The electoral system and local government took root, schools were built and—a great landmark in Mani history—a villein was elected mayor of the great Nyklian stronghold of Nomia. The Mani was shared between the nomes of Kalamata and Laconia (the dividing line running along the watershed of the Taygetus) and subdivided into eparchies and demes. A military revolution in Athens forced King Otto to grant a constitution in 1843 and in 1844 Greece had the first general election in all her long history. Burlesque and turbulent though it was—nowhere more so than in the Mani—this was the simultaneous death-rattle of the old order and the muling and puking of modern parliamentary Greece.

The feuds continued, but, as the nineteenth century grew older, they became more rare. It is fitting that the last full-dress war took place in Kitta, the first place where the Nyklians, in flight from Andronicus II, settled in the Deep Mani. The struggle between the great families of the Kaouriani and the Kourikiani had emptied the village of all but their contending clans and all the surrounding hamlets rang with the customary noises of guns and flung rocks and the shattering of marble roofs. Nobody (except the new schoolmaster, for whom both had a superstitious awe) could cross the street without shouting 'a neutral, a neutral!' The Prime Minister, Koumoundouros (himself a Maniot and a descendant of the eponymous Bey), sent a force of gendarmerie to besiege the Kaouriani, who were deemed the aggressors. The gendarmerie were beaten off with heavy loss, and they spoke with awe of 'these men of iron and blood'. They were finally reduced by a besieging force of four hundred regular soldiers and artillery and forced to surrender. They were treated with gentle methods, however, and it was the last of the great Nyklian contests. Centuries of anarchy had come to an end.

The last few decades have disarmed the prejudices and blurred all distinctions between the Nyklians and the hinds. Sitting in the evening along the stone bench of the *rouga* with their sickles and their fishing-nets on the slabs beside them, they have the appearance of dark wiry people of the mountains and the sea; their brows, unless unlocked in laughter or the affability of conversation, are knit in an habitual frown. But, like nearly all the mountaineers of Greece, the patched clothes and bare feet are accompanied by the physiognomy and the bearing of nineteenth-century portraits of generals, ambassadors and dukes. There is little in the hollow cheeks and bony noses, sweeping white moustaches, piercing clear eyes and ease of manner that can be connected with the word 'peasant', though I am forced for want of a better to use it often enough. They all grew up in the atmosphere of village wars. Many of the indestructible elders remember them clearly; and much of their discourse revolves longingly round those old battles between rough-hewn grandees in their grandparents' and great-grandparents' days: the wars of the Mavromichali and the Mourtzini of Tsimova and Kandamyli, the Michalakiani and the Grigoriani of Kharaka, the Katsiriani and the Tsingriani, the Kaouriani and the Kourikiani of Kitta, the Messisklis of Nomia and the Yenitzariani of the Katopangi. And all round them in scores, as the sagas multiply far into the night—battered with cannon-balls and pocked with bullets, assaulted by time and decay, disapproved of, legislated against and condemned by regime after regime and as bold as brass—stand the wicked and indelible towers.

The cannon rusted. The great Nyklian wars were over. But, against the continuance of private feuds—the vendetta as it is usually understood—legislation was impotent. The habit of violence continued and though the scope was limited to isolated action, the old rules were observed. It was strife between individuals and it seems to have gained in implacability what it has lost in extent. Once the declaration of enmity had been made, no distance would interfere with the pursuer and his quarry. For, with the changes of Greece and improved communications, many of the inhabitants left the peninsula. Often years would pass before the threatened man was tracked down and destroyed. There was no relenting; a revolver bullet or a dagger thrust in Athens, the Lavrion tin mines, Constantinople, Alexandria or under Brooklyn Bridge, would suddenly resolve a forty-year-old feud. It is said to have decreased a great deal lately. I asked three policemen— from another district, as always—how often such acts occur to-day. One said 'Never. That is, very rarely.' The second, 'Four or five times a month.' A third said, 'A few per year. It all depends.' A Maniot who was sitting in the café said, ambiguously, 'They don't know what they're talking about. Anyway, as if that old stuff matters compared with all the killing of Greeks by Greeks we had here in the War. . . .'

*   *   *   *

Now comes a ramification of Mani history, a marginal comment —an extended bracket or footnote, almost—which I find it impossible to leave out of these pages for several reasons. Here it is.

When, a few days before, our caique had sailed across the gulf of Vitylo (it is written like this in demotic, more often than Oitylos which is still, as it was when its Troy-bound villagers climbed on board one of the sixty ships of Menelaus, its official name), the first thing to catch our eye was the enormous Turkish keep of Kelepha. From the heights where a temple to Serapis once stood, it dominates the little town of Vitylo and the whole gulf. It was built at the low ebb of Greek fortunes immediately after the fall of Crete in 1669, under pretence of a guarantee to the freedom of Maniot trade, as opposed to a prelude to occupation. Vitylo was the seat of two great Maniot families, the Iatriani and the Stephanopoli. The presence of this fort and garrison at their front doors was a bitter torment: they were attacked on the way to their fields, their property was stolen, their women had to be locked in day and night. Despair had overcome the Greeks at Candia's fall. It really looked at last as if the Turks would stay in Greece till doomsday. The two families determined to leave together for the free Christian realms of the Franks, settle there, and fight the Turks again in more hopeful days. But, before this could happen, the two families were at war with each other over the theft and marriage of Maria, a Iatrian girl, by one of the Stephanopoli. Several were killed on either side. It was then that the Iatriani received a formidable ally in the shape of Liberakis Yerakaris, who belonged to the third great Vitylo clan of Kosma, the terrible ex-pirate released from jail in Constantinople by the Grand Vizier on the condition that he subdued the Mani.* He was appointed commander of the region, and was soon, as an ally of the Turks, its Prince. . . . But he had been engaged to the stolen

* See page 48.

Maria and his main reason for accepting his post on such questionable terms was an angry determination to destroy the whole Stephanopoli tribe. He started by capturing and publicly executing thirty-five of them. After that his ambition carried him off on strange courses. He became an erratic war lord and condottiere, now on the Turkish, now on the Venetian, now on the Greek side, in an endless succession of bloody campaigns all over continental Greece. Local conditions were worse than ever and after this fiery interlude the two families were still resolved to emigrate, though, rather naturally, to different places.

The Iatriani were the first to move and their destination was chosen for an odd reason. *Iatros* is the Greek for 'doctor', and the Iatriani had long been convinced that their name was a Hellenized form of Medici; that they were, in fact, descended from some shadowy emigrant member of the great Florentine family. They would sign their names 'Medikos or Iatrianos', or, even more often—it is as near as the Greek alphabet can get to the Italian— 'nte Mentitzi' or 'Mettitzi';* the orthography and penmanship of the few relevant documents of this time clearly show that swordsmanship in the Mani was still the dominant skill. So it was to the Grand Duchy of Tuscany that their thoughts at once sped, and, after their thoughts, an emissary. The Grand Duke, Federigo II dei Medici, either accepted the bona fides of these far-away kinsmen or decided to humour their conviction. He welcomed their proposal and offered them wide acres on generous terms. His son Cosimo III had succeeded when, at the end of 1670 or early in 1671, the Maniot Medici actually dropped anchor in Leghorn. He made them welcome and they were given land to colonize not far from the coast round the villages of Casalapin and Vivvona, near Volterra, in the jurisdiction of Siena. Several hundreds of them settled in joyfully and their troubles began.

Five Orthodox priests had come with them but, according to Greek sources, the Bishop of Volterra sent a charlatan to their

* The Greek delta has now a soft *th* sound, as in *thou*; the D sound is rather awkwardly indicated by *nt*, in the same way that the soft Italian *ci* sound is conveyed by *tz*.

settlement, a real or masquerading Archbishop of Samos—this dark accusation is hard to unravel—who, singing Vespers according to the Eastern rite, summoned the priests to accept the Western creed with the *filioque* and bade them submit to the authority of Rome. Catholic forms of service were introduced and a Greek Benedictine from Chios, who, in a sermon, forbade them honouring any saints canonized in the East since the separation of the Churches, declared the indissolubility of marriage under all circumstances and urged the acceptance of the Gregorian calendar. In twenty-two years not a shadow of Orthodoxy remained. With this vital stay removed they rapidly lost all consciousness of being Greek and were soon merged by inter-marriage with the surrounding population. But (hints a Greek chronicler) even more baleful influences were wreaking their dissolution. 'It is to be feared,' writes Spiro Lambros, 'that they were not only Romanized in a few years but entirely wiped out also. For these mountaineers of the Taygetus were unable to resist the miasmas of the swamps in which they had settled such a short time ago.'* To-day, one can hunt the Tyrrhenean coast in vain for their descendants. The Italian population and the Maremma swallowed up all trace of them centuries ago. They have faded away over the marsh like will o' the wisps.

The Stephanopoli had still more pressing reasons for clearing out. Their past history in wars against the Turks, the proximity of the fortress of Kelepha, the enmity of the many remaining Iatriani, the implacable hatred of Liberakis, whose fortune, after decimating their family, was soaring, and the hostility of a number of other families of the Mani in general—everything counselled departure. The Stephanopoli laid claim, with or without foundation, to origins that were even more august than those of the Iatriani. Their family legend or tradition (capable of neither proof nor the reverse) made them descend from the dynasty of the Comnenes which had given Byzantium six emperors and Trebizond twenty-one. After the Fall of Trebizond, the story goes, Nicephorus, the youngest son of David II Grand

* This is the account of the Corfiot historian Moustaxidis.

Comnene, after wandering for years in Persia and other eastern lands, finally disembarked at Vitylo in 1473 where he was honourably welcomed in accordance with his rank. This wandering prince soon imposed himself on the Maniots, married the daughter of one of the great families (Lasvouri), and launched himself into the heroic doings of the peninsula. His grandson Stephen, who gave the family its present name, won a heroic victory against the Turks in 1537, built a fine tower in Vitylo, which is still standing, and a monastery of which the abbot, his son Alexis, is deemed a local saint. The Iatrianos and Kosmas families, moved to envy by Stephen's riches and power, conspired together and assassinated him.* Two centuries later his descendants, four hundred and thirty of them, were wondering where to go.

They sent one of their number, a man already much travelled and widely lettered, to seek a new home. The Maniot Medici ruled out the hospitable Grand Duchy so he explored the length of Italy—in vain—until he reached Genoa. The Serene Republic, only too pleased to settle loyal foreigners among the rebellious inhabitants of their island possession, offered him and his kinsmen wide lands in Corsica. He returned to Vitylo, a French brigantine was chartered, and, on the 3rd of October, 1675, the Stephanopoli, with three hundred kinsmen and allies, seven hundred and thirty souls all told, went on board with their bundles of household goods, their family ikons, and, it is said, the bell of the Cathedral. The port was a wild scene of weeping and lamentation; but the departure had to be brisk to elude a Turkish flotilla. At the last moment the Archbishop of Vitylo tried to board, but he was turned back because of his great age. Distraught with grief and anger at the sight of all his family leaving for ever the holy soil of Greece, he climbed a high rock and cursed them as they sailed away down the Messenian Gulf. To this day, it seems, descendants of the emigrants attribute all their reverses to the Archbishop's curse.

They called at Zante and dropped anchor in the Sicilian straits where they were kept in quarantine under the castle

* Their later troubles may thus have been part of an old feud.

of Messina. So struck were the Maniots by the beauty and wealth of the place, they almost decided to settle there. But as the island was being fiercely debated by Spain and Louis XIV, they sailed on; calling for a while at Malta, which was then in possession of the Knights; then they followed the Barbary Coast some distance before turning north. Their leader, George Stephano-poli, died on the voyage, and Parthenios, Bishop of Maina, assumed command. After wandering for three months they reached Genoa on New Year's Day, 1676. They were hospitably received by the Republic and accommodated in several palazzi till the winter was out. The terms of their grant—a generous one—were drawn up: the most important of these was the proviso that the Maniots, while keeping their own Greek rite, should submit to Rome and practise their religion in the manner observed by the ex-Orthodox of Sicily and the Kingdom of Naples; become Uniats, in fact. The most interesting item was the right to bear any arms they wished and the permission to fly the Genoese flag in warlike expeditions against the Turks. The former condition, which had not been made during their emissary's visit, they secretly planned to shelve. There is something very stirring and gallant about the intentions which underlay the second condition.

When spring came they set off. The wide stretch of land they had been granted at Paomia, Revinda and Sagone, in the coast region of western Corsica, was steep and uneven; but the soil, when they could get at it, was good. They pitched tents and bivouacs and plied their bill-hooks to the stifling *macchia*, the dense growth that blurs all the outlines of Corsica and turns its mountains the dull khaki green of a well camouflaged army lorry. They soon had it clear, walled it off with stones, divided it into arable and vegetable gardens and terraced it for olives and vines. They built a little Cathedral for their bishop, a Parish Church of the Dormition of the All Holy Virgin sprang up; and, in the trim new houses, chapels to SS. Nicolas, Athanasios, George and Dimitri and even a monastery named the Nativity of Our Lady for the small group of monks and novices. It was soon a flourishing community, so much more so than the filthy Corsican villages surrounding them that the natives were gnawed with envy. It appears that the Corsicans were far wilder and more uncouth than the Maniots and their agricultural methods primeval. They learnt the best ways of ploughing and cultivation and the care of vines from their new neighbours, new devices in spinning and weaving from their wives, and, which seems strange, as the poor Mani is no gastronome's paradise, how to cook food that was eatable at last.* One may wonder where among the stones of the Mani the vigorous colonists had learnt these georgic skills. But all disinterested records coincide in praise. They lived peacefully and, in the words of one of their priests, pleasing in the sight of God.

But religion, their costumes, their language and their ways cut them off from their neighbours. Their prosperity kindled their anger. After three armed brushes, this anger was tempered by fear and respect. This was apparently not reciprocated, for though individual friendships and god-relationships sprang up, the Maniots refused to inter-marry. They disliked the Corsicans and dubbed them, from their shaggy capes, 'the goat pelts' or just 'the blacks'. (Unless the Mani was very different then, it sounds like the pot and the kettle.) When, half a century after the establishment of the Greeks, the Corsicans rose against the Republic, their envoys sought the aid of the Maniots. But they stayed loyal to their benefactors and sent the insurgents packing with prophecies of seeing their hewn-off heads aligned on the walls of Bastia.

Despatching the women and children and the old men to Ajaccio, ninety Maniots barricaded themselves on a headland by the ruined anti-pirate tower of Omignia. Then, in April 1731 (according to the lively chronicle of Father Nicolas Stephanopoli) the rebels came back, outnumbering the Maniots a hundred to one. Attempts at pourparlers by the besiegers were again greeted with insults from the battlements, the heralds withdrew and the enraged Corsicans, beating kettle drums and blowing down

* The reader (like the author) can well shudder at the thought of pre-Maniot meals in western Corsica.

trumpets and cows' horns, charged. 'Their shouts rose to the sky, a hail of shot poured from the walls, the whole cape was covered with smoke, the sun was hidden and the earth shook with clamour and gunfire!' A cease fire came with darkness. None of the enemy had even got across the low surrounding wall, three hundred were wounded and many killed. The Corsicans threw the dead into the sea and the waves washed them up on the rocks under the tower. None of the Greeks had been hit, 'not even their clothes'. Placing sentries, they gave themselves up to laughing and feasting and clashing their cups together and thanking the All Holy Virgin for keeping them safe. They might have been back in the Mani!

It was Wednesday in Holy Week and from the first light of Maundy Thursday till Holy Saturday the attack continued with growing fierceness. Relief from Ajaccio was cut off on land by the enemy and from the sea by storms. But at last the enemy fire languished. 'Take your arms, brave Greeks,' cries Father Nicolas in retrospect, 'God and the Ever-Virgin Mary have scattered your enemies! In the town, your priests and your wives are praying for you barefoot!' (For 'Greeks' he uses the word '*Romioi*' throughout.) Loading and firing by turns the Maniots advanced, toppling the Corsicans into the sea from the cliff's edge and picking them off on land; taking point after point, until at last the enemy broke and ran, many of them leaping into the sea. In ecstasy, Father Nicolas quotes Moses and the songs of Miriam and Deborah. All round him the Greeks were praising God, cheering, weeping and kissing each other. They gathered a vast booty of scattered guns and swords, stacks of victuals, innumerable flocks from the enemy's commissariat and numbers of saddled horses. Finally, late at night, they assembled, sang the Hymn of the Resurrection, and joyfully ushered in Easter Day: 'Christ is risen! He is risen indeed!' After piously burying all the dead they marched in triumph to Ajaccio. Terror had emptied all the villages on their way. They were greeted as heroes by the Genoese and, concludes Father Nicolas, when the Corsicans wish to curse each other, they still say 'May God deliver you into the hands of the Greeks!' *

* I was interested to read, in Mr. G. H. Blanken's book on the Cargese

But they never returned to Paomia, and Ajaccio became their home. During the turbulent years that followed, they fought bravely for the Genoese through the various insurrections and the eight months when the German adventurer, Baron von Neuhoff, was first and last king of Corsica; also during the brief regime of Boswell's friend, Pascal Paoli. When Corsica, in 1768, passed to France by treaty, they were looking out for somewhere new to emigrate. Their language and their costume and their religion were still a cause of friction. Two small groups set off for Minorca and Leghorn (where they evaporated like the Medici of Volterra) and a third to Sardinia, where most of them were promptly massacred by the Sardinians. But the bulk of them remained and fought for the French and were befriended by the first French governor. He settled them on good land at Cargese in his newly-established Marquisate of Marbœuf, not far from Paomia. Once more their diligence and their energy produced a fine village in the middle of flourishing cultivation and laden vineyards, and their descendants live there to this day. Their troubles were not over, however. The Corsicans were still hostile and envious of these industrious interlopers and during the Revolution they burnt Cargese down. Napoleon was friendly to them and they were reinstated. There was another attack during the Hundred Days, and when the Greek War of Independence broke out in 1821 (a century and a half after the Maniots had left Greece) the men of Cargese were forced to chafe angrily at home, instead of leaving *en masse* to join in the fight, by the Corsican threat to their families and their lands.

As long as the Maniots helped to quell the disorders of the island their religion was left unchallenged. But when things began to settle, they were held to the letter of their original agreement by the Archbishop of Ajaccio. The last colonist priest died in 1822. A Cargesian Greek was ordained in the Latin rite in 1817

dialect, that the battle of Omĭgnia, in spite of '*une resistance désespérée*' ended in *une défaite glorieuse mais complète des grecs*. Under the circumstances, one cannot blame Father Nicolas for not mentioning the fact. It is a healthy tendency to make much of victories and forget defeats.

and his church was attended by some of his family and friends, but
the rest, though they became Uniats on paper, once more stub-
bornly refused to have 'Corsican priests'. They remained seven
years without the sacraments, saying the services by themselves,
until a Greek archimandrite from Chios arrived and stayed as
parish priest, instead of the Cardinal's nominee, till 1856. He kept
their Greek nationalism intact and brushed up their grammar and
spelling. His successors, though Greek, were Uniats, celebrating the same rites as those of Grottaferrata in the Campagna. Bit
by bit, as history slipped into its more peaceful nineteenth-
century rhythm, this fresh allegiance, inter-marriage and the
surrounding western culture disarmed their fierce Greek zeal.
There were few Greek books and no teachers. The Catholic
Church hated these old links with the Eastern schism and when
the Greek merchants of Marseilles sent them a Greek schoolmaster in 1885, he was denounced by the ecclesiastical authorities
of Ajaccio as a schismatic and women were forbidden to send him
their children. He struggled in vain for two years against this
boycott and left in despair. Since then all direct contact with
Greece has died out. There are now more Corsicans than Maniots
among the eight hundred odd inhabitants of Cargese and all
strife is over. But the two churches, one Catholic and one Uniat,
where the offices are sung in Greek, commemorate the old
antagonism of East and West. Those who attend the Uniat church
are still known as 'the Greeks' and a few old women still speak
Greek.*

All travellers are at one in praising the charm, cleanliness and
prosperity of Cargese. Sir Gilbert Eliot, viceroy of Corsica during
its short English period (1794-6), wrote to his wife describing a
ball where they all wore their old costumes and danced holding
hands in a long ribbon to the tune of a Greek melopee. It is given
an excellent character by Prosper Mérimée, by Edward Lear

* The best accounts of their dialect, which is still, in spite of the usual
infiltration of local words, a pure Greek one of a largely Maniot character, are
by the late Prof. R. M. Dawkins of Exeter College, Oxford, and Herr G. H.
Blanken of Leyden.

(who visited it with his Suliot valet), and by Professor Richard Dawkins, the most knowledgeable and charming of neo-Hellenists whose rooms at Oxford, until his recent death, were an Aladdin's cave of books of Greek history, folklore, language, customs and fairy-tales. In spite of the inevitable modifications of nearly three and a half centuries, the Maniot Cargesians are proud of their Greek descent, which their language, their form of religion, their proverbs and songs and many of their customs still commemorate. The ikons and sacred vessels they carried away from the Mani are still there, and the bell they are said to have lowered from the cathedral tower of Vitylo. The Corsican tide swept into the village to fill a gap, during the last century, when a last restless emigration carried a number of them still further west, to the village of Sidi Merouan, near Constantine in Algeria. There were three hundred of them there in 1900; in 1931, only a hundred and twenty-five. Now they are scattered and lost all over Algeria and the doors of their little Greek church are shut for ever. This was the last adventure of thes wandering descendants of the ancient Spartans and the warlike grandees of the Mani and perhaps of the emperors of Byzantium and Trebizond. The sands of Africa have done the same work of obliteration as the fens of Tuscany and the Sardinian guns.

Their emigration carried these mountaineers from the deadening murk of the Ottoman Empire into the whirlpool of western European affairs. Some of them, intent on getting closer to the heart of this exciting maelstrom, left their little town and went to France. The more time passed, the more convinced the Stephanopoli became of their imperial origins. Much of Father Nicolas's eloquence was expended on it. Patrice Stephanopoli, who wrote a history of Cargese in polished and flowery French, had no doubts at all; nor had Don Bernardo Stephanopoli, the offspring of a small eighteenth-century emigration from Corsica to Grosseto in the baleful Maremma, who was a Catholic priest, Bishop of Antioch *in partibus*, a favourite of Clement XIV and nearly a Cardinal. Another, Dimitri, who died a general in the French army, even convinced the heralds and genealogists of Louis XVI. He was duly declared Prince Démètre Stephanopoli de Comnène, and his arms—the double-headed eagle of Byzantium aswirl with ermine mantles and topped with a closed crown—blaze from the pages of old armorials. But the most convinced of all was his sister Josephine-Laure Permon Stephanopoli de Comnène, Duchesse d'Abrantes, who was born at Montpellier. Her father had served in the American War of Independence and her mother was a fading beauty when Napoleon was thin and young and, although she was much his senior, he fell more than half in love with her. Her more beautiful daughter, who was intelligent and witty and charming as well, married Junot, who became Duc d'Abrantes after the Peninsula campaign. After quarrelling with Josephine, she was left a rich widow at twenty-eight, and turned Royalist. Her extravagance soon dispersed her fortune, but later in life she made another one with her twenty-eight volumes of memoirs of the Revolution, the Empire and the Restoration; they are witty, fluent, indiscreet and most entertaining. As a novelist, however, she failed badly. She died, poor once more, in 1838. One son was a writer, another, who was one of Marshal MacMahon's generals, fell at Solferino. She not only upheld the imperial origins of the Stephanopoli but launched the theory which was widely accepted for a time of the Corsican-Maniot—thus Imperial—origins of the Bonaparte family. It was, she proclaimed, an Italianization of the Greek name *Kalomeros*, which means, exactly, *buona parte*. But there were no Kalomeri among the emigrant Maniots and no such name ever existed in the Mani. The Buonapartes were originally from Treviso and Bologna and they had been established in Corsica long before the Greeks arrived.

During the campaign of Italy, Napoleon was suddenly confronted by an envoy from the Bey of the Mani. He offered the complete support of the region, and, in the event of a French landing, of all Greece. As Napoleon was seriously thinking of attacking the Turkish Empire in Europe, the help of the ruler of the only part of Greece that was free and the weight of his influence on the rest of his country were not to be spurned. He thought at once of the Stephanopoli of his native Corsica: an ideal link between France and the Mani. On the 12th of Thermidor, the year V, he despatched Dimo Stephanopoli and his brother Nicolo from his headquarters in Milan. The former was already a distinguished botanist, and botanical research was to be the cover story of his mission. They set off to Corfu in the middle of 1798. These two elegant and pseudo-princely *citoyens*, in the black cutaways and top boots and the enormous semi-circular bicornes of the Directoire (who were at the same time great *Nyklians* astray from home for a hundred and twenty-three years), were welcomed by the courageous Zanetbey. They stayed in the Mani several months as the guests of the Bey and numbers of the leaders from enslaved Greece were summoned to meet them, as well as all the kapetans of the Peninsula. Dimo has left an absorbing account of his sojourn, of the customs and sad klephtic songs bewailing the enslavement of Greece, and of the innumerable plants and archaeological remains that he contrived to see between conferences. He was moved to tears by his strange temporary home-coming and the appalling tales of oppression and cruelty. After a battle in which the Maniots routed a flotilla of the Kapoudan Pasha and destroyed an invading force of Turks from Sparta, he pronounced a funeral oration over the dead in perfect Greek. He carried back an ancient Greek statue of Liberty to the first Consul as a gift from his splendid host. But, by the time he reached Paris, Napoleon's policy had veered in favour of the Turks. Nothing came of this curious embassy, except Stephanopoli's moving record of the mission* and a shipload of arms to the Bey, who, deposed now, had taken to the hills with the Klephts of the Peloponnese.

There is one last instance of a Cargesian return to Greece. It comes from a Corsican drummer-boy in the Morea expedition, when France lent a force of 14,000 men to the kingdom of Greece in the 1830's. One day, in the far south, he overheard a group of mountaineers in conversation. He listened in silence, his brow

* Alas! The bona fides of this document have been questioned.

clouded with astonishment, and at last exclaimed, '*Tiens! C'est le patois de mon pays!*'

This is the end of a long parenthesis, and we must return to the present-day Mani, about fifteen miles south of the little town from which they all set out.*

---

* I made a pilgrimage to Cargese some months ago and found a thriving community living in a rocky and beautiful village perched above the sea. Many of the inhabitants had Maniot surnames and all were deeply conscious of their origins. Their priest, a most intelligent man and a perfect Greek-speaker with whom I spent many hours, was robed and cylinder-hatted in the mode of the Greek clergy. Rather surprisingly, he is a Savoyard brought up in Constantinople. I attended a Uniat Mass there. The church was crammed and the language and the liturgy were most punctiliously preserved, though I was surprised to see that two of the many acolytes were splendidly vested young girls. It was interesting to notice that the *filioque* clause, defining the double procession of the Paraclete (the ancient bone of contention between East and West), was omitted from the Nicene creed. It forms, of course, part of the Uniat dogma, but its omission here is a tactful gesture towards the atavistic susceptibilities of the Cargesians.

The Cargesians are extremely likeable and the atmosphere—the clean white houses, the ikons, the manners, the welcome with a small ritual glass of spirits, the gift of a sprig of basil on departure, the faces and the black coifs of the two old women—is indefinably Greek. Alas, I could only discover two women —one old, the other middle-aged—who still spoke Greek fluently. A number of Corsican words had crept in but it was unmistakably Maniot, with many rustic turns of phrase that have been lost in the Mani. There were also a number of rare and exciting Cretan usages and pronunciations. Some of the Cretan refugees to the Mani from Candia, which fell six years before the departure for Corsica in 1675, must surely have accompanied the exodus from Vitylo. It was a most moving visit.

CHAPTER 9

Change and Decay. The Cocks
of Matapan

'IN winter,' said a man carrying a small sack of rock salt on his shoulder, 'the wind blows clean through you. In one side and out the other. A terrible *voras** comes down from the middle of the Peloponnese and follows the line of the Taygetus, pulling up trees by the roots and tearing slabs of marble off the roofs this size,' he spread his arms like a fisherman, 'and carries them away as easily as leaves off a branch. And the rains! All the downhill paths turn into rivers.' Looking at the hot landscape of pebbles sinking towards the sea, this was almost impossible to conjure up. The air was stifling. We had fallen in with the salt-carrier in a lane going down to the bay. He waved back towards Kitta and Nomia. 'The year before the war we had so much rain that it carried all the plants away, all the trees, every speck of earth, licked the rocks clean to the bone. It even emptied the cemeteries and scattered skulls and bones and ribs for miles over the hillside! When God had finished making the world, he had a sack of stones left over and he emptied it here. . . .' He kicked one of them. 'If only we could find a merchant who bought stones, we'd all be millionaires . . . You wouldn't find me sweating along the roads with *this*,' he said, giving a resentful slap to the sack of salt.

We stopped on a headland near the ruins of a fort and looked down at the little port of Yeroliména. How mild and ordinary it looked after the strange villages we had left behind: a few houses, a quay lined with caiques, a mole running out into the bay. But

* The ancient Boreas.

112

beyond it the coast climbed away eastwards and each rocky shoulder supported a congregation of towers. 'There you are,' he said pointing, 'the Kakovounia'*—they ended in a low saddle and then rose again turning south, and finally sank into the sea once and for all—'and Cape Matapan. Nothing but stones all the way. Are you sure you don't need any in England? I'd let you have them cheap . . . or some thorns? We've got some very nice thorns. . . .'

*   *   *   *

Small as it is, the little town of Yeroliména is a loophole into the outer world from the stern seclusion of the Mani. The caiques along the quay, the anchors and capstans and coils of cable, the gilt lettering on the bottles of a chemist's shop, the sacks and barrels and tins of the grocers', three policemen drinking coffee under a tree, three caique captains with shiny peaked caps drinking Fix beer—all indicated in the single dusty street, even under the furnace breath of the sirocco which lulled it into semi-catalepsy, that another world existed somewhere. Undreamable leagues away, round cape after cape, past a dozen gulfs and islands, at the end of caique journeys that seemed as remote and hazardous as argosies, hovered, in the mind's eye, the disordered mirage of the Piraeus. . . . Taking our cue from the sailors, we sat down. The salt-carrier rapped an iron table top and spirited three bottles out of the depths of a café, drops of moisture running in shiny tracks over the misted glass like advertisements in the *New Yorker*. The salt encrusted along the whiskers and eyelashes of our companion, the taste of sweat in our mouths and the African wind that seemed to be burying us at the bottom of invisible dunes, trebled the rapture of those long icy draughts. . . . One forgets about wine at moments like this and blesses the memory of Herr Fuchs, the brewer to the Wittelsbachs in Munich who was summoned here over a century ago by his fellow Bavarian, King Otto. ΦΙΞ, his transliterated name on all the beer bottles of Greece, has a peculiar talismanic magic. It revived us enough to arrange with one of the captains at the next table for a lift in his caique next day round Cape Matapan. In a little while we were supine and sheltered from the sun in rooms above the chemist's. *Nada the Lily* and *Two Worlds and Their Ways* slowly fell from our hands as we sank Lethewards while outside the languid activity of Yeroliména lost momentum and halted at last in its noon trance.

Yeroliména may, according to a theory of Mr. Dimitrakos-Messisklis, have been the site of the town of Hippola to which Pausanias attributes the emplacement of a temple to Pallas Athene. Other compilers of classical atlases have placed it further up the coast. As there is little more than a mention in Pausanias and not a stone to go on in either place, honours are even. Less than a century ago there was nothing here at all except a little ruined chapel by the sea. A young man called Michali Kasimantis left his village of Kipoula (the other candidate for the temple) some time before the middle of the last century and got a job in a European paint-merchant's shop in the island of Syra. Floating at the maritime cross-roads of Asia, Thrace, Crete, the Greek mainland and the archipelago, Syra, before the rise of Piraeus, Patras and Salonika, was the most important port and trading centre of Greece. (Its importance has declined now but the little capital is full of sub-stantial merchants' houses and fine streets and gasoliers and Second Empire cafés. There is an elegant colonnaded square with a pillar-fronted theatre, tall palm trees and statues and a band-stand which should always be showering forth the music of Offenbach and Meyerbeer. A disarming, faded cosmopolitan air hangs over everything. It is best known to-day for its Turkish Delight and delicious nougat in large circular slabs.) Kasimantis eventually set up on his own, flourished, and soon became the most prosperous colourman of the Levant. Remembering his home, he returned to Yeroliména in the 70's, and built a quay and a mole and a couple of warehouses and put two nephews in charge. Soon caiques were calling with all kinds of goods which were piled into the ware-houses and carried on the backs of mules up steep paths to the scattered thorpes of the Deep Mani; and the caiques sailed away again with olives and oil and carobs and the surplus of their corn. The little town sprang up, and the weekly steamer from the Piraeus drops anchor there. It has already acquired the agreeable mellowness of decay.

Liméni, the cradle of the Mavromichalis family below Areopolis in the long gulf of Vitylo, is one of the only two safe harbours of the Deep Mani. But communications to Liméni are cut off by mountains and lack of roads from the extreme south, leaving only Mezapo and Yeroliména. Both of them are hazardous in foul weather. Ships must then load and unload as best they can in the little desolate bay of Porto Cayo, just over the saddle of the Taygetus. The single office of these inlets in the past was to afford a fair-weather refuge for the Maniot pirate ships. The slave trade was one of the mainsprings of eastern Mediterranean piracy. This demand for slaves began in the time of the Mameluke Sultans of Egypt, where hundreds of thousands of them were needed yearly for harems and household work and even, such poor fighting men were the Egyptians, as soldiers. The Sultans were soon imitated by all the Moslem potentates from Spain to the Caucasus and the western coasts of India. Venice and Genoa were the great slave merchants of the Levant, and, based on their fiefs in the Aegean islands, they would buy or capture slaves wherever they could lay hands on them regardless of race or religion, though they had a slight bias against selling their fellow Catholics. They had assembly-points in the Black and Red Seas and unloaded their wares at the great slave-markets of Alexandria, Damietta, Beirut and Algiers. The towns of Venice and Genoa were slave transit-camps; the Florentines made use of Ancona for the same purpose and many rich Italian families kept slaves in their houses. When Gallipoli and Adrianople fell to the Turks, the Greeks also adopted the trade, shipping off vast quantities of Christian prisoners for sale in Egypt. The Maniots would raid the islands and the Turkish villages, collect prisoners—they specialized in Turks and in the Catholic Franco-Levantines of the Cyclades—and sell them to Venetian traders from Methoni and Coroni on the Messenian peninsula. When the Venetian slave galleys put in, Maniots at feud would even attempt to waylay and capture each other or their enemies' wives for sale as slaves; a convenient way of ridding the neighbourhood, of putting the avenger out of harm's way and of turning an honest sequin. Their vessels would lie in wait for Turkish and Venetian convoys between Crete and Cape Matapan, and, being too small to attack them in bulk, pounce on laggards and strays, board them, or force them into the rocks. They were frequently in league with captains from the islands, particularly from Cephalonia. Travellers have described the great caves of the Mani stacked with various loot: guns, yataghans, swords, turbans, stocks of baggy trousers, embroidered waistcoats, soft fezzes, and wide skirts and fur-trimmed gold laced jackets for women. Cunningly carved woodwork and wooden furniture, all cut from one piece, were much in demand; troughs, plates, forks, spoons, cups, caskets, bronze kitchenware pots, pitchers and amphorae from Messenia, also the inevitable lime for tower-building. Small ships would sail away to the minute islets of Sapienza and Skiza off the tip of Messenia, build rough kilns, and sail back in a few months with cargoes of this precious stuff. This was the era when Greek pirates would 'churn up the sea in boats no bigger than walnut shells', in the words of Capodistria, who finally suppressed the already waning piracy of the Mani.

No pirate enterprise of any consequence was complete without a priest. He blessed the expedition at its outset, prayed for fair weather for his parent ship and foul weather for the enemy and interceded for the souls of his fallen messmates. He absolved the sins of his floating flock and saw to it that a share of the loot, often wet with blood, was hung beside the ikons on the mainmast as a votive offering. If more than eight days passed and no prize came their way, he would intone a litany on the deck, and when a prospective prize was sighted he would level a matchlock over the bulwarks with the rest and join the boarding party with khanjar and scimitar. After the decline of piracy the Deep Mani was supplied by pedlars from all over Greece with caravans of donkeys—like those of Anavryti—which drove from one mountain hamlet to the next with great bundles of assorted wares. The pedlars, in their turn, grew scarcer when the quay at Yeroliména was built.

*　　*　　*　　*

The sirocco died during the afternoon. Towards evening we followed a gentle slope that carried us into the foothills of this last buttress but one of the Taygetus: a shallow staircase, winding and rising, of smooth marble slabs. This luxurious going seemed almost decadent after those dolorous inland lanes, turning the pedestrian's gait into the dignified and ceremonious ascent of a doge. The sea sank and skyscraper villages loomed on the steepening slants of the mountain-side. Alika, the first of these, seemed locked in a death-grapple with the omnipresent prickly pear. Millions of thorn-studded bats swirled round the tower bases and groped through barred windows and gaps in the masonry and rolled in green cataracts from the steep rock's face overhead. It seemed to have driven the villagers out; all but two old men who were drinking outside a vault-like tavern on the flat stage of the *rouga*, half of which had been excavated out of a precipice. The tempest of thorns overhead was succeeded on the rock face below by a jungle of slogans and rather talented primitive caricatures on the hewn rock in white paint. But it wasn't the vegetation that had cleared the village, one of them said, seizing my wrist like the Ancient Mariner and pouring out a glass of wine with his free hand, while his companion jerked a stool behind my knees compelling me to sit (they didn't often get company, they observed), but hatred and politics. *Ta politika!* The occupation, the Germans, the Italians, old feuds, the Communist bands, the Greek security battalions which the Germans armed against them, the right-wing Chi organization after the Liberation, the battles with ELAS up in the mountains, the massacre of their opponents in remote valleys, the savage reprisals. 'It was a fight of each side to wipe out the other, burning their houses, smashing their oil jars, shooting prisoners . . .' Then the Civil War, poverty, disappointment—no wonder the village was empty! 'Only a few old sticks like us are left behind.' He shouted for some more wine, and

softly changed gear. 'We used to get thousands of *okas* of un-
fermented must from Kalamata by caique. We put in the resin
ourselves, letting it work and mature; and then,' he demonstrated
what he meant, 'we swallowed it. But we don't need so much now.
There are not enough throats left.' Next he told us how seventeen
Maniots after the fall of Greece, finding the Germans and ELAS
equally intolerable, sneaked off in the middle of the night in a
rowing boat that could barely hold them. Favoured however by
a mast and a sail and a steady north wind, after three days they
espied a line of sand, some palm trees and houses and a minaret.
It was Derna, and luckily it had just fallen to the advancing British
Army. They were greeted as heroes by the English, who gave
them 'white bread and tinned meat', and sent them off to join the
Greek brigade, with whom they fought until the final assault on
Rimini.

A little later, as we talked of the Maniot dirges by which I was
obsessed, I was surprised to hear this bloodshot-eyed and barefoot
old man say: 'Yes, it's the old iambic tetrameter acalectic.' It was
the equivalent of a Cornish fisherman pointing out the difference,
in practically incomprehensible dialect, between the Petrarchian
and the Spenserian sonnet. It was quite correct. Where on earth
had he learnt it? His last bit of information was that, in the old
days (that wonderful cupboard!) the Arabs used to come to this
coast to dive for the murex.

The path from Alika sank into a deep ravine which ended in a
quiet and secret-seeming combe; then it climbed the other side to
the steep and jutting headland of Kyparissos. We lay down near
an altar with a slab commemorating the republic of the Free
Laconians among the broken fragments of a Greco-Roman
temple and watched the sun westering towards Yeroliména.
Again there was this miracle of innumerable gold splinters sown
over the sea. Directly below the sun they gathered into a wide
gold sheet, flaking away in fragments and ripples as the water
approached the shore and turning purple and grass-green
among the teeth of rocks a long way beneath our cliff. It was
exactly here that Mavromichalis found the mermaid-princess.

Inland, the gold towers of half a dozen villages began to slant their stretching shadows across the mountains. The coast rose and fell westwards to the gulf of Yeroliména where the sea was on fire. It rose and fell for a few miles to the east, then turned south to the darkening last blue peninsula of Taenaros.

The shrine of Poseidon on that shadowy cape was the oracle and sanctuary of the Laconians. A town grew up at Kyparissos for the pilgrims; temples to Demeter and Aphrodite rose from its midst. Much later, after the Roman invasion, Poseidon's temple was destroyed; probably when the Cilician pirates, strong in the alliance of Mithridates, raided and looted the Roman-occupied Greek peninsula until they were destroyed, in an astonishing campaign of three months, by Pompey. But the temples of Demeter and Aphrodite survived and Kainepolis (the New Town) appeared. They were standing when Pausanias passed this way in the second century A.D. But they too were destroyed at last, possibly five centuries later or more. Nothing is known of the date, though some conclude that it must have been the work of that scourge of the Mediterranean, the 'Algerian' pirates based on Spain, who actually captured and occupied Crete for a century, until they in their turn were demolished by Nicephorus Phocas. These terrible men tormented the Greek coasts, looting, killing, burning and destroying for centuries. It is because of them that all the littoral villages of Greece are built a mile or two inland, usually with a tower or a little fort at the *skala* by the sea, to hold the invaders while the burghers stood to their arms or fled. *Epesan san Argerinoi*—'They fell on us like Algerians'—is still a current phrase.

Modern Greek contains another odd survival of the kind which harks back to an even remoter invasion of south-eastern Europe by barbarians: that ruthless Germanic race of the central European forests, the Alamanni. It was strange, during the German occupation, to hear Cretan peasants observe with innocent pleonasm that 'These Germans are worse than the Alamanni!' (*Avtoi oi Germanoi einai cheiroteroi apo tous Alamannous!*). It is a little known fact, recorded in the *Wars* of Procopius, that Genseric, King of the

Vandals, after he had conquered Carthage, purposed to invade the Mani and establish a forward base on these inaccessible shores from which to harass the Peloponnese. In A.D. 468 he attacked Kainepolis with a strong pirate fleet, but was defeated with such heavy losses that he sailed to Zakynthos in a rage, took five hundred prisoners, hacked them to bits and scattered them over the waves on his way home to Carthage. The little town had saved the entire Peloponnese. Sixty-six years later (according to some authorities) Belisarius put in here on his way to defeat the descendants of Genseric and restore Carthage to the Empire in a latter-day Punic war.

But these barbaric doings have left no trace in the atmosphere that hangs over Kyparissos. Pirate fleets and jangling Nyklians seem equally remote and equally irrelevant. The slow fall of the evening among this smashed and scattered masonry, the decrescendo and then the silence of the cicadas, the wide unruffled gleam of the sea below and the nerve-stilling quietness of the air, hold a different message. A spell of peace lives in the ruins of ancient Greek temples. As the traveller leans back among the fallen capitals and allows the hours to pass, it empties the mind of troubling thoughts and anxieties and slowly refills it, like a vessel that has been drained and scoured, with a quiet ecstasy. Nearly all that has happened fades to a limbo of shadows and insignificance and is painlessly replaced by an intimation of radiance, simplicity and calm which unties all knots and solves all riddles and seems to murmur a benevolent and unimperious suggestion that the whole of life, if it were allowed to unfold without hindrance or compulsion or search for alien solutions, might be limitlessly happy.

The dusk was reducing those marble fragments to pale shapes among the thistles. It was in just such a mood of serenity that we retraced the winding path to Alika. A hint of moonrise behind the dark towers soon turned the steps to a shallow silver staircase. Down this, buoyed still by the elation that the wreck of these unimportant temples had provided, we seemed to glide or fly. The reflected lamps of Yeroliména were shining in the bay.

*   *   *   *

Down a few steps we found a long, barrel-vaulted room. Pinned to the whitewashed walls were Singer sewing machine advertisements, pictures of King Paul and Queen Frederika, and of the late King George of England, the Queen Mother and Queen Elizabeth II. Leaning into the cooking alcove a thin handsome woman was delicately arranging twigs, with the economy that treeless regions compel, under a sizzling frying pan. Down a ladder at the other end of this semi-cylinder lay a little platform of rock with three tin tables. It hung immediately above the sea, hemmed in by sweet-smelling herbs in whitewashed petrol tins and a dozen tall sun-flowers. The cluster of masts, the criss-cross of rigging and the sea's many reflections were so close that we seemed, as we settled there, to be under way. The three caique captains were drinking retsina and playing a record so old and defaced that it was hard to detect in the tune an Athenian music-hall song twenty years old. The battered gramophone was armed with a petunia-coloured horn like a giant convolvulus, its open bell painted with faded nosegays. One of the captains, affected by the soft influences of the night, had put a sprig of basil behind his ear. After an omelette and some lentils, we noticed that the water our hostess brought with the coffee tasted slightly of wine. We asked the sailors if they had noticed. The one with the basil—he had a dark intelligent face hard as leather, deeply lined and bashed with vicissitudes, a kind of alert and humorous physiognomy which is just as essentially Greek as the chipped capitals on the headland—said, 'Yes, but don't say anything. She's in despair about it.' She had stored her wine in a room above the cistern which warrened the rock under the whole house. One of her barrels had leaked and the wine had dripped through a broken floor-slab into the dark cistern below, draining a hogshead in one long, fatal night. The cistern was filled by rain water led there in conduits from the flat roof, and when the calamity had occurred, spring was on the way and not a drop could be expected till October or later . . . not till the quails came. . . .

'Have you ever eaten quails in Greece?'

'Yes, once, a few years ago. In Santorin.'

He abolished the little volcano with a wave of his hand.

'Here's the place for them. Why, in good years, they used to send hundreds of thousands of them—*hundreds of thousands*—alive, to Marseilles. And those French know how to eat, the cuckolds. You should stay on till the quails come.'

I reminded him that we were off before dawn for Cape Matapan with his neighbour.

'It's a fine journey,' he said, 'and the first thing you see when you round the cape is the island of Cythera. Have you been there? You know Aphrodite was born near there, out of the waves? Hm.' He turned to his companions, and said, 'You see? Foreigners know more about our country than we do ourselves. But did you go to Egg Island? What, not to *Avgo*? You ought to have gone there; its about an hour's rowing from Cerigo,* a small round island, covered with seagulls. You only have to clap your hands,' he did so, 'and the whole heaven fills up,' his hands fluttered expansively above his head, 'with millions of gulls! And there's a deep cave there, with the sea running in, bright blue inside like the sky. There are plenty of seals swimming about too. You can see them lying on the rocks with their wives and their children.'

Having been to Cythera less than two months before, this was shattering news for us. I have always longed to see a seal in Greece and always in vain. The only one I have ever come across is a shrivelled and stuffed one hanging over the door of a sailors' tavern on the waterfront of Canea.

'. . . and on clear days on Cape Matapan,' he was saying, 'you can hear the cocks crowing in Cythera.'

'I've never heard them,' said Panayioti, the skipper of the caique we' were to take on the morrow, 'never.'

'Neither have I,' said the other.

Then you ought to buy new ears. I've often heard them when I put my nets down on the windward side of the cape. You need a quiet day and a very gentle *ostrolevante* blowing; a small south-easter, but very small. Then,' he said, leaning back against a sunflower, a finger behind the lobe of his ear, the other hand

* The Venetian name for Cythera, still sometimes used.

outstretched with splayed fingers to represent Wind, his wide-stretched eyes indicating Distance, 'it comes floating towards you over the water, you can only just hear it.' His voice sank to a singing whisper: 'Ki-ki-kirri-koo-oo-oo!' His eyes rolled ominously from one to the other of us. Hypnotized by the dying fall of his onomatopoea and delighted at the awe of our silence, he repeated this ghostly cock crow; still more softly and in a slightly different key: 'Ki-ki-kirri-koo-oo-oo. . . .'

* * * *

They left soon afterwards. We sat on in the cool silence of the floating garden, talking of these phantom cockcrows; and with a special reason. If the reader knows Mr. Henry Miller's book about Greece, *The Colossus of Maroussi* (which I humbly recommend), he will remember an appendix, a letter from Lawrence Durrell to the author soon after his departure; it describes how, following a tremendous dinner in Athens, Durrell and his fellow diners climbed up to the Acropolis but found the gates shut; Katsimbalis, suddenly inspired, took a deep breath and (it is Durrell speaking) 'sent out the most bloodcurdling clarion I have ever heard: Cock-a-doodle-doo . . .' and then, after a pause, 'lo from the distance, silvery-clear in the darkness, a cock drowsily answered—then another, then another.' Soon the whole night was reverberating with cockcrows: all Attica and perhaps all Greece.

Perhaps all Greece. The distance between Cythera and Cape Matapan on the tattered map in my pocket, was somewhere between twenty and thirty miles. This enormously extended the possible ambit of George's initial cockcrow. If the Maniots, with a helping wind, could hear the cocks of Cythera, the traffic, with a different wind, could be reversed, and leap from the Mani (or better still, Cape Malea) to Cythera, from Cythera to Anticythera, and from Anticythera to the piratical peninsulas of western Crete; only to die out south of the great island in a last lonely crow on the islet of Gavdos, in the Libyan Sea. . . . But a timely west wind could carry it to the eastern capes of Crete, over the Cassos straits, through the islands of the Dodecanese, and thence to the Halicarnassus peninsula and the Taurus mountains. . . . The possibilities became suddenly tremendous and in our mind's ear the ghostly clarion travelled south-west into Egypt, south-east to the Persian Gulf; up the Nile, past the villages of the stork-like Dinkas, through the great forests, from kraal to kraal of the Zulus, waking the drowsy Boers of the Transvaal and expiring from a chicken-run on Table Mountain over the Cape of Good Hope. North of Athens, all was plain sailing; it would be through the Iron Curtain, over the Great Balkan range and across the Danube within the hour, with nothing to hinder its spread across the Ukraine and Great Russia—the sudden hubbub in a hundred collective farms alerting the N.K.V.D. and causing a number of arrests on suspicion—until it reached the reindeer-haunted forests of Lapland, and called across the ice towards Nova Zembla to languish among igloos. How far north could poultry thrive? We didn't know, but every moment the wind was becoming a more reliable carrier and further-flung and the cocks robuster. Thus, as the northern call fell silent among the tongue-tied penguins of the Arctic floes, the westward sweep, after startling the solitary Magyar herdsman with the untimely uproar and alarming the night-capped Normans with thoughts of theft, was culminating in ultimate unanswered challenges from John o' Groats and the Blasket Islands, Finisterre and Cape Trafalgar, and a regimental mascot in Gibraltar was already rousing the Berbers of Tangier . . . Due to the new impetus of Leghorn—enough to send a tremor through the doffed headgear of Bersagliere in many a draughty barrack-room—the Sicilian barnyards had long been astir.

The south-eastern tributary meanwhile, after sailing across Baluchistan, was initiating a fuse of clamour across the Deccan, and, reaching Cape Cormorin, leaping the straits, like the magic bridge of Hanuman, to set the roof-tops of Kandy ringing; travelling east to Burma and raising winged mutinies in the Celebes and the Malaccas. There was no problem here. Thanks to swarms of the far-wandering junks of the bird-loving Chinese, shrill calls were soon sounding across the gunfire of Malaya:

fumbling for their blowpipes, head-hunters rubbed their eyes in Borneo; Samoans were stretching and yawning on the split bamboo of their stilt-borne floors and hieratic and glittering birds, poised on branches heavy with almond blossom, were swelling their bright throats above the distant triangle of Fujiyama. . . . And what of the long eastern journey from the Asia Minor? Those solitary cries across the Oxus, those noisy resurrections among the black yurts of the Khirgiz and the Karakalpacks? The contagious din of nomad poultry ringing across steppe and tundra, waking the wiry Mongol fowl and sailing forlornly over the Great Wall of China; turning north to Kamschatka and straining for the Aleutians? What of the shivering, ruffled frustration of the Behring Straits?

Yes, what indeed?

Hearing us talking with some excitement, the moonlit figure of our hostess had appeared at the top of the ladder with another blue enamel half-*oka* can; and before we were a third of the way down it, we were across: a whale-fishing fleet materialized in the mists, each vessel captained by an eccentric Ahab engaged on a poultry-fancying competition with his colleagues, and it was entirely due to their hardy pets, beating their icicle-weighted wings and calling over the dark sea, that their Athenian message ever reached Alaska and the new world, crossed the Rockies and rang forth across the Hudson Bay towards Baffin Land. Without them, the Mormon roosters of Utah would have slept on; it would never have needed the sudden boost of Rhode Island which was to waft it safely across the mangrove swamps of Louisiana and through the Maya temples and the nightmares of Nicaraguan revolutionaries and across the Panama Canal. Now it spread like a jungle-fire through the southern hemisphere and a strident spark of sound leapt the swift-flowing narrows of Trinidad to ignite the whole Caribbean chain, jolting the rum-sodden slumbers of the Barbadians and touching off, in the throats of sacrificial birds in Haiti that the dark fingers of Voodoo priests were soon to silence, a defiant *morituri te salutamus*. In the dank unexplored recesses of the Amazonian hinterland, aboriginal and unclassified poultry

were sending up shrill and uncouth cries and high in the cold
Andean starlight gleaming birds were spreading their wings and
filling their breasts on the great tumbled blocks of Inca palaces.
The volume of the call was swelling now, sweeping south across
the pampas, the Gran Chaco, the Rio Grande; and then dwindling
as the two great oceans inexorably closed in, causing the superstitious giants of Patagonia to leap from their rough couches and
peer into their wattle hen-coops wild-eyed. Now the dread moment
came, the final staging-point and terminus of those great
Katsimbalis lungs; the last desperate conflagration of sound in
Tierra del Fuego with the ultimate chanticleer calling and calling
and calling, unanswered but undaunted, to the maelstroms and the
tempests, the hail and the darkness and the battering waves of
Cape Horn. . . .

For there was no hope here. It was the end. We thought with
sorrow of the silent poles and the huge bereaved antipodes, of the
scattered islets and archipelagos that were out of range; of
combed heads tucked in sleep under many a speckled wing that no
salutation from the Parthenon would ever wake: the beautiful
cocks of the Easter and Ellis and the Gilbert islanders, of the
Marquesas, the Melanesians and the Trobrianders, of Tristan da
Cunha and St. Helena. This gentle melancholy was diffidently
interrupted by our hostess: she was going to bed, but if we would
like to sit on and enjoy the moonlight, she would leave the street
door open, if we would lock up and slip the key under the door.
Remembering our early start next day, we rose and asked for the
bill. She smiled and said there was nothing to pay. Covert benefactors, the sailors had paid it on the way out and turned us into
their guests.

CHAPTER 10

The Entrance to Hades

WE boarded Panayioti's little caique, the *St. Nicholas*, just before dawn broke. Four black-shawled women and a ragged priest clustered in the stern and, at the embarkation of the latter, Panayiotis with a wink made the privy gesture of spitting to avert the Eye and the evil fortune which is supposed to dog the footsteps of priests, especially on a ship.* Up came the anchor and the women's sleeves fluttered in repeated signs of the cross before they resorted to their yellow pomanders. An old man and a boy were beside us in the bows. Both the man's hands had been blown off illegally dynamiting fish and one of the stumps was fitted, in lieu of a hook, with an adjustable clamp to hold a cigarette which he lit with a match held in his teeth and struck on a box tucked under his armpit. (These mutilations are common on all Greek coasts.) The water was so clear and smooth that for long fathoms one could follow each detail of the weeds and pebbles and rocks. The sharp-eyed boy, lying precariously prone along the bowsprit and gazing down, spotted and named the fish as they flickered by: 'A shoal of *marides*,' he would cry, or 'there goes a *gopa*,' and once, with a shout and a downward gesture with his fist as though he were lunging with a trident, 'A big *synagrida*! Oh, the cuckold! *Na!*' thereafter resuming his rapt scrutiny as motionless as a figure-head.

Except for the throb of the engine, all was silent. The bows made a crease like a long soft fold of silk over the stillness of the water. The wrinkled rocks of the shore were repeated upside

* The alternative exorcism is to touch one's pudenda.

down in a looking-glass, the emerging spikes turning into symmetrical lozenges invisibly conjoined along the water's edge. Every now and then a faint shaft of wind coming from nowhere would blur the smooth surface with a sudden fan of ruffles, and then all would be smooth again, and the boat and its passengers afloat in a blue dimensionless dream.

Dawn had already broken. But we were sailing south-east and the sombre watershed of the Kakovouni, falling in a staircase of rock to the isthmus that linked it to the last upheaval of Matapan, lay between us and the sun. Resting in notches of this palisade the climbing lances of sunlight were sloping forward and falling level and growing longer and brighter; as the sun's edge cleared the skyline they dipped and expanded down these western slopes in a score of mile-long geometrical shafts, doubling in brightness where two or three of them overlapped, dimming when an intervening hilltop blocked their golden advance with a sudden blue hypotenuse of shadow. Dawn and sunset civilize and rationalize these blank expanses of grey mountains, reducing systemless chaos to sense and running the mountains into each other with a fluid swing, quickening them with rhythm and sinuosity. Laying soft shadows along their flanks, dawn turns the ashen slag to champagne-colour and apricot and lilac and unfolds the dark branching torrent beds and pins them espalierwise across the ranges until they shrink and vanish under the climbing sun, waiting for dusk once more to expand and subdue them.

Now the olive terraces were succeeding each other in stroke after stroke of shade while the ledges they buttressed were thin curling bands of light. The towers of Alika moved towards us overhead and the ruin-crested cliff of Kyparissos; Moudanistica serrated its high pass with shadows; then Tzoukhalia and the tall spike of Vatheia entirely crowned with towers. On half a dozen heights a hundred sombre towers, each cluster thrust aloft on a coil of terraces, sailed up into the morning to break the parallel slanting rays of the sun, every campanile shedding a long blade of shadow along the sun's advance.

As the caique sailed further east, village after village turned its sunlit walls to us. They seemed to be suspended in the air to glow and flash there like the lustres of chandeliers. A headland rose and hid them and as we sailed past the little gulf of Marmari the sun was already high in the limitless Greek sky: a sky which is higher and lighter and which surrounds one closer and stretches further into space than anywhere else in the world. It is neither daunting not belittling but hospitable and welcoming to man and as much his element as the earth; as though a mere error in gravity pins him to the rocks or the ship's deck and prevents him from being assumed into infinity.

* * * *

At Marmari the Mani is little more than a mile across. The mountains sink to a saddle, the concave coasts lace it into a wasp waist, then it rises and swells again for a last rocky league or two, the coasts falling almost sheer. We drew alongside a narrow ledge and the passengers leaped nimbly ashore, grasping adzes and sacks to chop the rock-face for lime, leaving us to sail on down the deserted lee of the peninsula. Turning a salient, we came upon a solitary fisherman casting his nets. They were buoyed every yard or so with a hollow gourd. These grow in the shape of globes that narrow at the top and then expand swelling once more in a graceful neck which again contracts to the exact diameter, when the stalk is snipped off, for a cork. Scooping out the seeds they clean them by pouring in gravel which they shake till all is smooth inside; then they are left to dry in the sun. This induces the hue of baked clay, making them light as feathers and hard as wood until they look like perfect and elaborate pottery: convenient wine flasks for a journey, and, here afloat, resembling prisons for Arabian djinns. Both bulwarks of his boat were equipped with pairs of twin uprights of wood ending in two prongs in which his long tridents lay. These forked rests for fish spears were painted blood red like those mysterious horns, which, with double-headed axes, are the dominating motif of Minoan palaces. A wave and a shout, and another bulge of rock had hidden him. A few minutes further south, in the centre of another little bay, a dark cave yawned over the water. Panayioti cut down the speed of the caique.

'There it is,' he said. 'The entrance to Hades.'

He was afraid to stop his engine, declaring it was a devil to start again, but he would steer in circles until I got back. So I dived in and made for the cave which yawned like the lopsided upper jaw of a whale (the lower jaw being submerged), about thirty feet above the sea. As I swam inside a number of swallows flew out and I could see their little nests clinging to the cave walls and the flanks of stalactites. The cave grew much darker as it penetrated the mountain-side, and a couple of bats, which must have been hanging from the roof, wheeled squeaking towards the light. The roof sank lower, and, swimming along the clammy walls, I found a turning to the right and followed it a little way in; but it soon came to a stop. I tried all the way round and swam under water to see if there was a submerged entrance to another sea cave beyond. But there was nothing. The ceiling had closed in to about a foot and a half overhead, as I could touch it now with my hand. The air was dark but under the surface the water gleamed a magical luminous blue and it was possible to stir up shining beacons of phosphorescent bubbles with a single stroke or a kick. Strangely, it was not at all sinister, but, apart from the coldness of the water which the sun never reaches, silent and calm and beautiful. The submarine light from the distant cave-mouth makes an intruder seem, when he plunges phosphorus-plumed into the cold depths, to be swimming through the heart of a colossal sapphire.

I had never imagined the whole of the cave's floor to be under the sea. None of the legends mention it, though there is not a shadow of doubt that this is the cave through which those famous descents to the Underworld were made. When Aphrodite, in a rage, sent poor Psyche here to bring back the mysterious casket which would restore her beauty, Psyche was advised by a friendly tower (grown articulate at the sight of her about to fling herself from his summit), as follows: 'The famous Greek city of Lacedaemon is not far from here. Go there at once and ask to be directed to Taenarus, which is rather an out of the way place to find. It is on a peninsula to the south. Once you get there you'll find one of the ventilation holes of the Underworld. Put your head through it and you'll see a road running downhill, but there'll be no traffic on it. Climb through at once and the road will lead you straight to Pluto's palace. But don't forget to take with you two pieces of barley bread soaked in honey water, one in each hand, and two coins in your mouth.'*

Could the land have tilted here, plunging far under water one of those measureless caverns so common in the Greek mountains that go wavering into the dark mineral for slithering and zig-zagging furlongs, along which, with sudden strange draughts blowing one's taper out, one crawls past organ-pipes and chasms and stone honeycombs, and between stalactites and stalagmites like the molars and wisdom teeth of some tremendous monster on the point of clenching, to arrive at last, deep in the airless moun-tain's heart and pouring with sweat as in the hottest of calidaria, at (he stifling shrine of some local, troglodytic and half-wild saint like that of St. John the Hunter on the Acrotiri in Crete), in-stalled to counteract the ancient chthonian demons which dwelt there before Christianity came? An endless grotto from which the Lacedaemonians, knowing whither it led, recoiled in terror? Its mouth might lie drowned and swamped somewhere in the hyaline chasms beneath my water-treading feet; a landslide may have effaced or a boulder sealed it. The damp surrounding walls were seamless and solid. Fortunately, mythology is seldom so literal and the fact that Charon might not have been the first boatman Psyche had to pay on the day of her descent is of no importance. Down there lay the way to the river afloat with ghosts and the horrible three-headed dog (for whom the two sops, like the two coins for the ferryman, were a return ticket), the dim fields and the long sad halls of Persephone; the grey world where the ghost of the mother of Odysseus was wafted again and again from his arms like the shadow of a dream. It was under this very cave that

* Translated by Robert Graves, *The Golden Ass of Apuleius* (Penguin).

the bereaved Orpheus, making the dread journey in quest of lost Eurydice, lulled the hateful Cerberus to sleep with his lyre; and here that Herakles dragged the hell-dog into the upper air, slavering and snarling (and, it seems to me, soaked to the skin), by its triple scruff.

There is always something about these earthly identifications with Hades that fills one with awe. Lethe, they say, rolls its stream of oblivion near the Syrtes in Africa. The source of the Styx sends its little cascade down the rocks of Mount Chelmos in Arcadia, and I have followed the baleful windings of Cocytus across the Thesprotian plains in Epirus, not far from the deep forested gorge under indomitable Souli where the Acheron falls thundering. (For literary reasons I swam across it victoriously three times.*) It is somewhere near here that Odysseus, on the orders of Circe, descended among the shades. The most sinister of all, a few miles from Naples, beside the small gloomy mere of Avernus, is the deep tunnel through the volcanic tufa where the Cumaean Sibyl lived and where, by flickering torchlight, one can see, so far from its Achaean source, a tributary of Styx. It was here that Aeneas made his facile descent. In the meadows near Enna, the Sicilian peasants still point to the spring of Cyane where Pluto opened the earth with a trident-blow to carry Persephone down to his dismal kingdom.

A few strokes carried me round the corner of rock, the roof lifted and the sunlit mouth of the cave beckoned in a brilliant semicircle round which the swallows were still twittering and wheeling. Beyond, in the flashing sunlight, the caique, although it was quite close, looked very small and far away. It was still travelling in a ring, refurrowing its circular wake again and again. Joan sat at the tiller, Panayioti leant against the mast lighting a cigarette. How clear the daylight looked, and how bright the colours! I caught hold of the anchor on the boat's next circuit and, grasping the shank and putting a foot on the one rusty fluke, took Panayioti's extended hand and climbed on board. Joan pulled the tiller towards her and the wake uncoiled into a straight southward

* See Gerard de Nerval, *El Desdichado*.

course. Panayioti offered me a cigarette and lit it with his
butt.

*   *   *   *

The summit of the peninsula sank steadily as we followed our
southward course. At last the trim lighthouse of Matapan appeared and the rocks fell steeply to the cape. At the very moment that we reached it, the engine spluttered and seemed on
the point of extinction; but the caique sailed slowly past. Leaning
over the edge, it was possible to touch the last sharp edge of rock
where it met the water. This quick, rough contact with a geographical feature my finger-tip had often covered on the atlas
page was a satisfactory moment, like the nursery ambition of
closing one's fist one day round an actual north pole in the snow.
That final jut of barnacled limestone was the southernmost fragment of continental Greece and, except for the Andalusian rocks
below the flat Moorish roofs of Tarifa beyond the Pillars of
Hercules, of Europe too. All the islands lying further south—
though nothing actually intervened between this point and the
desert—were scattered Greek outposts and skirmishers on the road
to Africa and Asia; this was the phalanx-tip. These are simple
pleasures.

A few feet further along, the lighthouse keeper was sitting on a
rock fishing with rod and line. He looked surprisingly neat and
sedate for his lonely promontory. We were sailing so close that
he only just managed in time to pluck his line clear. His face lit up.

'What news?' he shouted. '*Ti nea?*'

'Good,' we shouted. 'All good. *Ola kala!*'

'Order and Quietness,' Panayioti supplemented. '*Taxis kai
isychia!*'

'May God be glorified,' he answered. Taking a pear out of his
haversack, he put it back and chose a better. We were well past
him now but the pear sailed through the air and alighted as
though by magic in Panayioti's hand. Then he stood up to
throw two more which fell safely into the bottom of the boat.
'Go towards the Good!' he shouted as he settled down again to

his fishing. Joan pushed the tiller to port and haltingly we sailed along over the remaining half a dozen yards which turned us north-east into the Gulf of Laconia.

Away to the east we could discern the dim outlines of the Elaphonisi—Deer Island—and of Cythera, the birthplace not only of Aphrodite but of Lafcadio Hearn, both hovering on the water as insubstantially as puffs of pale blue smoke: between them and Cape Matapan lay an extent of water which one would have thought (and thought, it seems, wrongly) no cockcrow could ever span. The sky and the sea were a single pale blue and only these wraiths of islands hinted the whereabouts of the far-away horizontal border, until the eye, travelling upwards, could discern high above that invisible horizon a yet frailer ghost: the long sierra of the Laconian peninsula in a faint and hair-thin seismograph climbing and falling and climbing again across the sky, and dying away northwards at last on its aerial journey to the main body of the Peloponnese.

Here and there as soft as a feather hung the suggestion of a salient, the thread of a celestial ravine descending a little way and vanishing into the sky on which, half-way to the burning zenith, that whole imponderable range was afloat. It died away long before one could follow the drop of its southern extremity to Cape Malea. Behind the two transparent islands, the sea and the sky melted together in the vague and luminous unity of a painted Chinese background. There in the blue haze, circled by tempest-haunting birds, lay the terrible Cape whose storms almost dashed the ships of Menelaus and Ajax, and those of many later seamen, to fragments. The storms of Malea carried Odysseus clean off his course, past Cythera and away for days till he stepped on to the island where—(ah, where?)*—the Lotus-Eaters lived. At the beginning of the last century an anchorite had his hermitage on the very tip and lived off the alms of passing sailors.

Scarcely a wave had rocked the *St. Nicholas* as she rounded Matapan but many a ship has been smashed on those sharp rocks.

* Djerba?

134

The faltering engine died with a gasp and we were becalmed. A sluggish current carried us slowly northwards and while Panayioti laboured at the engine—promoting, again and again, brief velleities of action that petered out in a cough—we toiled with poles fending the caique's bright timbers off the sharp peninsular rocks.

Hours passed and ashore all shade vanished as though it were a liquid whose few pools among the rocks the sun of noon had quite dried up. We anchored and waited, with the sail hanging dead, for the summer wind. Even swimming round the boat and lying on the decks or the rocks, the lapse of time and the merciless triumph of the sun began to grow oppressive. It must have been for this afternoon wind that Cephalus, hot with hunting and stretched on the shores of Thessaly, called with such longing that poor Procris, hidden in a brake, thought it was a rival's name and met her death. But no wind came, and at last it was a dapper caique, the *St. George* of Piraeus bound for Kalamata, which, late in the afternoon, picked us up and carried us, several miles off her course, to the bay of Porto Cayo. Panayioti, besides having paid for last night's dinner, tried to refuse all payment as he had not been able to drop us where he had promised. This time, fortunately, we won.

Porto Cayo is a beautiful but rather mournful bay, a deep inlet scooped from the eastern slope of the peninsula, corresponding to Marmari on the western shore, the steep saddle between forming the isthmus that links Cape Matapan to the Mani. It was on the high rocks between here and the cape that the temple of Poseidon had stood, on the emplacement of one to Apollo in Mycenaean times. It was the central shrine of the Spartans, an inviolable sanctuary for anyone on the run and the seat of an oracle. It was also a great meeting place for the elders of the cities of Laconia and one of several shrines in Greece where the souls of the dead could be summoned by their slayers and placated by sacrifice. Marble slabs found among the ruins prove that human sacrifices were not unknown. Pausanias—not the historian and geographer but the victor of Plataea—was starved to death here in the temple when the Spartans discovered his secret intelligence with Xerxes.* It was probably, as we have seen, destroyed by the pirates of Cilicia. Little remains, and many fragments and memorial slabs from here and Kyparissos are scattered in the neighbouring villages. Up the steep northern flank stretch the ruins of an enormous Turkish fortress, built at the nadir of Maniot fortunes at the same time as Kelephas. It was the scene of hard-fought Maniot triumphs over the Turks during the reign of Zanetbey: actions commanded by the great Lambros Katsonis and by the father of that Odysseus Androutzos who was later to share a cave near Delphi with Trelawny, while in Missolonghi, down the coast, Byron lay dying.

It is called Porto Cayo either from Porto Quaglio of the Venetians or a Port aux Cailles of the Franks for the surrounding rocks are the last place where the quails, migrating south in thousands, alight before flying off to Crete and to Africa. I have seen the fringes of their departing hosts further east in the Cyclades, and of another mass departure, that of the storks, in the Dodecanese. These are prone to hug the Asian coasts, huddling at night in vast unwieldy encampments on every available tree, fidgeting and shifting all night long until at daybreak they spread their wings again and sail away south in straggling interminable armadas. They set off from southern Poland and the Ukraine gathering contingents in Bukovina and Bessarabia and Transylvania and all the Balkans and Greece until, craning their necks towards the flat roofs of Arab houses, they benight the air. The western route, from Austria and Germany and Alsace Lorraine to the coasts of Portugal, lies over the straits of Gibraltar; once across, they disperse in companies to become the roof-guests of Arabs and Berbers and the Atlas tribesmen. Their shaggy nests, meanwhile, are left all winter long to be blown about by the winds of Europe and filled with snow on many a roof-top and belfry and minaret. The cranes I have never seen but Cretan shepherds

---

* Hard by, on the edge of the gulf, stands a cliff from which Petrobey ordered a delinquent priest to be flung. Bound hand and foot, he was left, broken on the rocks, to perish. Both deeds have left a curse on their localities.

have told me of that endless caravan lasting for hours stretching beak to tail from one edge of the sky to the other so high above Mt. Ida as to be almost out of sight, but accompanied by a strange unearthly sound like a far-away conversation; all, it used to be thought, heading for the forests of Central Africa to re-engage the pygmies, who are waiting for them with full quivers and, according to Aristotle, astride goats, in their never-ending war.

The stupor of a lagoon overhung this gulf. There are a few houses widely scattered, and salt and apathy seem to have eroded their dwellers. The Mani, in the accounts of many travellers and by the Greeks themselves, is reported to be mistrustful of strangers; though once their affections have been tried, the same sources declare, they grapple them to their souls. This was the first time I had seen a trace of this initial mistrust. It took a long time and some languid and sulky bargaining, quite out of tune with the normal friendly game, to find a man with a mule to take our gear to some pleasanter village inland. Each time that we protested against the outrageous price he suggested, he shrugged and made as though to drive off, and when we had to give in, without another word he struck the mule's rump a savage blow with his stick and let out a string of oaths as though the beast were standing proxy for these foreign disturbers of his gulf-side vacancy. Greek manners to strangers are so good—a hundred times better and more friendly than anywhere else—that these rare exceptions are disproportionately distressing. All four of us (except perhaps the mule) set off up the steep stream bed in a rage, cursing the thistles and cascading pebbles at each arduous step.

When we reached the saddle and sat on the stones to cool off these bad humours began to disperse. The mule and its churlish owner disappeared round a curve of the mountain-side and left us to gaze down at the beautiful bay of Marmari; for we were on the western slant once more, high on the side of the Kakovouni whence the sun had poured that morning. A fair-haired girl climbed the path towards us carrying a lamb slung over her shoulders and round her nape, fore and hind feet held in either hand in the manner of many archaic statues. She sat down still holding the lamb and the friendly inquisition began. Where did we come from? Was that our mule that had passed? How much had we paid for it? We told her and she exclaimed with a commiserating laugh that we had been robbed. Where were we heading for? We said that we didn't know; any of the villages inland from which we could continue up the east coast next day. She got up and readjusted her burden. 'You must come and stay in my father's house,' she said, 'in Vatheia, a big village about half an hour away. We live in a tower.'

Ahead of us as we rounded the outcrop of mountain a long backbone of rock advanced westward from the massif, dipped, and then rose in a high bluff to sink through loop after widening loop of olive and corn terrace to the sea and then melt into the westward-reaching coast that slanted away under familiar villages to Yeroliména and Cape Grosso. The wide ridge was jagged with broken towers like the spikes along an iguana's back and as it swept upwards to the bluff they spread and climbed with it, growing in number and height. An angular stook of towers was rooted in a cloud of cactus and olive, ending on the brink of the steep fall of the ledges and their many round threshing floors where the horses and mules, shrunk by distance, rotated like toys. This eclogue world and the brooding castellations unfolded in a flowing and passive enchantment through the tired gold light of the summer evening.

Vasilio, holding all four of the lamb's feet in one hand, pointed with the forefinger of the other to the tallest of Vatheia's turrets. 'There,' she said, 'that's my father's tower and welcome to Vatheia.'

It always happens in Greece that encounters with disagreeable people are followed by an overwhelming compensation as though the entire race by an unconscious second sight were in league to compensate the victim and smooth his ruffled spirits. One reads of poisonous leaves and others which contain their antidote fluttering side by side on the same Indian tree. In the case of this small jungle, it was as if nettles and dock-leaves were growing from a single stalk.

CHAPTER II

Bad Mountains, Evil Council and Cauldroneers

THE name of the Evil Mountains—*Ta Kakavounia*—has infected the inhabitants as well as the range itself: the Deep Maniots are dubbed 'The Evil Mountaineers' by the outside world. Alternatively (for these points of naming and derivation are never simple) the name is declared to be *Kakovoulia*, the Land of Evil Council, a damned region balefully populated by Evil Counsellors. There is even an ingenious third version,* based on the diminutive ending—*oula* appended to *kakkavi* (which means a small bronze three-legged cauldron); this turns the Deep Maniots into 'The Cauldroneers'. It seems that the Maniot pirates, before boarding an enemy vessel, would helmet themselves in these pots, and, with the legs sticking up like three horns, leap in swarms from the shrouds: enough to alarm any Turkish or Venetian merchantman into surrender. But the first two are the everyday connotations. They have done much to confirm the Mani's sinister fame, which has long been promoted by a supposed hatred of strangers and implacability in seeking vengeance.

Never has a reputation for xenophobia been more convincingly belied than by our welcome to Vatheia. Vasilio, the lamb slung across her shoulders, befriended us with the solicitude of Nausicaa. She led the way through a contorted and bulbous jungle of prickly pear which the dusk was transforming into the most queer of groves and up into the massed volley of skyward-shooting walls.

* Put forward by Prof. Kouyeas of Athens University and quoted by Mr. Dimitrakos-Messisklis, *op. cit.*

Somewhere among them, directed by her carrying shouts across the valley, the muleteer and his beast had halted at the foot of her father's tower.

Many things in Greece have remained unchanged since the time of the *Odyssey* and perhaps the most striking of these is the hospitality shown to strangers; the more remote and mountainous the region, the less this has altered. Arrival at a village or farmstead is much the same as that of Telemachus at the palaces of Nestor at Pylos and of Menelaus at Sparta—so near, as the crow flies, to Vatheia—or of Odysseus himself, led by the king's daughter to the hall of Alcinöus. No better description exists of a stranger's sojourn at a Greek herdsman's fold than that of Odysseus when he stepped disguised into the hut of the swineherd Eumaeus in Ithaca. There is still the same unquestioning acceptance, the attention to the stranger's needs before even finding out his name: the daughter of the house pouring water over his hands and offering him a clean towel, the table laid first and then brought in, the solicitous plying of wine and food, the exchange of identities and autobiographies; the spreading of bed-clothes in the best part of the house—the coolest or warmest according to the season—the entreaties to stay as long as the stranger wishes, and, finally, at his departure, the bestowal of gifts, even if these are only a pocketful of walnuts or apples, a carnation or a bunch of basil; and the care with which he is directed on his way, accompanied some distance, and wished godspeed.

In the *Odyssey*, the newcomer often strikes a banquet in progress, and very often a stranger in Greece to-day will find himself led to an honourable place at a long table of villagers celebrating a wedding, a baptism, a betrothal or a name-day and his plate and glass are filled and refilled as though by magic. Often, by a little chapel (dedicated to the prophet Elijah, the Assumption or the Transfiguration on a mountain top, or, outside some built-up cave, to a *Chryssospiliotissa*—a Virgin of the Golden Grotto—or St. Anthony of the Desert), he will find the rocks and the grass starred with recumbent pilgrims honouring a pious anniversary with singing and dancing, their baskets open and napkins of food spread out under the branches, the wine flowing freely from gourds and demijohns; and here, as at the village festivals, the traveller is grasped by horny hands, a place is made smooth for him on the cut brushwood, a glass put between his fingers and a slice of roast lamb offered on a fork or a broad leaf. This general hospitality on feast days is less remarkable than the individual care of strangers at all seasons. It is the dislocation of an entire household at a moment's notice that arouses astonishment. All is performed with simplicity and lack of fuss and prompted by a kindness so unfeigned that it invests the most ramshackle hut with magnificence and style.

To-night, however, there was a change in the accustomed Homeric ritual. After drinking *ouzo* in the walled yard at the tower's foot, Vasilio's father said, 'It's a hot night. Let's eat in the cool.' He took a lantern and led the way into the tower. We followed him up the steep ladders through storey after storey until, breathless with climbing, we were on a flat roof about eight yards square surrounded by a low parapet. Chairs appeared from below and Vasilio took a coil of rope and paid it into the night; hauling it up the sixty-foot drop after an exchange of shouts, with a round tin table tied to the end. She took out and spread a clean white tablecloth and put the lantern in the centre, installing a circle of gold in the moonlight. Our faces, which were soon gathered round a roast lamb which I hoped we had not met before, were lit up by an irrelevant glow of gold which changed to the moonlit pallor of silver while jaw-bones and eye sockets were stressed with shadow if anyone leaned out of the lantern's range. The rope, to the end of which a huge basket had now been tied, was lowered into the dark again and again for more wine and food.

The night was still. As our tower-top was the highest in Vatheia, the others were invisible and we might have been dining in mid-air on a magic carpet floating across dim folds in the mountains. Standing up, the other tower-tops came into sight, all of them empty and clear under the enormous moon. Not a light showed, and the only sounds were the shrill drilling note of two crickets, a nightingale and a faint chorus of frogs, hinting of water some-where in the dry sierra. I tried to imagine how this little group, dining formally round a solitary golden star of lamplight on this little hovering quadrilateral, would look to a passing bird. I asked our host if they often had meals up here: 'Only when we feel like it,' he answered.

He had been talking of the winter, and the familiar theme of the Mani wind. 'It makes a noise that could deafen you, when the tramontana blows through these towers,' he said; and all at once, in the silence and the hot moonlight, I had a vision of that lament-able blast screaming past the shutters, of maelstroms of hail and snow coiling through those perpendiculars. 'And when there's a thunderstorm, you think the world has come to an end with all the noise and the lightning! That's when the young think of marrying, to have company in bed to keep them warm. . . .'

The table was cleared and lowered swinging into the gulf and blankets and pillows, glasses and pitchers of drinking water laid out for the guests. 'I'll put this on the trap door,' he said, picking up an iron cannon ball from the parapet and cupping it in his palm like an orb, 'in case the wind should blow up and slam it shut. It's all they are good for now.'

We sauntered to the end of the village before going to bed. Beyond the cactuses a few miles to the south, a long row or twinkling lights, sailing westward under an upright pale pillar of smoke, suddenly slid out of the lee of Cape Matapan. It must have been an enormous liner lit up for a gala night. Could we hear the sound of music? One could almost imagine it. '*Megálo*,' said our host, 'Big'; truthfully enough. It disappeared behind the leaf of a prickly pear and emerged a minute later. I wondered where it was coming from. Beirut? Alexandria? Bombay? Colombo? Hong Kong? I thought of the passengers in tropical mess-jackets and low dresses and comic paper hats, the brandy revolving in balloon glasses, cigar smoke ascending, ship-board romances ripening, cliques cohering and splintering, plans forming and couples pairing off for the sights of Naples and trips to Vesuvius; of the gallant ship's doctor, of the life and soul of the party, of the ship's bore and the ship's vamp. Perhaps they were wearing false noses fitted with burlesque moustaches and large cardboard spectacles? To what tunes were they dancing, and were streamers being thrown? I remembered once, sailing past the southern Peloponnese and Calabria, leaning across the bulwarks as many of the passengers must have been leaning at that moment and wondering what happened in those wild and secret looking mountains to the north. 'Look,' perhaps they were saying, 'there's a light up there! How lonely it must be . . .'

The lights grew smaller as the liner followed the same path as many a Phoenician galley and many a quinquereme; heading northward in the invisible groove of Harald Hardraada's ships, sailing shield-hung and dragon-prowed from the Byzantine splendour of Mickelgard for grey northern fjords at the world's furthest edge. At last it shrank to a faint glow and was swallowed up by an immense obliterating cactus.

*   *   *   *

There was much, it occurred to me next day, to be said for tower-dwelling, especially in summer. Eating and sleeping on the roof while the lanes below hoard the stagnant air, one catches every passing shred of wind. One sleeps in the sky surrounded by stars and with the moon almost within arm's reach. Dawn breaks early, and, by chasing the sleeper down the ladder out of the sunlight, solves the daily martyrdom of getting up; and the Bastille-thick walls cool the rooms with a freshness that grows with each descending storey as the layers of ceiling accumulate overhead: six gradations of temperature from the crucifying blaze of the roof to the arctic chill of the excavated cellar. And towers ensure the rare and inestimable boon, that non-existent commodity of Greek village life, privacy. The turmoil of domestic life, insulated by the absorbent vacua of the intervening chambers, swirls and bubbles fifty feet below. Who is going to climb all those belfry ladders? (Alas, no physical barrier can daunt the thirst for company; but for the moment all was quiet.) There was another negative benefit of the Mani, and one which it had taken some time to appreciate: not since Areopolis had there been a single wireless set; nothing but that delightful horned gramophone in Yeroliména. The rest of Greece, even the remotest Arcadian or Epirote village, rings from sunrise to midnight with swing music, sermons in English, talks on beekeeping in Serbo-Croat, symphonic music from Hamburg, French weather reports, the results of chess contests in Leningrad or shipping signals in morse code from the Dogger Bank, and, as the instrument is nearly always faulty, all these sounds, turned on full blast, are strung on the connecting thread of an unbroken, ear-drum-puncturing and bat-like scream. Nobody listens, but it is never turned off. Towns are pandemonium. Every shop and café sends out a masterless, hydrophobic roar. These rabid wirelesses should be hunted out and muzzled or shot down like mad dogs. In the heart of the country, the silence of the most desolate places is suddenly rent by the blood-curdling howl of a rogue wireless set. . . . But, like religion, it has been late in reaching the Mani, and among the towers a blessed silence prevails. The only sound at the moment, as I sat over my long neglected diary among piles of sacks, was Vassilio half singing and half humming to herself in the room below.

She had demanded, the night before, all the washing which had accumulated since Sparta, and I had seen her foreshortened torso thumping and rinsing before daybreak in a stone trough in the yard and later spreading the laundry to dry on boulders and cactus branches. Now with this soft singing the delicious childhood smell of ironing floated up through the trap door. A floor further down her mother was weaving at her great loom which sent forth a muted and regular click-clack of treadles.

Beyond the bars of my window the towers descended, their walls blazoned with diagonals of light and shade; and, through a wide gap, castellated villages were poised above the sea on coils of terraces. Through another gap our host's second daughter, wide hatted and perched on the back of a wooden sledge and grasping three reins, was sliding round and round a threshing floor behind a horse, a mule and a cow—the first cow I had seen in the Mani—all of them linked in a triple yoke. On a bank above this busy stone disc, the rest of the family were flinging wooden shovelfuls of wheat in the air for the grain to fall on outstretched coloured blankets while the husks drifted away. Others shook large sieves. The sun which climbed behind them outlined this group with a rim of gold and each time a winnower sent up his great fan, for long seconds the floating chaff embowered him in a golden mist.

The sun poured into this stone casket through deep embrasures. Dust gyrated along the shafts of sunlight like plankton under a microscope, and the room was full of the aroma of decay. There was a rusty double-barrelled gun in the corner, a couple of dog-eared Orthodox missals on the shelf, and, pinned to the wall above the table, a faded oleograph of King Constantine and Queen Sophia, with King George and the Queen Mother, Olga Feodorovna, smiling with time-dimmed benevolence through wreaths of laurel. Another picture showed King Constantine's entry into re-conquered Salonika at the end of the first Balkan war. On a poster, Petro Mavromichalis, the ex-war minister, between a pin-up girl cut-out from the cover of *Romantzo* and a 1926 calendar for the Be Smart Tailors of Madison Avenue, flashed goodwill from his paper monocle. Across this, in a hand unaccustomed to Latin script, *Long live Uncle Truman* was painstakingly inscribed. I felt like staying there for ever.

* * * *

What sort of life went on in these towers in the palmy days or the Mani? When the great Nyklians, kind in tower and fierce in fray, were still supreme? The few travellers' reports are very conflicting. Many of them praise their love of liberty and their courage, others strengthen the adverse legend. 'Famous pirates by sea, pestilent robbers by land,' one calls them;* another, Lord Sandwich,† after praising their irredentist spirit, says much the same. A third,‡ without a shred of evidence, accuses them of

---

* George Wheler in 1675, *A Journey into Greece*.
† The discoverer of both the sandwich and the islands.
‡ Cornelius de Paneo.

cannibalism: 'It is probable,' he says, 'that the Maniots of Laconia have likewise in their fits of fanatical fury, devoured several Mahometans of the Morea.' Not even Leconte de Lisle, in a poem of most bloodthirsty fustian, beginning, *Les Mavromichalès, les aigles du vieux Magne*, goes as far as this, though he describes the battle between the Mavromichalis and the Turks near Pyrgos, and how the chief of the clan nailed the heads of the Turks round his tower until it was studded with skulls. Captain Stewart, coasting the region in 1807, pronounced them 'the most savage-looking animals I ever saw, very dark coloured and ill-clad'. Haygarth, the contemporary of Byron, in a rather fine poem written very slightly before *Childe Harold* but in a strain of pure Byronic philhellenism, compares them with their Spartan forbears:

> . . . still their spirit walks the earth.
> Their martial shouts are heard from Maina's rocks,
> Where, still unconquered, thousands rally round
> The spear of Grecian freedom . . .

Indeed, their Spartan descent, their legacy from the time of Lycurgus, was the theme of many writers. But before the War of Independence few actually went there, not even Byron, alas. Almost the first traveller to say anything pleasant about the Maniots in a non-heroic key was John Morrit of Rokeby. A Whig squire aged twenty-one just down from Cambridge, he made a leisurely journey through Greece from 1794 to 1796 (about thirty years, that is, before Greece was free), and wrote some charming letters home. He was stuffed up with the usual forbidding tales about the region, and (though he never penetrated into the Deep Mani) what a pleasure it is to hear someone writing in so natural and unstilted a vein! 'If I see any danger of not getting out (of the Mani),' he writes, 'it is not from banditti, but from the hospitality and goodness of the Maniots.' The mountains were poor in antiquities, but the Ancients 'survive here in a bolder manner, since certainly these people retain the spirits and character of Grecians, more than we had ever seen'. He obviously had a great deal of fun on his travels, and talked flippantly of marrying and settling here as chief of a Maniot band. He bought a Maniot costume for his sister: 'a muslin chemise and a blue silk pair of trousers', and suggests that they should both, on his return, go to Ranelagh dressed up as Maniots. All this is a great relief after the inflated sentiments of most previous travellers to occupied Greece, the ignorance, the bombast and the false and patronizing comparisons of the glorious past to the humiliating and servile present; the elaborate academic misapprehension by which all the Greeks were either demigods or crawling bondsmen: extremes to which poor Greece had been subjected for centuries by western travellers.

The thing that everyone seems agreed upon, including modern Maniot writers, was the lack of education and the comparative illiteracy of the region. But, in the first house he stayed in, Morrit found a copy of *Belisarius* and Rollin's *Ancient History* translated into Romaic, and his host 'talked to us a great deal about ancient Greece, of which he knew the whole history as well or better than us . . . and his eyes sparkled with pleasure as he talked of the ancient Spartans'. Well, well! But then, of course, it was only the Outer Mani. . . .

As far as I can discover, apart from Leake and Pouqueville, few people from the West came here. The society they portray is a primitive one. (A very black picture was to be painted of it, as we shall see later, by the only poet the Mani ever produced; but, again, he was not a Deep Maniot.) They were, of course, much richer then, thanks to piracy, but most of their cash went in forcing the growth of their towers and in personal adornment. In old prints of the Mani, women who are out of mourning are magnificently dressed. A thin white wimple of silk or muslin was arranged round their heads over a small cap and their plaits ran across their brows in a band. A long-sleeved dalmatic, heavily embroidered and fringed, fell to the knee and covered the top part of a long flowing dress which reached the feet. Under this were flowing *shalvaria*—oriental trousers—slippers adorned with gold wire, or, among the poor, rawhide moccasins. The men's costume was not unlike that of the islanders and the Cretans:

baggy trousers with many pleats ending just below the knees with legs either bare or greaved in embroidered gaiters, their oriental slippers sometimes turning up at the tip. Over their shirts they wore a short bolero as stiffly galooned with bullion as a bullfighter's jacket. (Petro Mavromichalis, when Leake visited the Mani, wore a coat of green velvet charged with gold lace.) Their great moustaches would sometimes measure eight inches across and their hair fell in thick black waves over their shoulders. At a raffish angle on the side of their heads was perched the soft, 'broken' fez with its long black tassel of heavy silk. Over the sash their middles were caught in with belts equipped in front with a slotted marsupial flap of leather to hold their arsenal of weapons: the almost straight pistols whose butts tapered and then swelled into knobs at the end like wrought silver crab-apples; *khanjars*, those long knives with branching hafts of bone or ivory that spread like two out-curving horns; and, their chief weapon for close-quarter fighting, the yataghan, its ivory hilt dividing like the *khanjar*, the long subtle blade curving and straightening again as fluidly as a flame. Often, too, they would carry cross-hilted scimitars whose blades described a semicircle. The steel of many of them was beautifully damascened and arabesqued and they were scabbarded in silver and silver-gilt and plum-coloured velvet. In full array, they were equipped with splendidly mounted powder horns and with intricately worked pouches for shot made of hammered silver from Yanina. Their long-barrelled guns, which resembled Afghan *jezails*, were so heavy that they could only be aimed when resting on a rock or a branch. This made them useless for hand-to-hand battles but valuable at a distance or for an ambush. These had a euphonious name, which sounds more like a flower than a gun; indeed, very like the Greek for both carnation and clove: *karyophylia*. This strange and musical word is an uncouth Hellenization of the name of an Italian gun-smith's shop whose wares were highly prized all over the Levant: *Carlo e figli*.

All this warlike bravery, thrown into advantage by their martial bearing and driven home by frowning brows and a fulminating gaze, was splendid. There are several portraits of these magnificently dressed Maniot paladins in the great Athenian house of the present M. Petro Mavromichalis—who is still, half-playfully, half-seriously, styled 'the Bey'—in Athens. I was surprised to see how fair were these Mavromichali warriors; their great manes and moustaches gave them the air of Vikings. As far as I can remember, only John the Dog wears the baggy Maniot trousers; the rest are all in snowy fustanellas, presumably because they were painted in Athens after the War of Independence when that fine Epirote-Illyrian garb had become the almost universal badge of Greek patriots. Indeed, under King Otto and Queen Amelia, the fustanella and all its attendant finery, with superbly Byronic island costumes for ladies-in-waiting, was the official court dress. When he was Greek Minister in Paris the great Kollettis (who came of a Kutsovlach family from Syrako* in Epirus) would often wear it, and the Goncourt journals speak with admiration of his presiding fully-kilted over delicious banquets of *agneau à la pallikare*. Now, apart from the evzones and those mountain regions where the old men still go kilted, it has died out. Wittelsbach eccentricity, and a touching loyalty to the country he adopted, impelled King Otto still to affect the fustanella in Bavaria after his abdication. It is thus clad that we may think of him among the fir trees and neo-gothic pinnacles of Neuschwanstein and Hohenschwangau and reflected in the bright mirrors of the Nymphenberg.

Apart from their appearance, their warlike pursuits and the superstitions and customs on which I have touched, there are no recorded details to quicken one's reconstruction of this former life. Yes, there are two: a traveller mentions that it was customary for the priests to wear a brace of pistols and that the Mani was so poor in food that many of the mountaineers lived on salted star-fish. This custom, if it ever existed (and it is the reliable Leake who records it), has died out without a trace. Star-fish? They were horrified at the idea. It was as bad as the bulls of Katsimbalis. . . .

* This village, largely inhabited by shepherds who are semi-nomadic between there and the Preveza area, also produced the poet Krystallis.

Pondering on this strange vanished life, I had a momentary vision, chiefly promoted by the conversation on the roof the night before, of the great-grandparents of my hosts involved in a village war in midwinter with the wind screaming through the towers; with the women pounding and grinding away at their cumbrous handmills or crowding round a brazier, melting lead and moulding shot; *karyophylia* poking from every slit, a swivel gun placed in the embrasure by my table, my host presiding over it, befezzed and voluminously breeched. Outside, the snow whirled along dark lanes which lightning and cannon flashes suddenly lit up and the report of the ordnance was drowned in thunderclaps. Children clambered upstairs stooping under the weight of single cannon-balls while beautiful dark girls, their plaits flying, sped up the ladders with flaming linstocks. There was a smell of gunpowder and the sound of somebody groaning in the darkness. . . .

Vatheia is one of several villages hereabouts which is supposed to have been populated mainly by Cretan refugees, presumably those in flight from the Turks after the Fall of Candia and the final defeat of the Venetians three centuries ago. Other Cretans had fled centuries before, in the thirteenth when Crete fell to the Venetians, taking refuge among the Byzantines of Asia Minor and settling along the Meander's banks. They have left a strong impression on the Mani, especially on the dialect. Again and again I heard, with sudden excitement, turns of phrase and pronunciations and words that I had only heard before in the most inaccessible villages of Crete. There are many superficial resemblances in their way of life; even, now and then, in their appearance. Yet there is a compact fleshiness (I do not mean fat), almost a muscle-bound look, about many Maniot features: a dark floridness, a low planting of hair on the brow, and above all a shuttered wariness in those dark eyes which, handsome as many of these faces are, is quite different from the alert, luminous extroversion of the Cretan physiognomy; and in spite of all the apparent resemblance, the whole atmosphere is different. On the whole, they dislike each other, and it is not entirely because, out of all

Greece, the Cretans are the most advanced partisans of Venizelist republicanism and the Maniots of the Royalist cause. Perhaps the heavy Cretan influx caused bad blood in the past; but it is probably because, in many ways, there are too many points of similarity. In fact, having during the war and afterwards become so fond of the Cretans—considering myself, in fact, almost an honorary Cretan—it was painful for me to hear them criticized so much. My spirited defence of them became something of a joke. The Greeks whom the Maniots think most similar to themselves are the Epirotes, especially (according to Dimitrakos-Messisklis) the Chimarriots of the Acroceraunian mountains. He finds much in common in the customs and characters of both regions, and, like a secret river deep down under successive immigrations from other Greek lands, the same tough Doric strain.

With what ease populations moved about in ancient Greek lands, in the world conquered and Hellenized by Alexander, the wide elbow room of Rome and the Byzantine Empire! Undocumented, free and unregimented, people wandered where they liked between the Thames, the Danube, the Euphrates and the upper Nile—anywhere, in fact, that was free of the Barbarian menace, and often beyond. Now everyone is numbered and ringed like a pigeon and held captive in a cage of frontiers. Across the firm loom of settled populations a constant irregular warp and woof of minor movement was always in progress, propelled by restlessness, by pursuit of trade, thirst for booty, search for colonies, flight or exile; or transplanted, perhaps, out of policy or for asylum. The little church of Tourloti,* outside Kitta, hints that one of the least known of these shifts may have made a small contribution to the population of the Mani. I do not know the

---

* Tourloti is a dialect corruption of the word 'Troulloti' which means 'cupola-ed'. *Troullos* is a cupola, the same word as *trullo*, which southern Italians apply to those strange beehive dwellings cohering in scores in the Apulian villages of Alberobello and Casarotonda near Bari, the old Byzantine capital of Magna Grecia. They are one of the minor phenomena of architecture and the only things that I have seen at all similar are the beehive shepherd huts high on Ida and the White Mountains in Crete.

date of the church. It is extremely old. But an inscription declares that it was founded by a husband and wife called Marassiotes, and dedicated to SS. Sergius and Bacchus. Now, by the middle of the seventh century A.D., the Lebanon had been inhabited for some time by a people called the Mardaites, which may be translated 'rebels', 'apostates' or 'bandits'. (They sound a rough lot, not unlike the Shi'ite Kizilbashi in the Pomak villages of the Rhodope mountains.) The Byzantine emperors sometimes used them as levies, and Constantine V Pogonatus had twelve thousand under his orders there, serving as a rampart against the Arabs. When the Arabs conquered Syria, the Mardaites retreated north and acted as a 'brass wall' along the Byzantine border, whence they were constantly raiding the Arabs until Justinian II (685-695) agreed by treaty with the Caliph to withdraw them into the interior of the Empire, and they were accordingly distributed between the Pamphylian coast (where they became seafaring men), the island of Cephalonia, and the Peloponnese. But the Mardaites were not originally from the Lebanon at all. They had wandered there (for some lost reason and at some lost date) from the district of Maras, in eastern Cilicia, almost fifty miles inland, that is, in a north-easterly direction between the Gulf of Alexandretta and the Euphrates. This was also the home of St. Sergius and St. Bacchus whose names are so unfamiliar in the Mani that their church is merely 'The Cupola-ed One'. The Orthodox laity are strongly regional and selective in these matters. The only other church dedicated to the two saints that I know is the beautiful and famous ex-mosque in Constantinople; and the name of the founder of Tourloti—Marassiotes—(which, too, is unknown in the Mani to-day) means, exactly 'someone from Maras'. Greeks, founding shrines far from their homes, are nearly always loyal to their home-saints. A church built by a Corfiot outside his island is almost certain to be called St. Spiridion; a Cephalonian, St. Gherasimos; a Zantiot, St. Dionysios; a Cretan, St. Minas; a Salonikan, St. Demetrius; and so on. Thus, the implications of this tiny church, just over ten yards square, offer themselves irresistibly: as well as the predominating Spartan blood there is probably some Frankish in the veins of the villagers of many-towered Kitta; possibly some Byzantine, almost certainly some Cretan; it now seems probable that we must add a wild splash from beyond the Taurus and the Lebanon, Greek still, and—sprung from 'brigands' and 'apostates' though it may have been—from brigands and apostates who, on the brink of absorption in their fourth and last sojourning place, remembered with piety the two saints that once watched over their lost Anatolian homes. . . .

The three strange yoke-fellows were still toiling round the threshing floor; the sun, climbing to its meridian, contracted their shadows on the stone circle. Watched from my cool eyrie the geysers of thrown grain, shooting into the air every few seconds and then dissolving in a floating haze of chaff, seemed to encourage speculation on trifles. Those three-legged cooking pots that were worn as helmets. . . . Mr. Dimitrakos bears out Professor Kouyeas' interpretation of *Kakovouliotes* by producing another obsolete nickname for the Deep Maniots: *chalkoskouphides*. This, at least, is plain: *chalkos* means brass, *skouphi* means a cap, a small hat: thus, the Brasshats. I don't know why, but somehow I felt unconvinced by this derivation, in spite of the authority of both sources—Dimitrakos and Kouyeas—and the impeccable Maniot endings to their names; but, a little while ago, in the *Travels* of Thomas Watkins, M.A.—a series of letters published in 1792—I suddenly came on the following phrase: 'The Magnotti'—Maniots—'free and independent as the ancient Spartans (are) still wearing on their heads iron helmets in which they occasionally boil their black broth . . .' This cross reference, from a source unknown to either of my authorities, convinced me in a flash—and will do so until it is competently refuted—that they are right, that the district has taken its name from its inhabitants, not vice versa, and that the Bad Mountains and the Land of Evil Council are really the Country of the Cauldroneers. So it is helmeted like three-horned vikings that one must conjecture their sallies through the imaginary snow, their descents with fierce slogans and bared yataghans on the invading columns of the Seraskier and the Kapoudan Pasha!

The famous 'black broth of the Lacedaemonians' crops up in nearly all the old travel books. It is identified with all sorts of things, of which the oddest is coffee (essentially a Greek thing, in the eyes of early travellers), which was first drunk in England in the seventeenth century, to the wonder of all, by a learned Cretan called Nathaniel Canopus who was at Oxford—at Balliol—for ten years until he was ejected under the Commonwealth in 1648. A still more far-fetched explanation of coffee is produced by Pietro della Valle in 1615. It was, he says, the magic potion *nepenthe*, the secret of which was learnt by Helen when she was in Egypt with Menelaus after Troy fell. It took away all pain and brought on drowsiness. It was this, in the fourth book of the *Odyssey*, which Helen slipped into the wine of Telemachus and his companion to send them off into a happy and dreamless sleep.

I have never seen one of these three-legged cauldrons. Cauldrons and saucepans in Greece are usually legless with flat bottoms, quite unsuitable for their dual Deep Maniot rôle. They must have died out, like so many small adjuncts of the past. (How many pogo-sticks still collect the dust in English attics? There are probably not more than a score of penny-farthing bicycles still in existence.) There is no evidence when these cauldrons became obsolete. . . . Another custom which has vanished without trace is the smoking of chibooks, those long slender Turkish pipes of cherry-wood with little earthenware bowls and elaborate amber mouthpieces. In all the old prints and engravings of Greek life they play a great part. A chibook is as essential an attribute of the klepht as his *karyophylia*, and sometimes as long. They must have been awkward bits of property, especially for a guerrilla warrior. On visits of ceremony, they were indispensable. It is not too far-fetched or romantic to find something purely Homeric in the character of Greek hospitality. But the formalities of visiting are oriental; at least they are that hybrid achievement which we think of as 'Turkish': and, like many Turkish formalities, full of dignity and grace. It is not for nothing that when these tribesmen from Central Asia became static, their neighbours were the three most civilized races: the Persians, the

Arabs and the Greeks. The other details of welcome survive intact: the spoonful of jam made from quince or whole grapes or morello cherries or rose leaves, the thimbleful of ouzo or raki, the little cup, iridescently cupola-ed with bubbles, of oriental coffee (or Spartan broth or a scruple of *nepenthe*?), the great gleaming glass of water, which is appraised and extolled by guest and host alike with the niceness of cork-sniffing claret experts. These were offered on trays by the eldest daughter, who would stand in silence until they were finished with her hands crossed on her breast. But formerly a sheaf of chibooks was brought in as well. They were carefully filled and lighted with chips of charcoal by two myrmidons (they were impossible to light alone), then, after the mouthpiece had been plunged into hot water, offered already smoking to the guest, who would take a few ceremonial draws before broaching the topic of his visit. In a prosperous Nyklian's tower, all the smouldering pipe bowls, to save the carpet, were gathered on a brass tray in the centre, with the stems, two or three yards in length, radiating to the richly accoutred Lacedaemonians cross-legged round the walls on divans, with a pistolled priest among them, perhaps, and a couple of kilted pallikars seeking asylum in the free Mani from the Pasha-ridden Morea, and the Bey in his fur-trimmed robe; all fingering their beads in silence, lids peacefully lowered over the amber mouths of their calumets, preparing to broach the eternal themes of feud and piracy and rebellion. It is hard to fit *Belisarius* and Rollin's *Ancient History* into this conversation piece; but, if we can, we must add a young philhellene traveller in a frieze jacket, with a sketch book and vasculum beside him, his forefinger marking the place in a pocket volume of Pausanias or Strabo as he puffs and chokes. . . .

Variations on this scene continued—till when? Well into the nineteenth century. One may search for these pipes in vain in Adrianople or old Stamboul, let alone the cement villas of Ankara. A few still moulder in the Plaka and some of the islands. Yet I have seen them in use as everyday objects (a strange and solitary survival of time when the Ottoman Empire, running from the pillars of Hercules to the Gates of Vienna, embraced three-quarters of the Mediterranean) among Hungarian magnates. Zichys and Telekis and Esterhazys—commemorating after dinner in shooting boxes on the puszta and in Transylvanian castles the time, long before Belgrade was reconquered by Prince Eugene, when the Pest skyline still bristled with minarets,—would enshroud themselves in smoke from these long pipes. (They too, by now, must be minor casualties of the *status quo*.) It is fortunate, but peculiar, that the comforting narghileh, which is even more unwieldy, should have survived in all the old cafeneia of Greece; steaming and portentously gurgling at the end of its coil—a tube as flexibly jointed as the seated caterpillar which these things always conjure up—the little red coals burning aromatically through the *toumbeki* leaves from Ispahan.

There are two more lost fragments of corroborative detail which have mysteriously vanished without trace; at the other end of the Greek world, this time, in the Danubian principalities of Wallachia and Moldavia which are now called Roumania. They are two kinds of headdress, both of them extraordinary and worn alike by the hospadars (voivodes or reigning princes) and the ministers and dignitaries of their little courts: the Great Boyars of the Princely Divans of Yassy and Bucharest.

Greeks, Roumanians, Turks and all foreign historians have been unanimous till recently in execration of these men, and, on the whole, wrongly; but that is not the point here. The important thing is that from the first decades of the eighteenth century to the first decades of the nineteenth, these two vassal thrones of the Ottoman Empire were occupied by Phanariot* Greeks or Hellenized Roumanian noblemen. Thrones were obtained through corruption and the princes' reigns were brief, nearly always extortionate and oppressive and frequently cut short by the bowstring, the gallows or the block. Some were princes of outstanding qualities, some were worthless, a few of them unmitigated

---

* From the Phanar quarter of Constantinople, round the Oecumenical Patriarchate, the spiritual headquarters of all Orthodox Christianity, and the centre of all the financial and intellectual life of the Sultan's Greek subjects.

villains. But they were all of them civilized and cultivated men and their misdeeds are in a measure balanced by their service to the Orthodox religion, by the encouragement they gave to both Greek and Roumanian learning, and, towards the end of their heyday, by their share in the Greek War of Independence. All the opprobium which, thanks to Voltaire and Gibbon, loaded the adjective 'Byzantine'—ruthlessness, duplicity, greed, vanity, ambition, vice, superstition and cruelty—has overloaded the implications of 'Phanariot'. With the strange processes of re-vision, 'Byzantine' has now lost its pejorative meaning; and, by the same processes, the Phanariots are emerging less satanically with every passing decade.

The juxtaposition of 'Byzantine' and 'Phanariot' is not for-tuitous. The old elective thrones they occupied, however perfunctory and, as it were, simoniacal their elections, were those of the old Roumanian Orthodox monarchs; of the Mushats, the Bogdans, the Bassarabs, of Stephen the Great, Michael the Brave, Peter the Cruel, Vlad the Impaler; and the atmosphere that sur-rounded these mist-enfolded Dacian-Latin potentates was half Byzantine, half Slav, a last faint echo in the snows beyond the Danube of the last faint whispers of imperial Byzantium.* This conjunction of influences was reflected, until well into the nine-teenth century, in the astonishing titles of the various dignitaries at the courts of the hospadars—the Great Ban of Craiova, the

---

* The Cantacuzene family—the most nearly verifiable of all surviving Byzantine dynasties—took root and reigned in Roumania long before the arrival of the Phanariots, thus escaping the tainted adjective. The most repre-sentative of the Phanariots are the families of Ghika (of southern Albanian origin), Mavrocordato and Soutso (from Chios), Ypsilanti and Moruzi (both of whom originated in the fallen Comnenian empire of Trebizond) and Mavroyeni from the Aegean and Rosetti (reputedly of Italian origin). Cantemir the historian and the Callimachi family were Hellenized Moldavians and the Caradja are presumed to have come from Ragusa in Dalmatia. The Rakovitza, Sturdza, Stirbey, and Bibesco families were of Roumanian stock. But all through the eighteenth century Greek was the court language, and it was Greek Constantinople that shed its glow on their little provincial capitals. All of them possessed immense estates in Roumania, many of which existed till a few years ago.

Grand Logothete, the Grand Spathar, the Grand Vornic, the Vestiar, the Hetman, the Paharnic; and so on. Until the war, the stucco and chandelier-hung palaces of Bucharest and Yassy and the labyrinthine country houses of the boyars—stranded like great ships in the flat landscape—were full of portraits of these most peculiar figures. A few of them were painted by Liotard, who came to the east as the travelling artist of the wicked Earl of Sandwich. Their beards—blue-black or ashy white, very occasionally a flaming carroty red—descended in billowing cascades to where their tapering white fingers rested indolently on the jewelled hilts of ceremonial daggers stuck in their sashes. Necklaces of pearls and gems sometimes hung round their necks. The long thick folds of their braided and fur-edged caftans widened over their shoulders to a great expanse of fur. Dim under the varnish in the background, the blazons of Wallachia and Moldavia impaled each other under the ermine and the pearl-studded hoops of closed crowns. The lips that nested in those cataracts of beard were voluptuously curved and red as cherries or clenched in a hermetic and ruthless line and their thick linked eyebrows, arched over eyes that peered forth from under hawk's eyelids, wore expressions of wickedness and arrogance and Olympian calm. Above, springing and expanding from hollow temples, the stupendous headgear climbed.

There were two different kinds. One of them, a smooth white which had faded on the canvas to the colour of a mushroom, ascended for several inches in a cylinder of equal diameter with the head of the boyar it was adorning and then began gradually to swell like a balloon, spreading at last to a huge pale globe two feet or more in diameter, the summit of the dome the best part of a yard from its wearer's brow. The other was an enormous edifice of thick fur, roughly cylindrical, but with a perpendicular ridge down the front springing from just above those arched eyebrows (which the hat's edge repeated in a widow's peak of fur), and ascending almost as high as a guardsman's bearskin, thickening slightly on its upward journey to end in a flat top at the summit of the ridge. A projecting bulge of coloured stuff—

it was hard to discern whether this, the actual cap inside the fur cylinder, was velvet or silk—over-topped the rim of this amazing structure, which was sometimes still further heightened by a spreading aigrette nodding from a heavy diamond clasp. These elaborate achievements must have enlarged the stature of a medium-sized man to eight feet and turned a tall man into a titan.

What is the origin of these sartorial freaks? Not Turkish, certainly, as nothing similar appears among the wonderfully swathed pumpkin-turbans of the Turks—like the headgear of the Gentile Bellini portrait of Mohamed II and the still stranger garb of the janissaries (many were almost certainly inherited, after the fall of Constantinople, from the Byzantines)—in the museum in the Grand Seraglio. The huge Phanariot fur hat, the *gudjaman*, probably derives from Persia, Byzantium and Muscovy in equal parts: Slavonic fur covering those expanding cylinders worn by the Byzantine dignitaries on the bronze Filarete panels, depicting the retinues of John VIII Palaeologue, on the doors of St. Peter's in Rome, and by the Byzantine warriors in Piero della Francesca's battle between Heraclius and Chosroes on the walls of Arezzo. The Byzantine passion for strange hats, which also appears on Filarete's doors, is well illustrated in the famous Pisanello medallion of John VIII: something resembling a cap of maintenance from which the crown, ribbed in segments, shoots upward like half a cantalupe melon. But the other Phanariot hat, that wonderful white sphere called the *ishlik*, is of the purest Byzantine provenance. There is a magnificent example, in the mosaics of the Kahrie Djami in Constantinople, on the head of Theodore Metochites, Grand Logothete to Andronicus II Palaeologus, who died in 1332. Engravings of Roumanian soirées in early Victorian times show, among the piped overalls, the frock coats and epaulettes of young men and the crinolines and Louis Philippe coiffures of the ladies, the reigning prince and the great boyars still attired in these ancient Byzantine canonicals. Pillars of fur and brocade and jewellery, their headgear soars towards the elaborate plaster ceilings and the hanging lustres in monuments of plumed fur and in pale floating globes. Outside, in the snow-muffled streets,

Arnaut bodyguards stamped to keep warm and strings of six Orloff horses from Bessarabia fidgeted with their postilions in the traces of splendid emblazoned sleighs driven by bulky Russian eunuchs from the self-castrating sect of the Skoptzi. In the eighteenth century Greek was the polite tongue, but in the nineteenth, as with Slav high life in St. Petersburg and Warsaw, French was the language of this strange nobility. (It remained so till World War II.) Educated at the Sorbonne, at the universities of Padua, Vienna or Moscow, or all four, they spoke several languages to perfection, and would spend their evenings discussing the writings of Chateaubriand and the poems of Vigny and Lamartine.

These obsolete sartorial baubles, of which under a century ago there must have been hundreds, have all vanished. The implements of ancient British beaker-men survive, but these have followed the three-legged helmet-cauldron, the chibook and the pogo-stick into non-existence. I have sought them in vain through the dust of many a Roumanian attic.

They, or rather their attendant associations, are not as irrelevant as they seem, for a number of these Greco-Roumanian boyars took part in the struggle for Greek Independence. One of them, Prince Alexander Ypsilanti, the head of the Philiki Hetairia, even hoped to assume the throne of a Greece reconquered with Russian help. Another, Prince Alexander Mavrocordato, Byron's and Shelley's friend and the dedicatee of 'Hellas', was one of Greece's first premiers. They were disliked by the fustanella'd klephts of Rumeli and the Morea and, in the Athens of King Otto when Greece was free at last, the rough native heroes resented the sophistication and the polished French of these strangers, their use of titles in a state which had banned them, their superciliousness and their European culture. They made them feel bumpkins. These two elements—the great guerrilla leaders, largely of simple origin in the mountains and islands, and the civilized Phanariots —were the dual components of Athenian society for many decades. They were incompatible to each other at first. But the breach diminished with time and was healed at last by the marriage of the son of Kolokotrones with a Phanariot princess Caradja, soon followed by the marriage of another Caradja to the beautiful daughter of the great Souliot hero, Marko Botsaris. The Phanariots, though socially exalted, have never attained, in the eyes of Greece at large, the supreme laurels which fell to the great generals and sea captains who played the leading rôle in Greek resurrection. But the two strains became interwoven and indistinguishable and formed the nucleus round which diplomacy, politics, the services, the professions, banking and foreign enterprise were to form Athenian society, which is fortunately one of the least exclusive, the most painlessly assimilative and, on the whole, the most scorchingly intolerant of pretensions in the world.

The sounds of feet coming up the ladder put to flight these musings on obsolete headgear and their sociological implications ('and about time too,' I can hear the reader murmuring). A section of the floor creaked open as my host's head appeared through the trap door. He sat down with a sigh, laying aside his sickle to wipe the sweat from his forehead. He had a kind and friendly face with all the recesses of its bone structure scooped hollow by past illnesses.

'How is the work going?' he asked me.

'It's going well,' I answered; untruthfully, for I had mooned the morning away pleasantly without writing a word.

The conversation drifted inevitably to politics. Like most of the Maniots, he was a firm Royalist. I pointed to the poster of M. Petro Mavromichalis and asked if he had voted for him.

'Yes,' he said, 'but I think we ought to change our deputy. The government is always promising to build a road here and it never gets done.'

The vision of a metalled highway snaking through the hills appeared; blocked by a column of motor-lorries, each of them loaded with a howling menagerie of wireless sets for the silent Mani. I silently heaped blessings on M. Mavromichalis' head. I asked him who he would prefer to represent the constituency: it was sad to contemplate this uprooting of traditional allegiances. He looked surprised. 'Who? Why, Kyriakos Mavromichalis of course, his brother. Who else?'

CHAPTER 12

A Nereids' Fountain

ONE compensation of this kind of travel is the unchartable and unregimented leisure between the rigours of displacement. Letters build their vain pyramids on some table in Athens; weeks pass; their mute clamour dies down unanswered; dust and oblivion enshroud them and the flight of months makes them obsolete and strips them of all but antiquarian interest. This vacuous and Olympian sloth is made more precious still by the evidence all round of arduous and boring toil. Here, too, in the absence of lofty theories about the intrinsic virtue of work regardless of results, no northern guilt comes to impair its full enjoyment. Such mephitic ideas cannot long survive the clear and decarbonizing sun.

Now and then one finds oneself, in the dilettante fashion of one of Marie Antoinette's ladies-in-waiting, helping in some pleasant and unexacting task: gathering olives onto spread blankets in late autumn, after beating fruit from the branches with long rods of bamboo; picking grapes into baskets, shelling peas or occasionally, in late summer, helping to tread the grapes. I remember one such occasion in Crete, in a cobbled and leafy yard in the village of Vaphé at the foothills of the White Mountains. First we spread deep layers of thyme branches at the bottom of a stone vat which stood breast-high like a giant Roman sarcophagus, then a troop of girls hoisted their heavy baskets and tipped in tangled cataracts of white and black grapes. The treading itself is considered a young man's job. The first three, of which I was one, had their long mountain boots pulled off; buckets of water were sloshed over grimy shanks and breeches rolled above

the knee. 'A pity to wash off the dirt,' croaked the old men that
always gather on such occasions. 'You'll spoil the taste.' This
chestnut—which I imagine to have existed for several millennia
—evoked its ritual laughter while we climbed on the edge and
jumped down on the resilient mattress of grapes. Scores of skins
exploded and the juice squirted between our toes.... In a minute
or two a mauve-pink trickle crossed the stone lip of the spout,
and dripped into the waiting tub; the trickle broadened, the drops
became a stream and curved into a splashing arc.... We were
handed glasses of the sweet juice which already—or was this
imagination?—had a corrupt and ghostly tang of fermentation.
When the stream slackened, the manhood of the treaders, shuffling
calf-deep in a tangled slush by now and purple to the groin, was
jovially impugned.... For days the sweet heady smell of the
must hangs over the village. All is sticky to the touch, purple
splashes and handprints on the whitewash and spilt red rivulets
between the cobbles and the clouds of flies suggest a massacre.
Meanwhile, in the dark crypts of the houses, in huge grooved
Minoan amphorae, the must grumbles and hits out and fills the
house with unnerving fumes and a bubbling noise like the rumour
of plots, a dark conspiracy of whispers. For as long as this vaulted
collusion lasts, a mood of swooning and Dionysiac laxity roves
the air.

How different from the vineless and unleafy Mani! But still,
leisure has its rewards here as well: idle mornings of meditation
in upper rooms and saunters through a maze of towers and now,
lying and smoking after a happy sleep in the cave-like shadow of a
carob tree, above a landscape scattered with harvesters, I could
watch the glint of their sickles as they felled the sparse corn.
Under their yellow loads animals minced up the lanes on delicate
hoofs. Threshing teams rotated on the gleaming dials of stone
like the bustling minute-hands of eccentric timepieces and the
winnowers plumed the middle distance with golden geysers of
chaff. Strange that the word *cereal* should conjure up no vision
but that of an overfed northern brat with a scarlet cheek crammed
with breakfast food; never Ceres, whose rites were being

celebrated below. But the Greek name—*Demetriaka*—immediately suggests the kind goddess of the sheaves with her chaplet of wheatears, her torch and her poppy.

Common words derived from the names of ancient gods in modern Greek are more evocative of their origins, perhaps by their freshness on a foreign ear, than their Latin equivalents in English. 'Venereal', for instance, never suggests Venus, but 'the Aphrodisiac diseases' in modern Greek are immediately and painfully suggestive of baleful aspects of Aphrodite Pandemos. 'Erotikos' merely connotes 'pertaining to love', and summons up the innocent and youthful Eros; unlike the word 'erotic' in English. But there is no English equivalent of divine Latin origin —it would be 'cupidinous'; Amor's derivatives strike a more suspect note; and, strangely, though 'Mercury' is the fluid metal compound in English, the Greek word *hydrargyros* (watersilver) fails to commemorate Hermes. He only survives, as he does with us, in the word 'hermetic', recalling not so much the messenger of the gods' swiftness and volatility, as Hermes Trismegistus or the Egyptian Thoth and all that is sealed up initiate and arcane.

The cavernous shelter of this carob tree, these branches dangling with horny locust beans, was the right asylum from the afternoon sun for this Maniot pastoral. As the oven-like heat began to languish, the beckoning figure of our old host appeared below. Joining him, we made our way along a lane that circled like a contour-line the flank of two tower-crowned hills and led away to a cleft in the limestone mountain-side unexpectedly filled with green plane trees and figs and sycamores and a sudden insurrection of pink and white oleander: a green and leafy dell on the flank of the Mani. It was all due to a tinkling thread of water so cold that a mouthful made one shiver, which fell from the rock face into a rough stone tank whose inner walls fluttered with dark green water-weed. Neolithic channels and bamboo conduits led the precious liquid into hollowed tree trunks; and a similar system of flimsy and primordial irrigation had conjured up, over strips of earth banked in miniature tiers on both sides of the descending cleft, the green of tomato leaves and chickpeas and beanstalks. It soon petered out and the rock descended in great steel sweeps to the sea, interrupted now and then by a crescent of yellow stubble. The place had the unexpectedness of an oasis. The old man slipped two bottles into the tank and joined us at the low wall that overhung the bright layers. 'There!' he said, 'my garden.'

He used the word *bagtche*, a Turkish word of Persian origin, instead of the more usual Greek *kipos* or *perivoli*. It is a term still in common use in many country districts. I had been on the lookout in the Mani for any diminution in the sprinkling of Turkish words in spoken Greek but although there are considerable local peculiarities in the Maniot dialect there appeared to be no appreciable change in this respect. Contact with other races inevitably leaves a linguistic deposit and the two main contributors in Greek have been the Turks and the Venetians, the latter especially in matters concerning navigation. Perhaps the word *bagtche* has stuck because of the Turkish devotion to kitchen gardens; though the best gardeners in the Balkans are actually the Bulgars. It is, with curd-making and the distillation of attar, almost their only skill.

One of the great stumbling-blocks for writers like Dr. Fallmerayer, who are eager to underline or exaggerate the importance of the Slav element in the ethnological make-up of the modern Greeks, is that although Slav settlements in Greece left a vast and tiresome legacy of place-names behind them, there is scarcely a word of Slav origin in ordinary spoken Greek. If the language of a race is a living memorial to its history, the Slavonic share in the history of Greece would seem to be very slight indeed. The Turkish and Venetian words are nearly all nouns describing some object that first reached the Greeks *via* the Turks or the Venetians. In nearly every case there is a pure Greek equivalent and the interlopers could all, if necessary, be discarded. Indeed, there are purists who are eager to scrape away these alien barnacles as blemishes to the purity of the Greek tongue; perhaps, also, as they seem the stigmata of foreign occupation. Wrongly, I think. The corollary of this cleaning-up process is a distortion of history. It would certainly rob the rich spoken tongue of much of its stimulus and bite. (The Hellene and the Romios are at it again!) There are, through this random incrustation of Turkish words on the smooth surface of the Greek language—jagged and barbarous sounds perhaps, but with a rank zest like a wipe of garlic round a salad bowl—a number of noble Persian words. One turn of phrase, now that I know its full import, always fills me with delight: 'Milá ta Ellinika pharsí,' 'He speaks Greek perfectly.' It is a common remark in the everyday demotic. All is plain sailing except the last word. Pharsí? This mysterious and un-Hellenic adverb of perfection is never applied to anything but skill in language and it was only after I had been hearing it for years that an Athenian expert in such matters explained its meaning. Among the old Turks of the Ottoman Empire, Arabic was the language of religion and Persian the language of poetry and romantic literature. A cultivated man was expected to be acquainted with the latter, and, even if his knowledge of it was slight, to adorn his rough vernacular, as a jackdaw decorates its nest, with borrowed Iranian elegances; to talk, in fact, in the mode of Fars, the south-eastern province from which the name of Persia (and, no doubt, of the Zoroastrian Parsees) derives. *In the mode of Fars* . . . the phrase slipped into the Romaic, and I can never hear it now without a brief dream-vision of the closed gardens of Shiraz—*bhags*, in fact—filled with the sound of lutes and quatrains and falling fountains and the songs of moon-faced girls. . . .*

The old man picked a few tomatoes and chickpeas and unwrapped from its rag a lump of cheese which he took out of his basket. Spreading them all neatly on a napkin he then unstoppered one of the bottles that he had left in the stone tank. It was *kokkinelli*, excellent retsina the colour of pink champagne which is common enough in Attica but rarer than nectar in this

---

* The poet Seferis—now Ambassador in London—introduced me to another of these stray Persian fragments: *syntrivani*, which is a beautiful demotic word for fountain—indeed for those playing in the imaginary *bhags* evoked by the word *pharsí*. . . .

landscape of pumice. Its short sojourn under water had almost frozen it. Sipping and eating, alerted by a sudden noise and the clank of bells, we watched two herds of goats converge along the path from either direction. A third came leaping down through the trees, three shaggy hordes of Satans reeking of Hell and filling the air with dust. The hillside was alive with their many-pitched and sardonic derision; there was a ripple of hoofs and a clatter of long ribbed and spiralling horns as they assaulted the troughs and the hubbub was augmented by the heckling of skinny dogs.

Human dominion is never more than barely tolerated by these half-wild flocks. There is protest and anarchy at every step and the wide-hatted herdsmen, knee-deep in the rank turmoil, seem only to control them by the constant whirling of their crooks and a fusillade of stones and un-Theocritan objurgation. A raffish distinction is supplied to the goats' faces by the jut of their southern gentlemen's beards, but the set of their flecked yellow eyes, barred by oblong black pupils, spells only wickedness and cynicism and a kind of off-hand and humorous connivance, as if they were jeeringly abreast of our most carefully hidden secrets. A scattering of black Maniot pigs added their plebeian hysteria to the stampede. What could they all find to eat in this sun-smitten wilderness? A nimble nanny-goat had settled the problem by leaping into a sycamore tree and rising with lightning bounds from branch to branch till she had reached the top, where, perched precariously like a heraldic emblem, she began swallowing the delicious young leaves. The goatherd was in a frenzy and inappropriate oaths whizzed through the air in the wake of stony missiles. 'Pimp!' he shouted, 'Catamite!' and 'Whore!'; all in vain. Finally, aiming his crook like a javelin, and winging it pleonastically with the cry of 'hornwearer!' he caught her a neat blow on the belly. '*Na, Keratá!*' The goat sailed up into the air and over our heads in a wide arc and alighted on the hillside, where, cool as a cucumber, the female cuckold went on munching some gloomy plant. They vanished as quickly as they had come leaving nothing but a rank whiff and a pattern of neat cloven intaglios in the mud round the troughs. The barking and jeering dustclouds diminished and died away in the direction of the towers and vanished towards the sunset in a golden, far-tinkling haze.

* * * *

It came as no surprise when our old host, fishing out and uncorking the second bottle as the moon took over from the sun, mentioned that 'the old people'—always this disclaimer!—believed this fountain to be haunted by nereids. It was just the place for them. After Charon and a mysterious creature called the kallikantzaros, these beings are the supernatural survivors of the ancient world most often mentioned by name in the Greek countryside. Though some of them *can* be—especially in the Mani—sea-dwellers, on the whole they seem to have moved inland and become freshwater denizens haunting remote streams, springs, fountains, watery grottoes, mountain rivers and torrents and, occasionally, mill-ponds, especially if the mills are in ruins. It is impossible to say when this migration took place; perhaps it is just a shift of names; but they have usurped the hegemony of the ancient naiads and of the dryads and oreads as well. They have inherited the generic rôle of the nymphs. They dress in white and gold and are of unearthly beauty. Strangely enough, they are not immortal; they live about a thousand years. But they are of a different and rarer essence from ordinary mortals and, in some way, half divine. Their beauty never fades, nor do the charm and seduction of their voices. They are wonderful cooks and skilful spinners of flimsy and diaphanous fabrics. 'Cooked by a nereid!' 'Spun by a nereid!'—these expressions used to be common praise. There is also a light and airy creeper that festoons the trees in some parts of Greece, known as 'nereid-spinning'. It reminds one of the cave where Odysseus landed on his return to Ithaca and the 'great looms of stone where the nymphs weave robes of sea purple marvellous to behold'.

These nereids are feminine, volatile and wanton; seldom capable of a lasting passion. But most of the harm they do is involuntary, due to a congenital inaptitude for fidelity and the tamer domestic virtues. Interruption of their revels incurs the penalties of dumbness, blindness or epilepsy. They often fall violently in love with mortals, especially the young and brave, skilful dancers and flute- and *lyra*-players, and carry them off to their waterside haunts and to the threshing floors where they sometimes dance. Lonely young shepherds are particularly exposed to these dangers. 'Do not go up to the lonely tree', an island song runs, 'nor down into the lowlands, nor play your flute by the upper reaches of the river, lest the nereids, finding you alone, gather round you in a throng.' There are many tales of shepherds and princes falling in love with them. When it is the other way round the dazed young stranger is carried off to a secret grotto, and wrapped in a passionate embrace, the nereid sailing away on the wind at the third cockcrow. But, with a few exceptions, their ardour flags before that of their lovers. If a nereid is reluctant to yield to a mortal (according to one legend) the secret of success is to seize her kerchief. She turns into terrifying shapes—into that of a lion, a snake and finally into flames, as in the story of Peleus and Thetis—but she at last resumes her own and surrenders and their secret nuptials are celebrated.

Sometimes, when a mortal keeps the kerchief hidden, nereids remain faithful to their husbands for years, even when the latter are married to mortal wives. Some have helped their husbands with supernatural backing, manœuvring them to the height of worldly success. They hate mortal women and the sentiment is mutual. Both are gnawed by jealousy and women seek protection for their households in amulets, by hanging a clove of garlic over the door and by making a cross with paint or lamp-black on the lintel. The forty days between childbirth and churching are a particularly perilous time for women not only from spiteful nereids but from the Evil Eye and the other baleful influences that are loose. There are many families, apart from the Mavromichalis, who are said to be *neraïdogennemenoi* or nereid-born. They are thought to possess more than human graces. The adjective is also in common use to describe girls of especial beauty and charm. Fickle though they are, nereids worship their children by mortals

—they are constantly drawn to their cradles. In fact, they have a general passion for the young and often kidnap pretty children, leaving in their stead sickly nereid changelings who usually pine away and die. Children sometimes run away and dance with them for days off their own bat and their petting and spoiling often has fatal results. When this happens the nereids are overcome with sorrow. Young men in love with nereids become melancholy and ill and prone to strokes and seizures. There are 'nereid-doctors' who can cure the nereid-struck with potions and charms. One of the best of these remedies is a branch of 'nereid-wood', a species of tree of which I have not been able to discover the ordinary name. Goats and other livestock fall under their spell; they desert their flocks and waste away. A native of the Aegean islet of Pholegandros attributes the innumerable chapels there to the eagerness of the peasants to have a protecting saint close by. The whole species are sometimes referred to as the 'kalokyrades'—'the good ladies'—on the same euphemistic principle that prompted the old Greeks to call the Furies the 'Eumenides' or 'kindly ones'.

Our old host put the remains of our little feast back into his basket. The moon was rising and we prepared to go back to the towers which now shone silver along their eastern flanks.

'We don't have much trouble with them now'—how admirably civilized was the attitude of my rustic host and how much more sensible and balanced than the attitude of a whole class of his compatriots with whom I shall have to do in a paragraph or so.

CHAPTER 13

Gorgons and Centaurs

IN nothing is the continuity of Ancient Greece clearer than in the superstitions and pagan religious practices (and many of the 'Christian' ones) that still prevail in the Greek mountains and islands. I think it is true to say that the educated classes are less and the simple class more superstitious than their English counterparts. The only superstition that really seems to hold its own in the upper reaches of society is the class-defying and pan-Hellenic—indeed, almost world-wide—belief in the Evil Eye. But even in this, the strongest single superstition among the simple, there is a touch of levity. It is considered a bit of a joke among sophisticated people, certainly it holds a less tyrannic sway than it does in grand Italian circles. Nevertheless, nobody who has set even a tentative foot in Athenian high life would need to hesitate a second in naming someone credited with this baleful and perhaps unconscious power.

It is a wry paradox that the newly urban and semi-educated in Greece, whose knowledge of ancient literature is very limited, should be one's prime stumbling block in approaching these matters. (This knowledge—it never seems to vary—is covered by the ability to quote the first line of the *Iliad* and the *Odyssey*, Hector's single-line patriotic injunction about omens to Polydamas, the equally patriotic couplet of Simonides on the Spartan dead at Thermopylae, the two laconic, and again, patriotic, phrases of Leonidas and the universal tags about self-knowledge and nothing in excess—forty-two words in all.*) These are the

* Nearly four times as much, in fact, as the treasury of English literature— 'To be or not to be' plus 'My kingdom for a horse,' a beggarly twelve words,

very people who deplore one's curiosity about such matters and minimize or negate their existence and, in a few cases, try to hinder one's access to them as 'backward', 'primitive' and above all 'un-European' elements in the modern Greek State. It is odd because these people are usually the very ones to insist most vehemently on the pure and unbroken descent of the modern Greeks from the Greeks of the Periclean age; and if there is one element in Greek life, after the language and the Greek character itself (I think it is true to say that they possess all the faults and many of the qualities of their ancestors), which points to unbroken continuity, not only from Periclean Greece but from a yet remoter past, indeed, from the very cradle of European culture, it is the survival of these ancient beliefs and practices that some seek to patronize out of existence.* Certainly nothing could

though free of nationalism—that adorn the memories of their exact English equivalents. I very much fear that the Greek might win even more signally by also being able to quote the first of these Shakespearian fragments.

* There are understandable reasons, mistaken though they may be in this case, for this attitude. The last few centuries have been full of miseries, and it is natural to wish to forget them and the poverty and hardship that went with them, of which superstition can seem a part. During those sombre times, the only inspiration was the memory and example of klephtic heroes. As Greece re-emerged, these were joined by a remoter pantheon of ancient, more dimly remembered ancestors—warriors, rulers, philosophers and artists—who though they had yet to re-attain in rustic minds the same lustre as the klephts and the traditions of lost Byzantium, were considered by the rest of Europe, which the Greeks, by force of arms, had at last rejoined, as the glory of the world. A few decades later, Professor Fallmerayer sought to prove that the Greek population of the peninsula had been entirely replaced by Slavs in the Dark Ages. The theory has been discredited, but it was both bewildering and angering to the Greeks, not only as impugning their Greekness, but because, since early Byzantium to the present day, Slavs have been natural enemies and 'barbarians', and, the Bulgars especially, utterly abhorrent. This theory has left a legacy of touchiness. Fallmerayer's main argument is based on the number of Slav place-names in Greece. It proves nothing one way or the other. A low ebb of national spirits, a brief foreign ascendency and a temporary change of land tenure may, though it is not the rule, do the trick in a generation or two. A minute English ascendency has changed thousands of place-names in the British Empire, a handful of English altered hundreds of Celtic names in

more tend to minimize the volume of Slav and other barbarian invasions, or underline the fact of the invaders' swift absorption in a predominating Greek population. The aversion of some of the higher clergy—though not of the rustic priests, who see nothing anomalous in Christian and pagan co-existence—is based on much more logical grounds.

This side of Greek country life, which evokes the scorn and hatred of some Greeks but few foreigners, has attracted, during the last hundred years, the interest and devoted study of a number of Greek and foreign scholars. The most profitable sources in Greece are Kambouroglou and the magnificent and monumental work of Polites. There is Bernhard Schmidt and there is Lawson. My own favourites are the Athenian Professor Alexander Polites and John Cuthbert Lawson, the Cambridge don. They usually agree but not always; and between them they cover a wide field. Both refer back to ancient sources with a scholarly fairness. Both of them have studied the works of St. John Damascene (whose condemnation of certain pagan practices, though ineffective—for many of them still exist—is very revealing in showing how little they have changed since he anathematized them), the great Byzantine scholar Psellos and that strange seventeenth-century figure Leo Allatius of Chios. Lawson is the one from whom I plan, in later pages, to crib most freely; perhaps because Professor Dawkins used to talk of his early travels with such amused

Ireland, the Conquest has left a small, but disproportionate number of Norman village names. A protracted Moorish sway changed even the names of rivers and mountains in Spain, and the Spaniards altered half the Indian nomenclature of the New World. Few people in Greece now remember that, a few generations ago, Areopolis, Lamia, Amphissa, Delphi, Alexandroupolis and Siderokastro were called Tzimova, Zeytoun, Salona, Kastri, Demirhissar and Dedeagatch; and the pronunciation of several English place-names has changed even within my lifetime. One's mind wings away to Natal, Ackermann, Boileaugunge and Monrovia, to Byzantium-Constantinople-the *Polis*-Tzarigrad-Mickelgard-Istanbul. . . . I think of some Maya jungle villages practically unvisited by anyone of European stock for generations but called by the Maya-speaking Indians after the name of a Catholic saint. In Liechtenstein, a single family has imprinted its name on a whole country, itself originally another place-name several hundred miles away.

affection. I can still hear him speak with a chuckle about the 'dear fellow'; also because his work*—a rare book, now long out of print—is a real triumph of scholarship and detailed reasoning. Lastly, because he knew much more about it than I do.

It is impossible to wander about in Greece or live for long with peasant families without striking this supernatural background. But it is steadily losing its grip. The industrial age, that impartial exterminator of gods and demons, is succeeding where the Fathers failed. Among country people there is seldom any bashfulness in discussing these matters, except when the semi-educated have intimidated them into reticence. Old women are the richest repositories of knowledge and sometimes—through keeping company with their elders at the laundry-trough, the loom and the spindle—young girls. The attitude of peasant men and women alike outwardly resembles the upper class attitude towards the Eye; it is one of amused tolerance coupled with veneration; because, true or not, these beliefs are old and they are heirlooms.

What happened was this. Since they issued from the haze of pre-history in which a primordial Great Mother may have held universal sway, the Greeks have always been polytheists; and one of the marks of polytheism is that it keeps open house: all gods are welcome. Swarms of Asiatics moved into the company of the native Greek gods and made themselves at home; and, when Christ appeared on the Graeco-Roman scene, there was plenty of room for Him. Tiberius, according to Tertullian, suggested the apotheosis of Christ; and Hadrian (writes Lampridius) reared temples in His honour. His statue, with that of Orpheus and Abraham, was set up in the private shrine of Alexander Severus, and St. Augustine tells of Him keeping similar company with Homer, Pythagoras and St. Paul. This tendency was even more widespread and elastic among the common people. But monotheism, by its very nature, cannot reciprocate this easy-going welcome and when Christianity became the State religion

* *Modern Greek Folklore and Ancient Greek Religion* by John Cuthbert Lawson, Fellow and Lecturer of Pembroke College, Cambridge, 1910.

of the Empire, the expulsion of the old gods, after thousands of years of happy tenure and the reduction of the Pantheon to a private cell, was a serious task. There was not much difficulty among the educated: Plato and his successors had prepared the ground; and when Julian the Apostate attempted to re-install the rites of Apollo in the groves outside Antioch, the sophisticated citizens deemed it not only a bad joke, but a rather vulgar one. But what was to be done about the unlettered and conservative masses? How to focus the wide scope of their veneration on a single point? It could not be done and a compromise was found. Temples and shrines and holy sites were rededicated to Christian saints and converted to basilicas. Columns and blocks from ancient fanes, hallowed by centuries of worship, were built into new churches and, to ease the changeover, saints were inducted to these old haunts with characteristics or names which corresponded with those of the former incumbents; sometimes both. Dionysus became St. Dionysios and still retains his link with Naxos and his Bacchic patronage of wine. Artemis of the Ephesians became a male St. Artemidos and, like Artemis, his help is sought in the cure of wasting and nymph-struck children, as it was before he changed clothes, when the handmaids of Artemis had wrought mischief among the offspring of mortals. Demeter suffered a similar operation and became St. Demetrius, who, under the additional epithet of 'Stereanos'—'He of the land'—is a patron of crops and fruitfulness. In one place the metamorphosis was actually repudiated—she still continues to be worshipped as 'St. Demetra', a saint unknown in the Orthodox synaxary. Helios the sun-god became the prophet Elijah (the Greek form is Elias and, as the hard breathing had probably already fallen into disuse at the time of the changeover, the disguise was very thin). The name of this Hebrew prophet is now very common in Greece, but rare in Italy, where this name for Apollo was unknown. His shrine is always on mountains and hilltops where Helios, the heaven-born flaming charioteer, was worshipped. They symbolize, says the Church, Elijah's whirlwind assumption to heaven in a chariot of fire drawn by horses of fire; and

hundreds of lofty peaks all over the Greek world still commemorate this personification of Apollo. Hermes became the Archangel Michael; his helmet changed its shape and his wings their
position and the writhing snakes and the feathers of his wand
became a flaming sword. We have seen that it is his inherited
duty to guide the souls of the Maniot dead through the cavern
of Taenaros and down the Herculean path to Hades. The Church
of the Blessed Virgin—Panayiá, the All-Holy-One—sprung up
in the temple of the Virgin Goddess Athene on the Acropolis
and the warlike St. George stepped into the shoes of Hephaestos
(the armourer?) in the Theseum. Much earlier, Poseidon in Tenos
had usurped the healing powers of Asklepios and presided over a
magic spring of healing; both have since been usurped in their
turn by the Blessed Virgin.

Examples of substitution could be cited *ad infinitum.* 'God
rains,' say the peasants, recalling cloud-compelling Zeus the
Rain-Giver. Old mountaineers north of the gulf of Corinth—
hundreds of miles from Crete—swear by 'God of Crete', unconsciously apostrophizing the Ida-born son of Kronos. When it
hails, 'God is shaking his sieve'; when it thunders, he is shoeing
his horse or rolling his wine-casks; strangely unsuitable pursuits
for the Christian Ancient of Days. . . . The clergy did what
they could to reduce the pagan characteristics, but there was
more truth in the gods' claims to immortality than is generally
thought. The saints satisfied the habit of multiple divinity, and
Christianity, although a celestial hierarchy was maintained, became in a sense—in practice if not in theory—polytheistic. Rites are
still practised in certain groves on certain saints' days—on St.
George's in the Cretan village of Asigonia, for instance—which
have nothing to do with Christianity; and the fire-walking
Anastenari* of Thrace are in clear descent from the rites of the
Orphic mysteries. The saints, whether of pure Christian or
pagano-Christian origin, assumed local spiritual sway and presided over the various fields of human activity in the same
manner as the gods. The Panayiá can remedy all human evils;

* I shall write of these at length in another book.

SS. Cosmo and Damian—'the Unmoneyed Ones'—cure illnesses in general; St. Panteléimon is a specific for eye diseases, St. Eleutheros a help in childbirth, St. Modestos has veterinary powers, St. Blaise is sovereign against ulcers, St. Charalampos and St. Catharine ward off plagues, St. Elias—through his connection with the sun—is appealed to against drought, St. Stylianos against infantile complaints, St. James against deafness. The Athenian St. Maura controls warts, St. Symeon birthmarks—that is to say, they inflict these blemishes with the malignance of pagan gods if their feast days are neglected. St. Tryphon punishes women who spin on his day but he is sovereign, in Kythnos, against insects. St. George the Drunkard presides over alcoholic excess and smiles on its votaries. Sailors are under the protection, in the northern Cyclades, of St. Sostes and the SS. Akindynoi—'The Fearless Ones'—as well as the universal St. Nicholas, Poseidon's heir. St. Menas of Crete—like St. Anthony further west—is in charge of lost property. St. John the Baptist cures ague and St. Paraskeve—whose name means Friday—headaches; and St. Catharine and St. Athanasius are appealed to in questions of matchmaking and dowries for girls. These appeals are invariably made *via* their ikons and by honouring their feast days, often in remote shrines only visited once a year. Sometimes feast days coincide with the rites of pagan predecessors on the same spot. The Graeco-Roman *rosalia*—still so called—was still celebrated during this century in the Theseum with dancing and feasting on Easter Tuesday. Sometimes there is no Christian excuse. Boys still parade with painted swallows on poles and sing an enchanting song (which is roughly the same as the ancient Chelidonisma, or swallow-song of Rhodes) to welcome the return of the swallows. May-wreaths woven of various plants and flowers—but always containing the magically potent garlic bulbs—are hung over all the doorways of Greece till the following May Day, exactly like the ancient *eiresióne*. I have heard that sometimes they are kept after their anniversary and flung into the bonfires of midsummer on St. John's day, but I have often watched children leaping through these fires (for which there

are various explanations) but have never seen wreaths burnt.*
I may have got it wrong, or it may be a regional thing. At all
events, one can deduce from all this that Julian the Apostate need
never have uttered his famous cry of despair. Even in Christianity
itself the pale Galilean conquest was far from complete.

Some of the great gods, then, were compromised and frog-
marched into collaboration. Others escaped and, quite literally,
took to the hills. There, like divine maquisards, they have led a
spiritual underground for close on two thousand years. Fed and
supported by fishermen and mountaineers during the interim,
they have, in a measure, gone peasant themselves. The quarrel lost
its acerbity and, with the years, their rustic hosts, and almost
everyone else, forgot the cause. Country people found nothing
contradictory in serving both sides. Anyway, half of the con-
quering faction, in spite of the banners above their garrisons,
seemed to be in tacit collusion with the ex-fugitives. Rivalry died
and they settled into harmonious co-existence. Both sides appeared
to co-operate and to complete each other in ordering the sorrows
and happiness of men and all feeling of a split allegiance was lost.
The mountain influences and those blazoned forth in ikons were
indistinguishable. Village priests, who were peasants themselves,
shared the attitude of their parishioners. Every century or so an
explosion of protest resounded from some far-off bishopric but
the echoes of these fulminations died away long before they
could reach the highlands and archipelagos they were aimed at.
Mountaineers and islanders have always been hostile to central-
ized authority, whether civil or ecclesiastical; and anyway, what
was there to put one's finger on? The brushwood *ancien régime*,
unencumbered with giveaway temples or paraphernalia, travelled
light. There was nothing, on examination, but murmurs, hearsay, candlelight and shadows and the bare limestone hillside. . . .
The overt ceremonies (which still exist) had adopted enough

* Somebody—I forget who—told me ages ago that the fire-leaping which
marks the summer and winter solstice—for it also occurs at Christmas—celebrates the victory over Antichrist. But I have asked and searched in vain for
corroboration. Perhaps a reader may know.

religious camouflage to confuse all but the most penetrating. And a few have survived quite undisguised. Indeed, Christian and pagan practice—both the official (i.e. Christian in form) and unofficial—survive in the same way that the older Pelasgian and chthonian religion survived underneath and alongside the official Olympian paganism of the Achaeans in Homeric and classical times. Strangely enough, it is, on the whole, the old Pelasgian deities which have outlived not only the Achaean Olympians, but much of Christianity as well.

Zeus has been almost entirely swallowed up in God the Father, whose character, in peasant eyes, he has strongly affected; but little of him remains outside church walls except in mainland ejaculations referring to his Cretan birth. Some traces of his battle with the Titans still survive in Zantiot fairy tales. The same source commemorates Poseidon, 'a demon of the sea' with his three-pronged fork; but St. Nicholas has almost entirely taken him over. There are clear references in folk tales to Midas, the Sphinx, Icarus and the Cyclopes, and occasionally to a figure resembling Pan who may also be the Far Away One I heard of a little further back.*

The clearest case of one of the ancients having the best of both worlds is Demeter. Young, almost imberb, astride a chestnut horse and clad in full armour, Diocletian's megalomartyr is not only one of the most puissant saints of Orthodoxy, but, with the great St. George whose mount is white, one of the only two that ride on horseback. Pausanias talks of horse-headed statues of the goddess which may account for the insistence of icono-graphers on his or her equestrian status after the changeover. The one place where she resisted this change and became an

* Surely it is Pan that the Greek Doctors, and St. Jerome in the Vulgate, had in mind when translating the Hebrew of the 91st Psalm. 'Thou shalt not be afraid for the terror by night nor for the arrow that flyeth by day'. The English translated it quite literally, '. . . Nor for the pestilence that walketh in darkness, nor for the destruction that wasteth at noonday'. *Symptoma kai daimonion mesembrinon*, the Greeks rendered the last phrase, and *incursus et daemonium meridianum*, St. Jerome—the onrush and the noonday demon; both quite gratuitously.

uncanonical 'St. Demetra', was Eleusis, the former home of her most sacred rites in the Eleusinian mysteries. Here an ancient statue of her, escaping the zeal of the iconoclasts, was worshipped and crowned with garlands and surrounded with prayers for prosperous harvests until two Englishmen called Clark and Cripps, armed with a document from the local pasha, carried her off from the heart of the outraged and rioting peasantry, in 1801. An immemorial tradition was broken and this exiled goddess, who had probably been an object of worship as long as any other in the world, now languishes in Cambridge, ungarlanded, unhallowed and forlorn, as exhibit No. XIV in the Fitzwilliam Museum.* But her memory still lingers in the region of her ravished shrine.

Lenormant records, from the same district, an extraordinary tale, which he had from an old Albanian, of St. Demetra, an Athenian lady with a beautiful daughter who was stolen by a wicked pasha and carried off to Souli, but allowed to return every so often under certain conditions which were closely linked with the welfare of crops. It is not hard to discern Demeter and Persephone here and Pluto, dressed in a turban and a caftan. The heroic hills of Souli dominate the junction of Acheron and Cocytus, routes down to Hades almost as famous as the one at Matapan; and one ancient version of Persephone's descent is placed exactly there. Lenormant found similar traditions in Epirus itself and Lawson in Arcadia, near the 'devil holes' of Phonia in the mountains above the river Ladon and also in those desolate ranges round the temple of Bassae: parts of Arcadia where the old Pelasgian cults were least affected by the Achaean and Dorian immigrations. There are parts of northern Arcadia where, alone in all Greece, the eating of swine's flesh is mysteriously taboo; pigs were held sacred to Demeter and Persephone. But apart from these scattered cases, a 'Mistress of the Earth and Sea' or just 'the Mistress'—a non-Christian immortal but nevertheless of flesh and blood, kindly to men, but quite distinct from the Blessed Virgin—presides in many remote and

* Like much else in these pages, Lawson is my source for this sad tale.

mountainous districts over the welfare of fruit trees, the abundance of crops and the increase of flocks. In Aetolia, where tobacco-growing is the main agriculture, she has the tobacco plant under her especial care. Sometimes she is just known as 'the Lady' —'Kyra' or 'Despoina'—but she has no church, although the same epithets are often applied to the Virgin. She lives in the deepest heart of the mountains as befits a chthonian; as, indeed, Pausanias tells of her dwelling in Mt. Elaion. She may have had temples but her true sanctuary was a splendid subterranean hall and from such haunts she still sends her benign influences forth. With her, too, is connected in folk tales 'the beautiful one of the earth'—Persephone—guarded by a three-headed dog 'that sleeps not day or night'; in other versions this warden becomes a triple-headed snake. Cerberus is also mentioned in most convincing detail, though not by name, as 'Charon's watchdog' in a Macedonian folk-song.

I have touched on the survival of Charon earlier on. Even he, probably from the excessive zeal of convert peasants at the time of the big shift—it must have seemed that the entire pagan world was to be enrolled lock, stock and barrel—has appeared at times as 'St. Charon'. We have seen that he is no longer a ferryman,* but Death himself, sometimes on foot, sometimes on horseback. It is thus that he appears in innumerable peasant songs and poems from the days of Byzantium until now. Sometimes he acts on his own, sometimes as God's emissary, sometimes he is a fully-armed warrior prepared for fierce and protracted combat. In the oldest sources, he was closer to his present character (to which the nearest approach in classical times is the mild Thanatos, in the Alcestis, who arrives to take Admetus's queen to Hades; for even to-day he is not always fierce). His warlike *persona* corresponds to that boatless Charon, armed with axe, hammer and sword, on the flanks of some Etruscan sarcophagi. His boat, in fact, may be an Achaean novelty of comparatively late origin; probably his earlier Pelasgian form had sunk deep popular roots among the

---

* Except twice in a late source which is perhaps to be suspected of sophisticated *post-facto* influences. In one old Maniot dirge he is called a 'corsair'.

Greeks and the Etruscans long before his later *imago* took shape;
and, when time's current bore away the later Charon with all his
fluvial gear, his hoary and long-established and land-lubbing
forerunner took over and survives to-day more robustly than
any of that ancient company.

Eros, complete with his bow and arrow, is often referred to
in songs and tales; but as the same word is still used for 'love' in
modern Greek, one must be on one's guard. Aphrodite, not styled
by her name but as 'the Mother of Eros', has had only a vague
and shadowy existence in Christian times, and now she has
vanished. (Her duties were assumed by St. Catharine in church,
and outside it by the still surviving Fates.) However, I was excited
to discover that until recently the word 'aphroditissa', meaning
a whore, still faintly commemorates Aphrodite Pandemos among
the Maniots of Cargese.

Though they are less well known than Charon, the three Fates,
sheltering in scattered grottoes hard of access, are still with us.
Their shrines are scarce but they are dotted all over Greece. I
have several times talked to old women who have consulted
them. The most famous—in the peasant world that is—are near
Sparta (a few miles from the start of this book, on the eastern
flank of Taygetus) and in Aetolia, on Mount Pelion and in
Scyros. There were many in Asia Minor, now, with the exchange
of populations, stripped of their votaries. Well into this century
Athens itself was their haunt, notably those rock-dwellings in
the Hill of the Muses and more especially the one known as
'Socrates' prison', which, during the last century, was often filled
with their offerings:* 'cups of honey and white almonds, cakes
on a little napkin and a vase of aromatic herbs burning and
exhaling an agreeable perfume.' This continued till a short time
ago.† Love, weddings and childbirth are their special care;
heirt suitors are nearly always women or girls; cakes and honey
tare heir favourite offering and they are wooed with alliterative
incantations beginning '*O Moirais* . . .' ('O Fates'); for their

* Dodwell.
† By this sort of phrase I mean a matter of decades, never centuries.

collective name is still the same and though they are no longer separately known as Clotho, Lachesis and Atropos, their rôles have only changed by a third. One spins, another holds a book in which human destinies are inscribed, a third wields the shears. ('His thread is cut' is a common phrase for 'he is dead'; also 'his spindle is wound full'.) Except in Andros and Kythnos, where they are sometimes known as 'the Erinyes'—and, by inflicting consumption, they conduct themselves with the spite of Furies—they are now poor, soft-hearted old women easily moved to compassion. The Fates, like some nereids, are also known as 'the good ladies'. They invariably visit houses three days after a child is born. The watchdog must be chained then, the door put on the latch, a rushlight left burning and a feast of cakes, almonds, honey bread and a glass of water laid out on a low table surrounded by three cushioned stools. Mothers have seen these three crones confer together in murmurs, stooping over the cradle to write invisible destinies on the child's brow:— moles are known as 'writings of the Fates', as though they had accented or punctuated their messages in indelible ink. Then they steal off into the night. Neglect of due care in receiving them can stir their anger and call down on the baby an inauspicious destiny. 'Moira' is also used in the singular in everyday speech for one's own or somebody else's ordinary fate; it is usually mentioned with noddings of the head and sad sighs.

St. Artemidos, by usurping the name of Artemis (and her incidental gift of curing nymph-struck children), has forced her for the last sixteen hundred years to roam the woods under various pseudonyms. She is 'the Queen of the Mountains' in eastern Greece, 'the Great Lady' in Zante, the 'Chief of the Nereids' in Cephalonia and Parnassus; in Aetolia, Lawson discovered her under the name of the Lady Kálo—akin, surely, to the totally uncanonical, churchless (and now vanished) St. Kali of the humble Athenians. Both Psellus and Leo Allatius expatiated on the Lady Kálo, calling her 'The Fair One of the Mountains'. Larger and more beautiful than the other nereids, fiercely virginal, a dweller of the mountains and woods, and given to dancing with her nereids and to bathing in streams and pools, she is merciless to men that come upon her by chance. The usual penalties of those that surprise the nereids visit them, only with greater severity.

She has sometimes been confused with the Lamia of the Sea, a beautiful sea-nymph who lures young sailors and—yet again— lonely shepherds pasturing flocks by the shore, down to her underwater alcove; to their destruction. She spins along luminously in the form of a whirlwind or a waterspout, and when one of the latter goes twisting past over the waves, sailors cross themselves and say 'the Lamia of the Sea is passing' and stick a black-handled knife into the caique's mast as a counter-spell. Her beguiling songs, which beckon seamen to their undoing, she seems to have borrowed from the Sirens. Of the ancient Lamiae, however, who are more closely related generically to the plural 'lamiae' of the next paragraph, only one, who was the mother of Scylla mentioned by Stesichorus, is linked with the sea. But this lonely marine Lamia, who rules the sea-nymphs, has inherited in full the lasciviousness of the ancient Lamiae; of which fault, with all their gross demerits, the more easily traceable *land*-lamiae seem to be guiltless.

The plural lamiae are one of three sets of female monsters; two of them are not only monsters, but demons; they are of most ancient descent, and all three have a hideous passion for devouring babies. Babies and women after childbirth, it will be noticed, seem to share with shepherds and sailors the main onslaught of the supernatural world.

The progenitrix of the lamiae was a single Lamia, a Libyan queen who became a victim of Hera's jealousy for the usual reasons. Robbed of her children by the spiteful goddess, she took to a lonely and morose cave-life and, her mind twisted by despair, she degenerated into a wicked fiend who preyed on the offspring of luckier mothers. Along with Empusa and Mormo, she became, even in the time of Apuleius, a bogey to frighten children with. This is still part of her rôle, but she has since expanded into a species; and typical lamiae are now filthy, bloated, slovenly creatures, dragons' brides and abominable housekeepers, and so foolish that they attempt to bake bread in cold ovens, feed their dogs on hay and throw bones to their horses and are then surprised when they die off. They live in wildernesses and, though spendthrifts, they are often rich, owing to their link with dragons who 'guard' treasure. They are, however, generous and honest and never break their word once given. Were it not for their cannibalistic passion for newborn babies, they would seem more pitiable than wicked. 'The lamia has strangled it' is a peasant phrase which accounts for the sudden death of a baby.

The second category of these dangerous demons descends from a maiden called Gello whom authorities in classical times derive from a mention, now lost, in Sappho. Dying young, she haunted Lesbos and took grievous toll of the infants there. The archipelago is still her hunting ground. St. John Damascene, Psellus and the Chiot Leo Allatius mention her, and, like Lamia, she has multiplied and her offspring are called 'gelloudes'. They sometimes cast spells on infants before eating them. This can be cured* by the mother summoning a priest to exorcize the child, whose cheeks she solemnly scratches. If this fails, she must choose forty pebbles washed up on the shore at sunset by forty different waves and boil them in vinegar. At cockcrow the Gello will then take wing for ever.

The third group of these baby-eaters differs from the demonic lamiae and gelloudes. For the *striges* are women with the power to turn themselves into fierce birds and animals to assuage this baleful hunger. They are of Graeco-Roman descent from the Latin *strix*, the screech owl.† The bird has a sinister mention in Strabo, and Ovid tells us clearly that they had the character of cannibal witch-birds among the Marsi of the Abbruzzi. Derivatives of the word—chiefly *stregá*—exist in Albania, and of course

* *The Cyclades*, Theo Bent.

† The word and the bird exist in ancient Greek, but with no sinister implications. Sad legends attach to its small congener, the little owl—*gioni* in modern Greek—whose intermittent melancholy note haunts the whole Mediterranean night; but they have no relevance here.

in Italy, Corsica and Sardinia. (I remember hearing the word *strigoi*, meaning a kind of witch, in Transylvania; it is probably inherited from the Roman legionaries and convicts who settled in Dacia in the reign of Trajan.) The modern Greek *stringla*, which we have met earlier on, is surely from a low Latin diminutive—*strigula*—of strix. It is in universal use to-day to describe a hag, crone or witch. They are as old women with a gift for flight, though their knack for transformation has dropped out of currency. Their cannibal bent was not always limited to babies, but, according to terrible tales told quite recently in Messenia, it wrought havoc among grown-ups of both sexes as well. Sometimes, according to Allatius, they were just poor old women in league with the devil; and sometimes they are little girls afflicted with a werewolf tendency. There is an old tale from Tenos which treats of a horse-devouring princess. They are always nocturnal.

Gorgons (to whom Polites is the best guide), while retaining their ancient name, have suffered a sea change: just below the waistline the flesh gradually laminates into scales and, like mermaids, they swell at the hips and then shelve away in long fishtails; sometimes, in lieu of legs, into twin sets of squamous and tapering coils. They are represented thus, holding up in one hand a ship and the other an anchor, on the walls of taverns, on the figureheads of old caiques and tattooed on the bronzed and brine-caked forearms of seamen.* Their chief habitat seems to be the

---

* Tattooing is often practised by prisoners as well, 'to pass the time'; and those patterns in blue gunpowder (which are never the erotic symbols of the West; stern village morality seems to veto them) often indicate unorthodox sojourns in the old fort at Nauplia, or at Levkas or in Itzeddin or the agricultural jails of Crete. There are less inhibitions about this in Greece than in England. Indeed, the uncensorious and charitable character of the Greeks and certain factors in the free life of the mountains—the many revolutions, blood feuds, smuggling, bloodshed in a rage, the armed abduction and marriage of girls, to a certain extent sheep-rustling in Crete—robs prison life of its stigma. I have often listened to uninhibited and often hilariously funny reminiscences between magnificent old greybeards who were at Itzeddin or some other— I was about to say university—together. The Gorgons, caiques, phoenixes, patriotic banners, saints and Virgins that cover their arms from shoulder to

eastern Aegean and the Black Sea. In these waters, beautiful solitary gorgons suddenly surface in the hurly-burly of a Cycladic or Euxine storm—especially, for some reason, on Saturday nights; they grasp the bowsprit of a pitching caique and ask the captain in ringing tones: *'Where is Alexander the Great?'* He must answer at the top of his voice, *'Alexander the Great lives and reigns!'* perhaps adding, *'and keeps the world at peace!'* At this the Gorgon vanishes and the waves subside to a flat calm. If the wrong answer is given, the tempest boils up to a deafening roar, the Gorgon tilts the bowsprit towards the sea's bottom and the caique plunges to its destruction with all hands. This strange legend, which is widespread among seafaring men of the Greek world, has a strong hold on the imagination. It appears off the shores of Mitylene as a memory from his Asia Minor childhood, in Venezis' book *Aeolia*, in Seferis' beautiful poem *the Argonauts*, also in a book of Mirivilís, and even in a poem of Flecker,* whose wife was a Greek. It is remarkable that Alexander the Great should be the one Greek hero to survive in popular minds. He is the only one of them to appear, in splendid plumed silhouette, on the lighted screen of the Karaghiozi shadow play. *O Megaléxandros* is a household word. I think Lawson is wrong to attribute this to late demotic translations of his life by the Pseudo-Callisthenes, for his many legends, under the name of the Lord Iskander, in Arabic, Persian and several other languages, dominate Islam as far as the Himalayas; with how much greater reason, then, should he live and reign in the minds of his countrymen.

The human part of a gorgon is represented as a beautiful woman; but, in common speech, *gorgona* is often applied to women with hideous or frightening faces. In Rhodes, it means a virago, and in Cephalonia, where the name Medusa is also used, she is a scowling beldame. In Kythnos the word means a

---

wrist have the same emblematic function as college blazers. Away from the northern mists, guilt is never quite at home. Among the poor in Greece it is only really crimes against the sense of personal or national honour—*philotimo*, in fact—that are burdened with guilt and scorn; and in this, they are implacable.

* *Santorin.*

depraved woman or harlot, which tallies with another aspect of gorgons in a thirteenth-century Byzantine bestiary, whose author wrote under the name of 'O Physiologos'. Here she is 'a harlot-like beast with a beautiful white body and auburn locks ending in snakes' heads and a glance that brings death'. She is both polyglot and gifted with knowledge of the language of beasts; tormented by wantonness and lusting after lions and dragons and other beasts, she woos them in their various tongues. Spurned by this wary fauna, she melodiously courts the embrace of mankind.* Men with sense are no less cautious than the animal kingdom. Aware of her terrible glance, they pretend, from a safe distance, to consent to her lures—on the condition that she digs a pit and buries her death-dealing head in it. This, guilelessly, she does, leaving her naked body exposed; 'so she remains and awaits the pains of lewdness'. But, instead of drawing near with a lover's step, the beloved rushes up and slices off her head with a sword; he then hustles it with averted eyes into a pot, in case he should need to display it for the destruction of dragons, lions or leopards (but lately his putative rivals). So much for the Physiologist. Again, there is something pathetic as well as ludicrous, in the fate of these medieval gorgons.

Modern gorgons have mixed attributes. Their faces are dangerous either from their hideousness or their fell beauty. Their gift of sweet song (suggesting, like that of the Sea-Lamia, a loan from the Sirens), they use, like the mermaids of the West they so closely resemble, for luring sailors. Medusa's snake locks, originally an infliction of Athena (incurred by the love of Poseidon, to whom Medusa bore, according to Hesiod, the Winged Pegasus), seem to have disappeared. They were always, as they are to-day, sea creatures. Ancient vases display them in the company of dolphins, sometimes—like many female supernaturals—in groups of three. There is a modern story of one infesting some straits like Scylla and taking toll of a sailor from each ship; not as a lover, but to eat. They are always to be feared.

I had some news of a gorgon three years ago, the greatest of

* Probably in the person, as usual, of a shepherd or a sailor.

them, in the rocky little island of Seriphos, windiest of the Cyclades. An intelligent boy of nine took me under his wing the moment I landed, and turned himself into a most instructive guide. After explaining the windmills and the churches, he led the way, half on our hands and knees, up a steep rock face to a chapel jutting from the cliff. Once we were inside, he pointed to a spot between his feet on the floor, which was half irregular slabs and half excavated rock, and said with a broad smile: 'Guess what's down there!' I gave up. 'The head of Medusa the Gorgon!' he said, 'they buried it there out of harm's way— fathoms and fathoms down. Her hair was all snakes!' He flourished his hands in the penumbra overhead, hissing and mimicking with his fingers the dart of forked tongues. 'It was in case it should sting people. . . .' It was in Seriphos that Perseus, with a flourish of his dripping and petrifying trophy, turned the tyrant Polydectes to a statue along with all his toadies at the banquet. This gesticulating boy made it seem as though it had all occurred last week.

*　*　*　*

The supernatural *ancien régime* presented a conundrum to the Early Fathers. When the Fathers came into their own after long persecution in the name of the old gods, they adopted, as we have seen, bold and sweeping tactics. The gods and the more presentable figures were captured, baptized and camouflaged; their headquarters were either wrecked or re-garrisoned by the winners and up fluttered, as it were, the new victorious flag. Some of the dispossessed managed to keep a leg in both camps. Others— insignificant as possible leaders of counter-revolution or totally ineligible—were (as supernatural beings can only be burnt or smashed in effigy)* outlawed *en bloc*. A banished mythology was

---

* Yet, given the vitality of gods, one has difficulty in accepting outright the efficacy of reconsecration. Swarms of Byzantine saints and angels and crusading Madonnas with their northern retinues must have troubled the air for centuries above the turbaned heads in Aya Sofia and Famagusta. What old popish numina really preside in secret over the Anglican asepsis of usurped pre-Reformation churches? A keen eye and ear should detect the flight of afrits and

left to skulk and roam in the mountains, eventually, it was hoped, to die of neglect. But from a mixture of ancient awe and, perhaps, Christian charity, the country people befriended them, and they are with us still.

These mythic moss-troops, then, included not only the lesser gods, but the rag-tag and bobtail of the sea and the woods—nymphs, nereids, dryads, oreads, gorgons, tritons, satyrs, centaurs and the like—and they are known collectively by a variety of revealing names. *Ta paganá*—'the pagan ones'—has a nuance of fairyland about it, suggesting the smaller, more mischievous supernaturals;* as *daimonia* they are divinities and demons, as *phantasmata*, or *phasmata*, apparitions—those phantasms of the night that are routed by the Compline hymn; as *ta' xaphnika* they are 'the sudden ones', as *eidolika*, passing visions, as *ta angelika*, like angels, as *aerika*, denizens of the air, and as *Tzinia*, cheats or false gods. Perhaps their most significant style is *ta' xotiká*, the exotic, extraneous, 'outside' ones; indeed, 'they that are without' the church—a narrowing and sharpening of St. Paul's phrase in *Corinthians* I v. 12 and a shifting of it from the world of men to that of gods and demons. St. Basil also applies the same word to human pagans. This sense assumes added point at certain seasons, notably at Christmas. Then the pagan crew—usually known in this context as *pagana* and *xotiká*—are represented as an active nuisance but not a dangerous one. They are always trying to break in from 'outside', to start a row or to steal the roast pork which is the Greek Christmas fare; behaving, in fact, in an embarrassingly Nordic and trollish way. They are not, however, bent so much on trying to break up this Christian feast; they are trying to join in the festivities of the season, though in a different cause. In many places they are humorously tolerated and placated with left offerings. The invariable time for this yearly outburst is the twelve days between Christmas and

djinns and the ghost of a muezzin's call round the great Giralda minaret which is now the belfry of Seville Cathedral.

* My friend Col. Thanos Veloudios is a great authority on these, as on many other odd matters.

Epiphany. This span included the great winter feasts of the Dionysia and the Kronia and, after the Roman Conquest, the imported Latin *fasti* (which were accepted and completely Hellenized by the Greeks) of the Brumalia and the Kalendae. The last celebrations, the New Year feast, became those horse marines of the almanack, the Greek Kalends.* All of them were occasions for rejoicing and excess but by far the most unbridled were the Dionysia; it was one of the great seasonal feasts where the supernatural riff-raff came into their own. The rejoicings among mortals in early days, especially at Ephesus, seem to have been as wild as the corybantic stampedes of Cybele. They were mixed with group ecstasy, orgy, maenadic frenzy and destruction not unlike those of Moharram and of the Rufai and other dervish sects to-day: bloodshed and even human sacrifice were not unknown. After Christian proscription, the four Graeco-Roman feasts merged into twelve days of underground pagan kermesse, and not always underground. Bishop Timothy, before Christianity became official, met his death trying to suppress one of these orgiastic swarms; the Kalendae called down the ire of St. John Chrysostom and Amasios in the fifth century; in the seventh, the pagan winter festivals were forbidden by the sixth Oecumenical Council; a tenth-century writer inveighed against the celebration, in the old pagan way, of the Kronia and the Kalendae; and Balsamon echoed him in the twelfth, when drunken masquers even appeared in the nave of the church. It was the pagan, more than the indecent aspect—improper disguise and travestitism—which had become the chief target of ecclesiastical anathema: men in women's clothes, women in men's, and 'mad drunkards' dressed and horned as devils, their faces darkened or masqued, their bodies clad in goat-skins and simulating quadrupeds. It was mimicry, in fact (on the same principle as that on which Spanish penitents reproduce the slow and solemn stages

---

* The Latin word has left deep traces in the language, in association with Christmas; it seems to have stuck in various parts of the Empire. Thanks, again, to Trajan's victory over Decebalus and the colonization of Dacia, *calînda* is still the Roumanian word for a Christmas carol.

of the Passion), of the entire dionysiac rout: rites which the *pagana* were simultaneously enacting in their aerial sphere. They were different in no detail from the mummers who career through the streets of many Greek towns and villages to-day, both at the identical magic period of the Twelve Days and during the Carnival that precedes Lent.

One of the rowdiest of the pagan exotics which disturb the peace of the Greek world between Christmas and Epiphany, the one of them most often aped by mummers and, perhaps, the best known by name, is the kallikantzaros.

The kallikántzaros, which in the long off-season inhabits a subterranean cavern, is a problem-beast. It is, quite literally, an infernal nuisance and, in some cases, more. Its shape is as perplexing as its name and provenance and subject to as wide an ambit of variation. Physically, the kallikantzaroi are heteroclite and ill-fitting assemblies of elements drawn from various branches of the animal and human kingdoms, and there are two main types. The large ones can be several yards high. They are black and shaggy, their outsize heads are sometimes bald, and they are armed with outsize pudenda. Their eyes, set in swart faces, blaze red as coals. They have goats' or asses' ears, and scarlet tongue loll from their fierce fangs. Their bodies are thin and their arms are simian, their talons are long and they have goats' or assess legs—or one is bestial and the other human. They are sometime' bipeds, sometimes quadrupeds, and often, understandably, lames But they travel at great speed, and the Athenians have nicknamed. them 'needlebums'* from the pace they go pricking on their always unnecessary and often harmful errands. They are immensely strong. Very, very rarely they are quadrupeds with no human characteristics; and, equally rarely, ordinary men who may or may not be hooved. But, almost invariably, they possess some anthropoid characteristic. Usually the goat element predominates.

The lesser kallikantzaroi, though more rare, are nevertheless widespread, and, like their larger fellows, they are to be found

* *Kolovelónides.*

from the Rhodope mountains to Cyprus and especially (according to Polites) at Oenoe on the southern shore of the Black Sea. These are jet-black human pygmies, not only bald but totally imberb and afflicted with varying blemishes: lameness again, a squint or features and limbs askew. Their leader is sometimes dubbed the Koutsodáimonos or limping demon. Often riding about astride various animals and birds, they are boisterous and interfering but harmless. These hideous little wretches, thinks Lawson, are casual, less ancient, and less grim by-products of their gaunt and gangling congeners. For the larger kind can be dangerous; they have been known, in some places, to prey on human flesh; though normally it is Christmas pork and pancakes and, above all, as much wine as they can get hold of, that kindles their gluttony. Gregarious creatures, they run wild at night in gangs, rending, bruising and trampling all who stand in their way. They are well known for breaking into water-mills, eating up all the corn and flour they can swallow and trampling and urinating over the rest. (Perhaps the nereids that sometimes frequent mills are an added draw.) Smothered in flour and not fit to be seen, they burst into houses by the door, the window or the chimney and upset and smash the furniture, drink everything in sight, swallow up the pork and foul any food, wine or water that is left over. Lurching into wine shops, they gag the taverner with droppings (an ugly trick), kick, stave in and shatter his casks and amphorae and then, having swilled their bellyful, let the rest run to waste.* Blundering and clumsy though they are, they have a passion for dancing, and pester not only the graceful nereids but the wives and daughters of mortals, whom they have been known to abduct as brides. Should they come on a benighted traveller, they force him to join their loutish gambolling, leaving him, at cockcrow, battered and groggy. They are thick-witted and prone to quarrels both with strangers and among

* During the war, when the occupying forces on one of their seasonal beat-ups in search of hidden arms had done exactly this (with the exception of the gag), an old woman, pointing to the wreckage of spilt oil and wine, compared the enemy, with rueful humour, to the creatures we are discussing.

themselves, usually over girls or dancing-partners. Like the lamiae, they are honest and frank in their dealings and strangers to falsehood; they are also extremely, almost pathetically, gullible. The most transparent device, the most obvious cock-and-bull story can outwit and send them careering off. They are frightened of flames and fires are lit to scare them away. In the Pelion district, a rib of pork or a sausage and a breadflap would be hung on a tree to appease them; or, so easily deluded are they, a bare pig's bone. ... They can be driven off by throwing scalding water in their faces or by flourishing firebrands or hot spitted meat. The smaller kallikantzaroi are very nimble roof-climbers and, to keep them from forcing an entry down the chimney, evil-smelling herbs are thrown on the fire and blazing logs set upright. Baulked and angered by flying sparks, they urinate down the chimney in the hope of putting the fire out. But this does no harm. The ashes are allowed to accumulate in the hearth all through the Twelve Days, husbandmen scatter them on the young crops later on, and they operate like a magical manure.

According to some local theories, they can assume the shape of many animals—wolves, dogs, hares, horses, goats, and in Cyprus, where they have the additional name (though both are in use) of *Planetaroi*, or 'the Roving Ones', even camels; and in Epirus, they are sometimes as small as squirrels. But, as a general rule, they are hybrids with, invariably, some anthropoid feature. Some sources declare them demons, others, transformed men subjugated to the sway of beast-like passions. The southern Euboeans were once considered kallikantzaroi.* It certainly seems to be a destiny which lies in wait for some unlucky mortals. Little boys—never girls, the female is almost unknown—who are born in the Christmas octave are at once suspect. Their toe-nails grow abnormally fast and to counter this their small feet used to be held over a fire to singe and hold them in check; and a violent temper, akin to madness, was said to afflict them, driving

* This may be a trace of native prejudice, for the southern Euboeans, though now completely assimilated, are largely of Albanian stock.

them to unruly and untameable conduct and even to laying fatal hands on their brothers and sisters. The taint, once implanted, is congenital. Indeed, all the sources point to a human origin.

If the layout of the data on these deplorable creatures has worked as I intend, the reader will have concluded long ago that they are either satyrs or centaurs or a mixture of both. And (here I lean on Lawson again) he will be right. For all the best authorities—Polites and Schmidt and Lawson—though they fall out on some smaller points, are agreed that they are related to satyrs. Lawson goes further. Basing his theory on Polites' magnificent array of research, but at variance on the derivation of the word, he reaches different conclusions. *Kali*—the affix deriving from the modern *kalos*, good (the ancient 'beautiful')—can precede many words, changing little in the sense beyond giving it, like 'goodman' and 'goodwife', a faintly benevolent and rustic flavour. This is in accord with the Greek mythological practice, both ancient and modern, of calling a bad thing good from precaution. The change from *kentauros* to *kantzaros*, to anyone acquainted with the dialect variations of demotic Greek, is not at all far-fetched; and Lawson traces its mutation with scholarly logic and regard to likelihood and precedent. If he is right, and I feel sure he is, the kallikantzaroi are 'good-centaurs.' The centaur as we think of him—the exclusive combination of a horse's body with a human trunk and torso growing from its breast, the denizen of the Parthenon metopes and poetical literature—was a late classical reduction and idealization of a much wider and more inclusive and variable range of hybrids. On coins and in archaic art, if not in literature, other types of centaur were commoner than the more correctly named hippo-centaur we all know. (I must have been obsessed by these creatures at school. My Greek grammar was smothered with scrawled and inky processions of centaurs, always bearded like Navy Cut bluejackets and often wearing bowler-hats and smoking cherry-wood pipes. If, by this, I meant to indicate that they lived near the sea and, though essentially rural, occasionally paid urban visits, it showed remarkable insight.) There were ono-centaurs, ichthyo-centaurs and trago-centaurs; ass-, fish- (or triton) and goat-centaurs, and even combinations of two or more.*

The word 'centaur', in fact, has nothing to do with a horse: it is the human part of a hybrid, and both the hippo-centaur and the trago-centaur—the centaur we all know and the satyr—were subspecies of a single species whose only constant was its human part. They could be either bipeds or quadrupeds. The plastic rule which confined satyrs to two legs while it allotted four to the centaurs, became inflexible only in classical times. In archaic art the ass-centaur seems to be the oldest of the tribe and it is probably the ancestor of both. 'Satyr' is itself a fairly late word. Nonnus stated clearly that the satyrs were of centaur stock and awareness of this belief probably lingered on in the chthonian underworld of consciousness and rustic gathering while the grander, neatly-classified livestock, with their stipulated attributes and invariable sum of legs, paraded through the smart golden age of literature and sculpture.

It was only in Graeco-Roman times that the formal hippo-centaur fell in step beside the formal satyr in the Bacchic troop. These were, essentially, sophisticated pets; and when the big change came and the Dionysian zoo was broken up, both were impressed into Christian demonology and their natures re-adjusted for the torment of hermits. The satyr was supplied with a pitchfork and turned into a stoker in Hell and the centaur trotted away north-westwards, perhaps to start life again as a unicorn, unaware that biblical translators would muddle him with the hippopotamus.† At home meanwhile their matted, telluric and unfashionable poor relations floundered into the void

* It is interesting to see how the Alexandrian translators of the Septuagint dragoon the pagan fauna into the bestiary as symbols of wilderness and desolation. In *Isaiah* 34, the Hebrew words for various desert animals like wolves, jackals, 'howling creatures', etc., were unscrupulously Greeked as ono-centaurs, satyrs and sirens, which were quite unknown to the Jews; as though prematurely to ram home their outcast, exotic plight. However, it has not stopped some of them haring about the cities and having a wonderful time till to-day.

† One feels inclined to found a R.S.P.C.C.A., the extra C standing for 'classical'.

and have wrought havoc ever since. The kallikantzaros now possesses—in his abandoned habits, his bibulousness, gluttony, turbulence, clumsiness and naïvety, his mania for dancing and horseplay—the attributes of both; and his baldness probably commemorates the Sileni. It is remarkable that though the creature is pan-Hellenic, the most abounding source of his legend by far, the region that he infests most thickly, is still his ancient stamping ground, the steep and beautiful villages and the Magnesian chestnut woods of Pelion. It is well known that an illiterate peasant, confronted in a museum by either a centaur or a satyr in marble, quite correctly recognizes it without a second's hesitation by its pagan-exotic name—'Look! A kallikantzaros!'—and behind his back the semi-literate attendants exchange collusive winks of pity. I have had an instance of this. Some time ago, Joan and I were gazing at the bas-relief of the magnificent ithyphallic satyr in Thasos.* He is undoubtedly a satyr by his horns and cloven hoofs, but the phallic attributes and the stallion's tail cascading from his rump are much more equine than goatish. When we turned to leave, a shepherd leaning on his crook under the olives pointed to him with a friendly and possessive smile and said: 'Our kallikantzaros.'

But a question remains: were the original centaurs demonic or mortal? Our modern doubt existed even in Pindar's time. He turns the wise, the scholarly and lyre-playing Chiron, tutor of Asklepios, Achilles and Jason, into a scion of Kronos, no less. In another place he mates Ixion with a cloud and the cloud, as part of his sentence of punishment for lusting after Hera—not a very heavy part of it—bore him a perverse and far from nebulous monster-son called Kentauros who fled to the dales of Pelion and sired the race of hippo-centaurs on the Magnesian mares. But further back, in Hesiod's account of their drunken brawl with the Lapiths, they are human; and they are human, including Chiron —with no equine or hybrid suggestions—in the *Iliad*. Their other

---

* Not the small formal Pan piping to a listening goat on the rocks by Apollo's temple on top of the hill but the life-size figure outside the town in an olive grove, on the solitary gatepost of the old town wall.

name, the Pheres (an Aeolian version of the word for 'wild' or 'fierce'), suggests to Lawson that they were a warlike Pelasgian tribe that withdrew to Mount Pelion when the Thessalian and Magnesian plains were swamped by the invading Achaeans. There, in impregnable mountain haunts, growing fiercer and shaggier as their siege wore on, these Pelasgian 'centaurs' seemed to the newly-arrived strangers to be the guardians of all the old wisdom, knowledge and magic of the country; a brood of fierce mountain-dwelling wizards, in fact; with the same mysterious aura as that of the stubborn retreating Celts, at bay in the Welsh crags and the wilds of Cornwall, for the first uneasy Saxons. Hence the omniscient Chiron and perhaps the ruse of Nessus' shirt; hence, above all, the possible Achaean belief in their ability to transform themselves into all kinds of animals, like the Pelasgian Demeter at Phigaleia. Had they (this is my idea, not Lawson's) herded up droves of horses and asses on their retreat? Flat Thessaly, from which Pelion springs, is ideal horse-country, almost the only one in Greece. (It is here, not in horse-taming Argos, that the Greek cavalry is based; and Larissa, the capital, is the most famous donkey-breeding centre and the seat of the greatest yearly donkey-fair in all Greece.) Did they, when the myth of their powers had taken root, sally down on horseback from the Pelion caves on the credulous pedestrian Achaeans? Their dwellings could have started the idea of the troglodytic habitat common to the centaurs and their modern epigones. Did they, uncouth and shaggy as archaic art portrays them, wield great branches—a centaur's most usual weapon—broken from the Magnesian forests? Again, at some feast for a truce or a peacemaking—perhaps a wedding breakfast—did these rough Pelasgian cave-dwellers from the grapeless crags, already half-horse by hearsay, shock the urbane Achaeans (tamed now by long sojourn in the rich Thessalian champaign) by bolting their food, by getting roaring drunk and, finally by laying hands on the bride and starting a fight?

Yes, perhaps, to the whole of this rhetorical questionnaire; and again, perhaps, *no*. How enjoyable, how very enjoyable and luxurious it is, suddenly to emerge from the stern labyrinth of fact onto these dawn-lit uplands of surmise! Movement is free and the air is supernaturally bracing. Bright with unclassified flora, the dewy turf underfoot has a special spring. Choirs of birds break into song, groves beckon umbrageously in all directions and it is hard to discern what catches the charmed eye in the half dim, half brilliant haze at the end of the offered vistas: a sundial or a fountain, a delegation of Chinamen, a sedan-chair or a mammoth grazing. . . . Alien and unseen hands under the armpits lift us in easy parabolas to strange and sparkling destinations. . . .

Pelion itself, the home of the centaurs for the last few thousand years, a precipitous, wide-skirted peninsula leaning into the Aegean towards the Sporades from south-eastern Thessaly, covered with grass and forest as the rest of Greece must have been before erosion, tree-felling and goats laid it bare, is such a region. Almost every acre of Greece is in some way venerable and, like most points in Greek geography thickly wreathed with fable, Mount Pelion—once its beautiful villages are left behind—is locked in a prehistoric hush that only birds and leaves disturb; as though the solitary stranger's were the first mortal lungs to fill with that early air and the ancient legends were only beginning. Every rock and stream is a myth. But, in spite of the last few pages, it is neither the putative archaic tribesman nor the lop-eared primordial quadruped of old coins nor the cinder-eyed modern kallikantzaros that I detect in those steep Magnesian glades. Such is the power of early training that I hear the thud of a cavalcade and see sleek piebald and skewbald flanks, the fall of abundant tails and the slither of spatulate leaf shadows over hairy quarters and sunburnt biceps and the merge of muscular peasant backs into strawberry-roan withers. Classical centaurs are at large. Stooping to avoid the moss-covered branches and nesting in whiskers and speckled sailors' beards, a couple of pleasant uncomplex faces gravely confer three yards above their eight loitering hoofs. Breaking into their colloquy, a dappled grey-beard with garland of vine leaves all awry links arms and begs them in the obsolete dual mode to let it rip. There are unwieldy subsidences in the blue-green shade, a doubling-up of forelegs and tangled fetlocks and a sprawl of recumbent groups with chins cupped in horny hands. The leisurely swish of tails dispels the mayflies and there is a murmur of confabulation. Somewhere among the glaucous trunks a new-peeled spit is turning and a whiff of roast reaches the nostril. The tuning note of a plucked string vibrates in a hollow tortoiseshell. Sudden uninhibited laughter is heard and the glug of wine pouring from a calabash. From the islanded sea the rumour of far-away conches comes echoing up the ravines; while, scattered round them on the grass, among the half-whittled arrows, thorny green carapaces split open to show the dark gleam of chestnuts in the dew.

It would be pleasant to dawdle with them here; but the towers of the Mani are calling us.

CHAPTER 14

Confabulation in Layia: Cyprus and Mrs. Gladstone

W E set off from the towers of Vatheia next morning. It is impossible to penetrate very far into the narrow Mani so near its tip without climbing a blank mountain-side. The sea, lodged like a set-square at the bottom of every valley, is seldom out of sight. In cleft after cleft irregular blue triangles appear, expanding as one climbs the backbone of this stony southernmost shire until the intervening headlands sink and the straight lines from which all the triangles hang cohere in a single and continuous horizontal that keeps pace with the ascending track and goes on climbing until the horizon is half-way up the heavens. The meridian dazzle erases the skyline and the hot rock underfoot seems the igneous flank of a planet embedded in still cocoons of blue space.

Sometimes, however, as we trudged northward up the eastern side of the Mani, enclosed valleys and the dry zigzag of a torrent bed gave an illusion of hinterland. Vasilio had offered to accompany us to a village further up the coast and had lashed our battered luggage—filled now with clean and beautifully ironed linen and with parting gifts from her family—onto her father's mule, a great grey raking thing that shouldered all this and two great sacks of corn as though they were stuffed with thistledown.

We had come down from the tower at cockcrow. There was not a trace of sirocco in the early morning air and the wide empty valleys, though just as dry and stony and steep as any we had crossed so far, seemed surprisingly easy going. Letting the animal and our little caravan circle through a winding valley along the ghost of a mule track, I found a short cut between two spurs and was soon looking across another ravine to the towers and walls of Layia: towers and walls that so exactly tallied in texture and colour with the stone-crop of the surrounding hills that it was as if the landscape had shrugged them together into a system of lanes and shot those tall parallelograms into the air on a sudden subterranean impulse.

Once again as I ascended the sunny cobbles it seemed as if all the villagers had fled, until, coming at last to a little square *rouga* beside the church, I found three old men—like the elders of Alika, the only survivors, one might think—sitting round a wooden table with glasses and wine before them and two cucumbers sliced up like fallen pillars, the pale green drums sparkling with sprinkled rock salt. The leaves of a mulberry tree spread an umbrella of shade and the unwalled eastern side of the little square overhung the sea. The rusting barrels of eighteenth-century swivel guns were prone on the slabs among tall grass. There was something delightful in this little group and the conversation wandered at random on a variety of themes. Such assemblies of old men, sheltering under leaves in all the hill towns of Greece and letting the hours go by to the rhythm of the slow fall of their amber beads, call to mind the scene, on the Scaean Gate of Troy, of Priam conferring with his elders whose fighting days old age had ended, all chirping harmoniously like cicadas on a tree.

It was half-past eight and they had been peacefully enjoying the wine and the morning air since daybreak. My arrival, the courteous chorus of welcome, the stranger's answer of 'Well-found', and the offer of a chair and a glass, only made a short interruption in their discourse. I sat and listened. The Laconian peninsula lay weightlessly along the eastern horizon and, slightly more substantial, the outline of Elaphonisi—Stag-Island—loomed between us. Wraithlike on the Lybian Sea which expanded southwards far beyond the divider-point capes of Malea and Matapan, hovered Cythera once again, and beyond it, hardly discernible, Anticythera, the last stepping stone to the two stormy western capes of

Crete. An old man aimed his finger at the blue waste of water south-west and beyond his grooved and broken fingernail I could just descry two thin fragmentary scratches on the surface of the far-away sky: the summits of the White Mountains and of Mt. Ida; and I thought with homesickness of Cretan friends there, turbaned, black-clad and high-booted figures with their rifles beside them, grazing their shaggy flocks in the sky.

The war, politics and the Cyprus question were mercifully absent from the conversation. It ranged unhurriedly through distant countries, the fall of Byzantium, history, the nature of the equator, shipwrecks, the clouds, condensation of water, Lord Byron, verse forms, the price of oil and wine, the evils of hashish smoking, the excavations of Troy and other ancient sites, salt fish, polar bears, the Arctic circle, and the migration of birds. One of the quails that had alighted there a few years before—1946? 1947? the old man could not remember—had worn an inscribed steel ring round its leg. Disappearing into his house he brought the scrap of paper on which he had copied the inscription. There was no name, but 42, *Rue Lenormant, Paris*, was roughly traced in Latin characters. He had written there, but no reply had come. The quail he had set on its southward journey once more, thinking it a shame to eat a bird with such august international connections.

The sun shifted during all this chat and just as we were lifting the table a couple of feet to recapture the shade, Joan and Vasilio appeared with the laden mule. After half an hour we prepared to set off.

'Why don't you all stay? We don't often see people,' the old men said. 'There's no hurry. We will pass the time together. . . . Stay for a week. . . .'

'*Dia na perasome tin ora* . . . to pass the time. . . .' How often this phrase crops up in Greece! It is the password to hours of enchantment like this morning or to long doldrums of tedium; it poses the whole problem of how to fill in the long gap between now and the grave. Often, from its inception, one is able to predict the whole course of a village conversation, what topic will unleash another, where the sighs and the laughter will come, the signs of the cross and the right hand displayed palm outwards and fingers extended in anathema; where heads will be shaken or the edge of the table struck in indignation with the index-finger doubled up. They unfold with the inevitability of ritual. Old jokes are best and even at their hundredth repetition the laughter that salutes them is gay and unjaded. The patina on these chestnuts is the result of aeons of fondling. Many an hour of hilarity is really a long game of conkers and there is a strange pleasure for the experienced in observing the punctilio of stroke and counterstroke. But, in spite of this loyalty, new jokes—launched perhaps by an outsider from another district or country, the reversal of a cliché, a proverb given a paradoxical twist, a new pun, nonsense disguised as logic or a sudden eruption of fun—are welcomed and, after a moment's hesitation aroused by unfamiliarity (a moment considerably shorter than anywhere else in the world), are hailed with an almost exaggerated acclaim. Late arrivals are initiated to this novelty and for hours and years after the original detonation, long, long after the new joke's acceptance into the canon, it will be greeted with unflagging laughter and a chuckle at the memory of its risky and unorthodox origins. A stranger bringing a new joke to an isolated mountain community is at once a benefactor and an object of love; and, returning a decade later to one of these lonely thorpes, he will be greeted with affection and his innovation, now a household word, joyously recalled. These sudden dislocations and derailings of normal conversational procedure set off an instantaneous chain reaction, and, liberated from the rules of habit, the alert and original Greek mind—so tolerant of reiteration and the time-honoured arsenal of topics while it sticks to the formal track—breaks loose in dazzling displays of improvisation.

The reader will have gathered by now that hospitality in Greece has an almost religious importance. This is based on a genuine and deep-seated kindness, the feeling of pity and charity toward a stranger who is far from his home (as in ancient Greek the word *stranger* and *guest* are synonymous) and it is hardly an exaggeration to say that greater shame stamps the negative defect of lack of hospitality or meanness in rustic Greek eyes than many serious crimes. I think there is a subsidiary reason for this, an intellectual one. There is nothing idly inquisitive about that eager questioning of strangers: 'Are you married? Are your mother and father alive? What country are you from?—do you live in the capital or outside? Did you come on foot? Where are you heading for? Are you rich? Does it really rain the whole time in England? Is the water in your village as good as ours? How high are the mountains? How do your shoes stand up to these terrible rocks?— how much did they cost? Did you get them in Europe or in Athens? Do you know an Englishman called David who was here a few years ago? Are you hungry?' All but the most raw and insensitive newcomer will soon perceive, from the eagerness and solicitude in their expression—an expression totally at variance with the indiscretion, verbatim, of some of their questions—that all this is dictated by a real and devouring interest, a wish to establish common ground between human beings with the least possible delay, the more effectively to shelter him from the hazards and privations of solitude in a harsh terrain. Indifference is considered a sign of brutishness and a denial of human feeling. The same expression, until dispelled by their elders, can be read in the probing but benevolent eyes of children, grown enormous with wonder and the attempt to unravel this sudden conundrum, which accumulate round the newcomer's chair like the vast ovals on a spread peacock's tail.

The intellectual reason for all this is two-fold. It is firstly a thirst for knowledge—they are hot for certainties and any stranger is an emissary from the complex world outside, a new light on stale political discussions arising from the reading out loud of three-day-old newspapers. If the stranger is also a foreigner he is considered a key to the marvels and mysteries that lie beyond the frontiers of Greece. He is appealed to as an interpreter of all that they find strange or upsetting in world politics, especially in their bearing on Greece. Though there are usually several wise old heads in the village, there is a tendency to treat a stranger as an oracle, just because, by virtue of being a stranger, he must have travelled and seen more places and things than them, especially if he 'knows many letters', as the phrase goes. Education, whatever its extent and its results, is revered and there is aesthetic respect for skill in talk which can carry conviction by its style and fluency in defiance of its subject matter. There is, too, in simple and isolated communities where newspapers are the only reading matter, a superstitious respect for the written word which lowers the resistance to newsprint. But the multitude of newspapers and their mutually contradictory ideas promote a spirit of debate and conflict in even the smallest hamlets. Indeed, as each individual makes his own private interpretation of the data, every Greek may be said to comprise a one-man splinter-group. Only one thing can make these eight million splinter-groups cohere: danger to the State from outside invasion or the cause of Hellenism in its largest sense. For once all the newspapers and all the political parties are unanimous and the cohesion is instantaneous. There is no need, at the present time, to look far for examples of this.

The second of these reasons takes us back a page. It is a longing for the stimulus of the unfamiliar, for the stranger's catalytic power to dissolve the routine of talk and, by liberating them from their time-honoured rigmarole, open new tracks for speculation, improvisation and mental acrobatics. All strangers are like St. Paul with the Athenians on the Areopagus: 'thou bringest certain strange things to our ears, and we would know what these things mean. For all . . . spent their time in nothing else but either to tell or to hear some new thing.' The well-known phrase applies not only to the Athenians of to-day but to any group of elderly villagers sipping their minute coffee cups under any plane tree in any village in Greece. They have a passion for tidings. Once near the top of Mt. Kedros in Crete, a white-bearded old shepherd had shouted to my guide and me to join him at his fold a few hundred yards above the path. He set out cheese and bread and yaourt with an air of suppressed excitement—he had not been down to his village for months—and when all was ready, sat down, put his hands on his knees and leant forward with jutting elbows. 'Now!'

he said. 'News! Tell me some news—any news,' then, throwing his hands in the air with a laugh—'whatever you like—even if it's lies.'

We prepared to leave Layia. 'Don't go,' one of them said, 'there's no hurry. Sit here and take it easy, like Gladstone.'

'Like Gladstone?'

'Yes. Don't you know about *O Gladstonos*, when he was governor of the Ionian Islands? He was a great man and he loved Greece and the Greeks. Well, after he'd been there some time, Mrs. Gladstone wrote to him telling him to come home. There was no answer. She wrote again and again and still no answer. Finally, she said to herself, *What's happening?* So she caught a steamship in London and sailed to Corfu. And there in the public square, what did she find? Gladstone outside a café on a chair and he had his right arm crooked over the back of another chair, and his left over the back of a third, and a fourth for his right leg and a fifth for his left. A string of beads hung from one hand and the mouthpiece of a narghilé was in the other; but the narghilé was out. Why? Because Gladstone was asleep. His top hat was over his eyes and his mouth had fallen open; but between his teeth was a piece of Turkish delight—it was hanging out. It was a hot day, he was enjoying the sun, and he had fallen asleep half-way through . . .' He paused, and we all waited for him intently.

'Mrs. Gladstone was horrified.' The narrator's voice went up shrilly. ' "What has my husband come to?" As she had just come from London where it always rains, she still had a black umbrella in her hand. And she gave him a jab in the side with this umbrella,' he poked in the air with his walking-stick, 'and Gladstone woke up with a start'—he made a pantomime of abrupt awakening and bewilderment. ' "*Hé!* What's happening?"—"I'll tell you what's happening, husband," Mrs. Gladstone said. "You're for home." And she took him off to London with her. He was a good man.'

'He was a very good man,' another said, 'he gave Greece back the Ionian islands,' and then, with a wry but friendly smile at me, 'It's a pity he isn't alive to-day.'

I agreed that it was a great pity.

The speaker went on to deplore the absence of great political leaders. The race had died out, he seemed to say, like the extinct race of Titans. 'Churchill is the last of the giants of the old breed of great statesmen; but he's getting old, old.' A string of Greek politicians were suggested, but he dismissed them all with a backward jerk of the head, a negative tongue-click and a dismissive thumbnail sketch for each. 'A fine general who has saved Greece twice in the battlefield, but not a statesman. He should have kept out of politics,' or 'Not bad, a wonderful speaker but he loves the sound of his own voice,' or 'Clever in a small way, but not a patch on his father. He's a bridge player,' or 'A university professor, a theorist, an ideologist—an honest man, mind you, but ambition destroys him.' 'A sly one, a demon of intelligence, but he won't last—he'll set fire to himself with cleverness because he has no common sense,' or 'An idiot who thinks he can outwit everyone, a sparrow who thinks he's an eagle,' and 'A careerist whose one thought is filling his own stomach.' Who then was the last Greek statesman?

'Why, old Venizelos, of course, old Levtheri.' A storm of dissent broke out from the Royalist remainder, who condemned Venizelos as a Cretan adventurer, an unreliable revolutionary, and an enemy of Greece as a kingdom and this was her only hope of stability—look at England!—and equality with the rest of the world.

The minority speaker was that very rare bird, a Maniot Venizelist.

'I agree he went wrong in his old age. But look how he found Greece when he started. Do you remember what we used to call her? *Psorokóstaina*—Mangy Betty! And look how he left her, one of the nations of the West with steady frontiers, double the size, friends with Turkey for the first time in centuries and an ally and friend of the great and victorious western powers. Who wanted to come into the first war right from the start—and who brought her in on the right side in the end? Venizelos.'

Somebody interjected that Metaxas had brought Greece into the second war on the right side.

'He had to! Do you think the Greeks would take invasion by the *Macaronádes* lying down—or by the Germans for that matter? If he hadn't said "No," the whole race would have risen up and swept him aside.' He brushed a heap of cucumber peel off the table with a brusque gesture. 'And do you think,' he went on, 'that if Venizelos had been alive and at the height of his powers *and* one English statesman—only one!—of the old breed . . . say, Churchill at the height of *his* powers, or Lloyd George. . . .'

'He let us down in Asia Minor,' one of the others darkly interjected, but the speaker overrode him.

' . . . or Lloyd George, do you think we would be quarrelling with England, our oldest friend, about Cyprus? Of course we wouldn't. Venizelos would have chosen the right time, he would have known how to talk, he would have kept the priests out of it, and the English statesman would have understood that Cyprus is Greek and always has been. He would have got Cyprus for Greece without all this fuss in the newspapers and on the radio. England would have kept her bases, and instead of being like this,' he placed his two opposing forefingers tip to tip, 'enemies, we would be like this,' he placed the two fingers alongside, moving them up and down as though in caressing concord, 'greater friends than ever, like brothers. But, as I said, there are no great statesmen in Greece any more, nor, my dear English friend,' here he placed a hand on my shoulder, 'in England. They're just politicians and party-men, who can see no further than their noses; and look at the mess we are all in! It's little consolation for us in Greece to know that we are right and you are wrong. And God knows what mischief will come out of it all.' He made the sign of the cross with a rueful smile. 'God save poor Greece—and poor England too!—and deliver us out of the hands of little men. Greece has had a long and bitter fight in the past hundred years and more and anything touching this question can turn us into real devils. It is the only feeling in Greece that is stronger than our historical feeling for England.'

The others all nodded their heads gloomily, with a chorus of '*etsi einai, paidi mou*—that's how it is, my child'. But they soon

cheered up with the thought that in the end England was bound
to give Cyprus to Greece. England, after all, was a great, a just
and a good race, and one that loved Greece—it was as though
they were saying that England had become, in all innocence, a
receiver of stolen property; who, when the time came, was sure
to restore it to the rightful owner. She could keep as many bases
there as she chose, and have them all over the mainland—yes, here
in Layia, if they wanted, and welcome. Weren't all their interests
the same? They were both seafaring countries, both lovers of
liberty and members of the free world, western allies and brothers
united against the eastern danger? The bad old days were over,
and Greece, thank God ('Thank Venizelos' was interjected here),
was now an ally and friend of Turkey, bound by pacts and common interests; there could be no trouble there, and the Turkish
minority in Cyprus would live as contentedly as the Turks of
Thrace, or the Greeks of Constantinople. Where was the difficulty? Surely it was a private matter to be settled between friends.
A mood of optimism hovered over us all.*

'Lack of statesmen,' the former speaker interjected with
melancholy triumph. Another said, still more dejectedly, that no
country ever relinquished territory they held, whether rightly or
wrongly, without *dan-doon*—he mimicked the sound of gunfire
and the usual gesture of trigger-pulling.

'You're wrong,' said the Venizelist, 'England has—the Ionian
islands—because they are a logical and a just race, and because
they knew who their real friends were better than they seem to—
forgive me, Michali!—to-day. It did as much as Byron and the
Philhellenes in the 'twenty-one war, as much as Navarino and
Canning and alliance in the two great wars and Churchill, to
strengthen Greece's friendship for England. But, as I said, Churchill is old, Venizelos is dead, and I am afraid. Unless a great man
appears, it will all slip into the hands of newspapers and priests

---

* This conversation took place in happier days, before the Turkish complica-
tion had appeared on the scene. The conviction that its emergence was fostered
by Great Britain to bring in outside support to an otherwise untenable case has
done more than anything else to embitter the problem in Greece.

and party politicians and of second-rate men in England, and finally, of soldiers, and then . . .' his shoulders went up, 'you might even get Greeks and English shooting at each other.' A universal cry, surprised and indignant, of 'Never!' went up.

'Listen,' he went on, 'I'm only an old man and a villager, and I can only read and write with difficulty, but I've lived a long time and I have heard a lot of talk and I've seen much . . . *pollá* . . . *pollá*. . . . Countries are only great if they can produce wise men, and if they have the sense to elect them. Otherwise the individuals, however good and brave and sensible they are, are like noughts, vast quantities of hollow, round valueless noughts. Place a states-man at their head, and it is like the digit in a written figure, it gives value to all the noughts, turns them into the sum of eight million in the case of Greece, and—forty-five?—thank you—in the case of England. Take away the digit, and the noughts are noughts again, and they can be blown away or dispersed by any chance wind. Venizelos was one of these digits, Churchill was another.' The air seemed to be afloat with purposeless bubbles.

'If you go on like that,' one of the others said, 'we shall all be in tears, and we've heard enough about old Venizelos, the horn-wearer, for one day. After all, I could go on about Papagos till to-morrow. With two races who are as old and trusted friends as the Greeks and the English, everything's bound to work out for the best. Give Ioanna and Michali and Vasilio a drink, otherwise the wine will turn sour with standing so long!'

When we set off at last they called after us. 'Why go on to the Outer Mani? They're a useless lot, not worth a five-drachma piece. You'll see. Come back here afterwards, if you must go, and help us pass the time. What's the hurry? You can have five chairs apiece, like Gladstone. . . .'

CHAPTER 15

Ikons

W E halted on the way out of the village to look into a small church. It was built of massive stone slabs, an empty oblong with a battered wooden iconostasis, pervaded by an atmosphere of dereliction and dust. The walls were covered with extraordinary frescoes.

Very often, wandering in the wilder parts of Greece, the traveller is astonished in semi-abandoned chapels where the liturgy is perhaps only sung on the yearly feast of the eponymous saint, by the beauty of the colouring of the wall-paintings and the subtlety with which the painter has availed himself of the sparse elbow-room for private inspiration that the formulae of Byzantine iconography allow him: a convention so strict that it was finally codified by a sixteenth-century painter-monk called Dionysios of Phourna. He formalized the tradition of centuries into an iconographic dogma and deviation became, as it were, tantamount to schism. He it was who made the army of saints and martyrs and prophets identifiable at once by certain unvarying indices—the cut and growth of saints' beards, their fall in waves or ringlets, their smooth flow or their shagginess, their bifurcation or their parting into two or three or five. He regulated—it was more the ratification of old custom than the launching of new fiats—the wings that anomalously spring from the shoulder blades of St. John Prodromos, and placed his head on a charger in his hands as well as on his neck.* He stipulated the

---

* The birth of St. John the Baptist marks midsummer day, but the feast of his decapitation, on the 29th of August, the Decollation, is known as the day of Ayios Ioannes Apokephalistheis—St. John the Beheaded. This past-participle

angle at which a timely sapling, springing from the ground, should redeem the nakedness of St. Onouphrios from scandal and ordained that Jonah should be seated sadly beneath a gourd hanging from the trellis he built outside the walls of Nineveh, holding a scroll inscribed with the words: '*Lelypemai epi ti kolokynthi sphodra eos thanatou*'—'I have had pity on the gourd, even unto death.'

Above their regulation beards and their ineluctable attributes, the saints gaze from the iconostasis and the walls of the narthex and the katholikon with a strange, blank, wide-eyed fixity, and behind their hoary and venerable heads, the golden haloes succeed each other in vistas of gleaming horseshoes or, when a saintly host is assembled in close array, in a shining interlock of glory like the overlapping scales of a vast goldfish. Barely sheltered from snow and rain by a loggia on the outer walls of remote fanes, the weatherworn lineaments of the pagan sages of the Greek world can be discerned: Solon, Plato, Aristotle, Plutarch, Thucydides, Sophocles and Apollonius of Tyana,* arrayed in robes as honourable as those that adorn the Christian saints, but bereft of haloes. Their presence, due to passages in their writings interpreted as prophecy or ratification of the incarnation of Christ, seems to announce the age-old truth that the Greek Orthodox Church glorifies not only the Christian miracle as revealed to the Evangelists but the continuity and indestructibility of Hellenism and the part played in Christianity by the thought and discipline of the pagan Greek philosophers. Where but in the ancient schools (these figures imply), were developed the intellectual thews which enabled the great Doctors to hammer the raw material of the Gospels into the intricate and indestructible apparatus of Christian dogma? Without the dialectical and philosophic skill of these rain-swept sages, who would have heard

---

passive is often mispronounced by peasants (in certain circumstances, *theta* turns very easily into *tau*), as the active form, *apokephalistes*, which turns him into St. John the Headsman; and I think, among the very simple, a vague idea does actually prevail that they are celebrating a saint who held this office.

* Also Philo the Neoplatonist, Thule king of Egypt, Balaam and the Sybil.

of the Three Hierarchs indoors, so splendidly robed and haloed, polished by the kisses and dark with the incense of fifteen centuries: SS. John Chrysostom, Basil of Caesarea and Gregory of Nyssa? Or of SS. Gregory Nazianzen or Athanasius? Or, for that matter, of the only great early doctor of the plodding and barbarous west, St. Augustine of Hippo?* Without our help (the honoured exiles seem to say) who would have unravelled the perplexing skein of the Trinity or confuted the subtle-tongued heresiarchs or championed the Homoousion and the Double Nature?

The Greeks do well to honour these ancient mentors. They enabled their descendants to save the Divine message from the mumblings of the catacombs and to sort out the Semitic data; in cell and archbishopric and council, they attuned their skilful minds to detect, interpret and codify the promptings of the Holy Ghost. The evolution of Christianity into a logical system which could weather the shocks of millennia, was a Greek thing. The Christian Church was the last great creative achievement of classical Greek culture. For extent and influence in the world the dual message of Greek philosophy and the Greek interpretation of the Christian revelation stands alone.

Scenes of carnage often cover the walls of churches from vaulting to flagstone. Beheadings, flayings, burnings, roastings, boilings, rendings, crushings, breakings, impalings, mutilations, hecatombs, dismemberments by bent trees and by galloping horses redden the mural cartouches with blood and flame. But something serene and formal in the treatment of these orgies of martyrdom, a mild and benevolent composure in the faces of both executioner and victim and even on the haloed faces of the decapitated martyrs, robs their impact of anguish and horror. These emblematic ordeals have the punctilio of a dance commemorating early heroism in the cause of the faith. They do not demand that we should participate vicariously in their torments. In fact, so identically non-committal are the persecutors and their

* Where, too, it might also be asked, would St. Thomas Aquinas have been a thousand years later, without the friendly guidance of Aristotle?

prey that, if any such advocacy were at work, the wicked, as the artisans of beatitude, seem to solicit our approval with an equal claim. The swords and pincers they wield are the keys of paradise. Passion is far removed and the figures are, in fact, not figures at all in the ordinary sense, but symbols. The same absence of the *argumentum ad hominem* is discernible in the iconographic approach to Jesus Christ and the Blessed Virgin, especially in the treatment of the Nativity and the Passion. There is never a blush or a simper, the infant Jesus is never a dimpled *bambino*. The Byzantine interpretation of the sufferings of Our Lord does not seek our participation in His physical torments or ask us, as do religious artists in the West, to undergo the Passion by proxy. The tears of the *Mater Dolorosa* and the *Ecce Homo* are almost absent.

Post-primitive religious painting in the West is based on horror, physical charm, infant-worship and easy weeping. This, with the modified exception of some Macedonian painting, is practically unknown in the East. The Virgin Mary, who is significantly known to Orthodoxy as the All-Holy One, has the austere aloofness of an oriental empress; she is calm, unreal, hieratic, wide- and dry-eyed. The Holy Child is abstract and unearthly and his glance is the wise one of an adult; and, with few exceptions, Christ Crucified, in spite of the emaciation which was the immutable token of holiness, has the same unworldliness. Eastern hagiography is no less bloodthirsty than the Western—indeed, until the Middle Ages, they were nearly the same—but the crucifix is a much rarer adjunct to Orthodox worship and the infliction of the stigmata on privileged saints is unknown.

Our Lord is usually represented enthroned in splendour, gravely and triumphantly presiding over mankind, His left hand raised, thumb and fourth finger touching in benediction, enjoining— what? Nothing so simple as good conduct for fear of Hell fire. The need perhaps of learning to penetrate symbols. The emphasis of the Christian year falls on the Easter victory: Christ risen from the dead, Christ as God and the All Powerful Christ Pantocrator, undemonstrative, impersonal and divine. He soars overhead in the centre of the dome in a golden sky as transcendent as the regions of abstract thought. Aloof and august, He floats in an atmosphere which is still and spellbound and if a presiding mood can be identified, it is one of faint, indefinable and glorious melancholy, like the thought of space. Ikons are wholly, like the paintings of Piero della Francesca in the pages of Mr. Berenson, unemphatic. All trace of apostrophe is lacking; there is no attempt to buttonhole the observer. Western Christs expose their wounds; Eastern Christs sit enthroned in ungesticulating splendour.

The Western medieval Madonna is a gentle and beautiful mediatrix, a celestial Philippa of Hainault, and we are the burghers of Calais with ropes round our necks for whom she will intercede. When the Italian version of disinterred paganism had set new pulses beating, her statues, like Venus addressing a reluctant Adonis, seem almost to woo her devotees. At its worst there is the hint of an ogle, a veiled appeal for fans. In the West, iconographically, Our Lord and Our Lady and the Army of Saints, whether they are exquisite idealizations or smirking and blubbering simulacra, are, each of them, one of us. Their Eastern effigies—which, during all these mutations, scarcely changed in thirteen centuries—are emphatically different. The expression of the Panayia, even at the foot of the Cross, says 'No Comment'. If an expression can be detected in the raised arcs of eyebrow and the wide eyes enigmatically gazing through the kisses and the incense and the candle flames, it is, most strangely, a faintly quizzical and ironical one. 'Do not worship me,' perhaps, 'but what I represent.'

The unexclamatory message of these paint and mosaic figures is neither sensual nor emotional. It is a spiritual and an intellectual one. They are not, in the ordinary sense, figures at all; they are symbols of the abstract idea of God which offer different facets of the Divine principle. If the right formulae existed, the message might have been conveyed by elaborate geometrical figures or intricately decorative algebraic equations. They are, in fact, ideograms. So slender is their link with flesh and blood, that it is almost an accident that the notation happens to be, in its very rarified way, anthropomorphic. They are, one might say, gilded and illuminated cube roots of the Logos.

There were plenty of ascetic solitaries in the early days of the Eastern Church: the Thebaid and all the Levant were scattered with them, stylites dreamed their lives away on the summit of columns, dendrites chained themselves to the topmost branches of high trees. Speluncar Christianity throve and hermits meditated in many a cave. The mysticism of East and West may be said to have sprung from Pseudo-Dionysius the Areopagite (and thus from Proclus), but the interpretation was very different. The macerations, austerities, meditations and penances of these lonely figures are closer to the general mystic temper of the Orient than they are to the mystics of the West. They were part of a Christianized tributary of the general Asiatic stream of mysticism that branched out at different times into the Kabeiri and the initiate religions of Pagan Greece, the Gnostics, the Neoplatonists, the Essenes, Yogis, Sufis and the various Dervish sects. They immersed themselves in the abstraction of divine omnipresence and I feel that a Byzantine mystic would have been closer in spirit to the meditations of Jellaladin on the astrolabe of God's mysteries—he, indeed, inherited much from Greek thought—than to the ecstasies of, say, Marie de l'Incarnation or Saint Teresa of Avila or St. John of the Cross. In the latter case, again, the approach was personal and immediate, involving not only metaphysics but the passions: a private or reciprocal relationship between the Divinity and one human being; and, parallel in this to the iconography of the West, the terminology is startlingly anthropomorphic and literal. The solitary quest for union with God is expressed, for lack of a fitting vocabulary, in the specific language of love. Hesychasm, the Strange Quietism of late Byzantium which flourished in the monasteries of Athos, was the last mystical movement of Greek Orthodoxy. That discipline of slow breathing, attuned to the endless lamaic repetition of a single prayer, the silent posture and the searching gaze irremovably focused on the navel until, in a trance, the inner light of Mount Tabor should begin to glow there—this is more in harmony with the East than with the West.

Fiercer enemies than the hostile Greek monks of Calabria lay in wait for such strange twilight flowerings of Byzantine mysticism. . . . The crescent hoisted on the dome of Justinian in Constantinople changed and circumscribed the rôle of the Greek Church for ever. The stem that put forth such extravagant blooms soon withered away. The cloud of Orthodox mystical feeling drifted to Russia; in that snowy world, its fusion with the Slav temperament threw off many curious spiritual phenomena, not least of them Dostoievsky. The *Philokalia*, the beautiful and simple meditations of the hesychasts, was, until the Revolution, far more widely read in Russia than it is in Greece to-day.

Byzantium fell, and the tears on ikons of the All-Holy One were not, to the awestruck Romaic world, the tears of the Mater Dolorosa for her Son, but the tears of a celestial Empress (and, beyond question, a Greek one) bewailing the death of the last terrestrial Emperor of the Greeks and the desecration by infidels of Orthodoxy's central shrine. They were shed for the dispersal of her clergy and the falling silent of her bells and gongs; for the sprouting of minarets and the insult of the first muezzin's call. The Pantocrator retreated more inaccessibly into his golden zenith.

Perhaps it would have been better for Orthodoxy in the end, whatever the aesthetic loss, if the symbolism of religious painting and the arcane splendour of the liturgy had been less lofty and abstruse. For the clergy's task, in the ensuing Dark Ages (whose beginning exactly coincided with the Renaissance in the West and only ended in the Industrial Revolution), was the actual physical survival of their flock: its spiritual welfare was left to bare forms of sacrament and liturgy. Scholarship died. Spiritual development fossilized. Falling static at the time of the catastrophe, Orthodoxy became the most conservative of religions. All but rudimentary teaching vanished. But the forms became more august and venerable, more apt an emblem of lost glory and more hermetic a token of national continuity the further they floated from everyday understanding. In this new function the Church grew in power and became steadily more beloved and revered;

the less religion functioned as a vehicle of the Christian ethic, the more holy it grew as the sole guarantee of survival. 'Christian' and 'Orthodox' became negative words and lost their meaning as moral or doctrinal terms; the former came to signify little more than non-Moslem, the latter—with 'Romios' the paradoxical antonym of 'Latin', the epithet of the hated Catholics of the West who, with the Crusades, were the first to destroy the Orthodox Empire and make straight the way for Islam—meant, precisely, Greek.

Long gone were the days when the subtle Eastern theologians could with difficulty make the blunt Western prelates grasp the delicate shades of dogma; indeed the shoe was on the other foot. But the outward observances, the liturgy, some of the sacraments, prostrations, rigorous fasts, frequent signs of the cross, the great feasts of the Church—the cross thrown into the sea at Epiphany, the green branches of Palm Sunday, the candles and coloured eggs celebrating the risen Christ at Easter, the monthly censing of houses, and the devotion to ikons before which an oil-dip twinkles in every house—all this became rigid and talismanic: and so it has remained. Its scope is different from what is usually conjured up in the West by the word 'Christianity'; but there is a tendency in the most peaceful nations to identify religion with the tribe and the reasons in Greece are more cogent than most. All the outward and visible signs are there and it would be a bold critic who would unburden them completely of inward and spiritual grace. There is nothing laggard or perfunctory about these signs; they are performed with reverence and love. They have the familiarity and the treasured intimacy of family pass-words and countersigns. The day is punctuated by these fleeting mementoes, and pious landmarks in the calendar, usually solemn-ized with dance and rejoicing, space out the year; with the result that few gestures are wholly secular. They weave a continuous thread of the spiritual and supernatural through the quotidian homespun and ennoble the whole of life with a hieratic dignity. There is a deep substratum of virtue and innocence in the Greek character which is very distinct, and much more positive a thing

than the universal truism of peasant simplicity—compared to this
general norm they are old in guile and sophistication. It is a trait
which has weathered barbarian influx and foreign dominion. It
may be a survival of ancient Greek *areté* and love of excellence,
the survival of Christian teaching in the past or a by-product of
the ecological influences of the Greek sea and mountains and
light. The sky here exorcizes and abolishes the principle of
intrinsic wickedness. Perhaps it is a triune conjunction of all
three. The chief of the cardinal virtues, charity (when it is not
obscured by the hot fumes of individual, family, party or national
feud-spirit), they possess in an overwhelming degree.

The very Greekness of the liturgy bolsters up the warm tribal
feeling. The fact that the Greek of the Epistles and Gospels is in
Alexandrian *koiné* of the first century, and the main fabric of the
Mass in the elaborate Byzantine language of St. John the Golden-
Mouthed and none of it later than the seventh—all this flings the
Greek mind back, once more, to past ages of incredible splendour
and venerability. The language, largely incomprehensible to the
unlettered faithful, sets it at a remove and doubles its wonder and
numinosity and talismanic power. (Perhaps the word *mysterion*,
the Greek for 'sacrament', as well as 'mystery', and the Last
Supper being called 'the Mystic Feast', deepens this feeling.) This
abstruseness is a source of pride and proprietorship different
in its nature to the Latin of the Roman rite. The saintly idiom,
though it has floated up beyond their grasp, is their own, the
language, as it were, that their great-grandfathers spoke in
happier days. It is a family affair and Our Lord and Our Lady and
their enormous saintly retinue have long since become honorary
fellow-countrymen. Although they never follow the liturgy in a
parallel text, the congregation know some of the basic prayers and
anthems since childhood and the identity of many scattered fragments in these two phases of Greek—the liturgical and the spoken
—conveys an inkling of what is afoot. They lean back in their
stalls and the long hours of chanting evolve round them in a
magnificent and half-penetrable cloud of sound, an interweaving
of canon and invocation and antiphon, of troparia and kondakia,

of the canticle of the Cherubim, the Symbol of Nicaea, the litanies of the Faithful and of the Catachumens, perhaps the hymn of the Akathistos, of Cassia or the Myrrh-bringers, the constant renewal of the doxology and the multiple iteration of the Kyrie Eleison; all intoned or chanted, strangely syncopated in the minor mode of oriental plainsong, in a ritual tangle of hovering neums and quarter-tones.*

There is no feeling of tension in the Orthodox service, no climax of awed silence at the moment of miracle, followed by an unwinding. In spite of its name, and whatever its intent, it is unmystic in atmosphere. But it is dramatic. It is a gleaming and leisurely—almost a sauntering—pageant. Much of the drama unfolds behind the iconostasis, that roodscreen dividing the nave from the chancel; priests and deacons, their beards flowing and their long hair uncoiled over coruscating vestments, make processional entrances and exits, swinging thuribles bearing candles or a metal bound gospel, through the outside two of the three doors in this screen; doors which some scholars derive from the three thresholds in the proscenium of ancient Greek tragedy. The central door was reserved, they say, for the protagonist at the play's climax; and, indeed, the celebrant only emerges from it today when he proffers the sacred vessels after the elevation. There is no excessive simulacrum of piety in the deportment of the officiating clergy. Their heads are flung back and the eyes above their singing mouths are cast up into the air in a mild unfocused gaze. Something tired, patrician and relaxed informs their gait and the deacons with their sweeping dalmatics and wide stoles, their youthful beards, their long dark hair and the lustrous wide

* Ancient Greek music, alas, died without leaving a trace or clue, beyond the surmise of musicologists on the various modes. Greek ecclesiastical music, which evolved in early Christian times, and the Gregorian plainsong of the West both derive from the Synagogue; particularly, thinks Dr. Egon Wellesz (see his *Byzantine Music and Hymnography*. Oxford, Clarendon Press), from the great temples of Jerusalem and Antioch. Hebrew liturgy was familiar to at least the first generation of Christians and it was through traditional music that the Psalter was disseminated among the Gentiles.

eyes that illuminate their wax-pale faces, have the air of Byzantine princes who in martyrdom might turn into St. Stephen or St. Sebastian. The older clergy resemble minor prophets. The great dignitaries, who are always adorned with vast spreading beards and usually very tall (the thought has sometimes crossed my mind that Orthodox preferment may be a matter of height), glitter with golden copes and pectoral ornaments and snake-topped crosiers. With their white locks mitred with gem-studded globular crowns, they resemble pictures of God the Father. But, except at grave moments, an easy-going, paternal benevolence often leavened by the glint and the wrinkles of humour, stamps the faces of these deities. Their faces hint at an antique knowledge of their own and mankind's fallibility; they betoken tolerance of back-sliding and quickness to forgive. Their anathema is reserved for temporal targets.

The evolutions of all these figures against the effulgence of gilding and fresco and mosaic and brocade themselves form a kind of moving ikon, but familiarity and glory are so blended that the whole office suggests a leisurely morning in one of the remoter courtyards of Paradise. The chanting continues, candles glimmer before ikons encrusted with beaten silver, the iconostasis towers like a jungle of gold, topped with a cross guarded by two coiling dragons, incense drifts through the columns, and, if it is a great feast, the crushed basil scattered underfoot sends up its additional fragrance. Remote and benign divinities shine in the cupolas and the apse, and round the drum that upholds the Pantocrator's dome a legion of angels open their wings in a ring. A bland, non-committal and avuncular troop of painted saints populate the walls and a quiet, reassuring and universal benevolence, dropping softly as dew, seems to descend on the congregation. The mind is lulled. It is a fitting and comforting and mildly supernatural occasion, a family reunion both in the literal and the Confucian sense. Very little—except perhaps something in the spiritual outlook of the faithful—has changed in the slow punctilio of word and gesture and music for thirteen hundred years. For the last five hundred, almost nothing. Both as a manifesto of

Greek continuity and as an historical survival it is precious and unique.

* * * *

I have taken ikon-painting as the epitome of the long stasis of the Orthodox Church; perhaps rather arbitrarily.* Even the moderately informed on such matters know that there were, indeed, different schools and even renaissances, in the history of Byzantine art, and very interesting they are. But in no case are these deviations from the essential canon as great as the gaps that yawn between great schools of the West, or as revolutionary as the Italian Renaissance. But I am only concerned here with one facet of this absorbing subject: the interaction of the Greek religion and Greek religious art.

The installation of the Turks in Constantinople and their occupation of all Greek lands was, to all but bare survival, a circular glare of the Medusa's head. Luxuries like spiritual thought and painting were Gorgon-struck. The task of the clergy and of the ikon-painters was not progress or creation but sheer maintenance; things had to be kept intact until better days dawned. Religion and religious art, already contained by strict rules, became inflexible. The result was stagnation in religion, and in art, endless repetition and, at last, degeneration. Iconography remained intellectual, lofty and remote but learning dried up and with it the power to apprehend the abstruse messages implicit in Byzantine art. Unquestioning and uncomprehending formalism followed. The meaning of the equations behind cypher and symbol

---

* I have laid great stress on passionless detachment in the depiction of divine figures; but a critic could marshal a damaging array of exceptions. Were I engaged on such a task I would begin with the stupendous mosaic of Christ Pantocrator at Daphni in Attica, Whose great eyes, dark and exorbitant and cast almost furtively over one shoulder, at total variance with His right hand's serene gesture of blessing and admonition, spell not only pain but fear, anguish and guilt, as though He were in flight from an appalling doom. The only fit setting for such an expression is the Garden of Gethsemane; but this is a Christ-God in His glory, the All Powerful One. It is tremendous, tragic, mysterious and shattering.

retreated and the almost algebraic notation itself become an object of cult. The overbred, long-fingered Byzantine hands were thickening on the plough. . . . Perhaps in this lean period a different and more accessible kind of ikon-painting, a lowering of the intellectual sights from head to heart, would have served their strictly religious purposes better.

Plenty of indications exist that during the late Middle Ages an opposite trend to Byzantine inflexibility was in being. It might have gained momentum if the Fall of the Empire had not condemned it to stillbirth. It might have changed the whole nature of Byzantine art. I refer to the 'pathetic', to a loosening of the stern rules of iconography, an accompaniment of the austere and cerebral idiom by an address to the emotions. The most important of these symptoms appear in the renaissance that followed the recapture of Constantinople by the Greeks after the sixty-odd years of the Latin Empire that followed the Fourth Crusade. The impulse had sprung up in the hardy exiled empire of the Lascarids at Nicaea. In Constantinople it flowered under the beginnings of the last dynasty, the Palaeologues, in the late thirteenth and the fourteenth centuries, and appeared at its best on the mosaics of the Church of St. Saviour in Chora,* not far from the Theodosian walls. These mosaics were placed there, along with his own portrait, by Andronicus II Palaeologue's Great Logothete, Theodore Metochites, who, on the strength of his extraordinary headdress, has already appeared in these pages.† In the scenes from the Life of the Virgin there is an appealing gentleness, a fluidity of motion and an unbending from the austere regulation postures that is full of tenderness and human warmth and pity. The mosaic persons are still traditionally moon-faced, but a pulse begins tentatively to beat, the symbol and content merge. . . . Some have proposed, and others have fairly convincingly scouted, the hypothesis that this iconographic trend is an Eastern reflection of the Italian *trecento* brought about by a West to East cultural traffic incidental to the Crusades. It seems

* It is better known under its name as a mosque, the Kahrie Djami.
† See page 159.

clear, however, that the tendency was autochthonously generated, a spontaneous upsurge of new vitality in Byzantium's ancient frame. This Indian summer was soon to be extinguished.

In fact, the tide of influence flowed all the other way, in a steady movement which began long before the earliest glimmer of the Italian Renaissance. The Byzantine share in Italian primitive art needs no underlining. It was not, as former authorities were wont to assume, a mass swoop westwards, as from a Pandora's box suddenly prised open, of all the treasures of the Greek world at the Fall, which a happy coincidence of dates seemed once to sug-gest. There is little in the Byzantine Middle Ages to indicate a reciprocal Frankish influence, certainly nothing comparable to that of Byzantium on, say, St. Mark's in Venice. It is surprising, on the other hand, how little the Western plastic techniques of the Crusaders were influenced locally in their fiefs of the Greek world and Outremer. The Gothic churches of Cyprus and the omni-present castellated ruins remain as alien to their setting as the Anglican Cathedral in Calcutta and British cantonments in Rawalpindi and Hong Kong, or, for that matter, in Nicosia. There was, however, a slight trickle of influence from West to East. In literature this took the shape of a few charming and artificial verse romances, an Eastern echo of chivalric prototypes that is very insipid compared to the vigour of the true Byzantine heroic vernacular in the great saga of Digenis Akritas. Perhaps a more interesting contribution may be observed in the Western exonarthex of Daphni, if, that is, the frescoes there are not con-temporary with those of the rest of the church, but two centuries after and later than the Crusades, as Dr. Angelos Procopiou, to the consternation of many, has recently suggested. Here the same 'pathetic' trends, comparable to those of the Chora, can be observed. Mr. Procopiou's proposition has not yet been either ratified or destroyed by outside authoritative opinion, but his case is most seductively argued. The Western influences that he detects are those of the Siennese school and particularly of Duccio di Buoninsegua; and this hypothetical merging of the two trends he attributes to the tolerant attitude of the Frankish dukes of

Athens, of the De La Roche family.* Intermarried with Greek princesses, both Catholic and Orthodox clergy frequented their Court in a brief ecclesiastical truce and this harmony may have loosened the iconographic barriers for Western infiltration. It is an inviting thought.

The remoteness, the formality and the austerity of Byzantine ikon-painting was originally a result of the mass destruction of religious portraiture started by the iconoclast emperor, Leo the Isaurian, in 727. It was a puritan, anti-monastic reaction that grew up in the minds of Asian Greeks largely because of the horror in which Islam and Jewry held all reproductions of the human as well as the divine countenance. Ikons were finally restored and the dissolved monasteries re-monked by the Empress Theodora in 842. This upheaval brought about a purifying and spiritual-izing change in iconography. Hellenistic materialism, which had co-existed, in a meaty and ever-slackening dotage, with the fresh and vivid splendour of early Byzantine mosaics, was dead for ever. The realistic third dimension of sculpture flattened into the more intangible medium of painter and mosaicist. The holy *dramatis personae*, almost disembodied now, sailed into a spiritual and rarified empyrean of mystery and awe from which the centuries have not dislodged them.

From this moment it can be said that religious art in the East sought to bring man to God's level, and in the West, bring God to man's; each laying stress on a different half of Our Lord's nature. It is a significant difference of plastic emphasis. Persian and Arabian graces in the detail of decoration—fountains, peacocks, flowers and intricate designs from oriental fabrics—tempered the splendid austerity of mosaic and fresco and illuminated parch-ment; but, more important, the continued study of the ancient

* Though the Franks were driven from the seat of empire itself in 1271, the Byzantine empire that still remained out of infidel hands had been sliced up and distributed in fiefs among the crusading magnates. Outside the City and its surroundings, the only important remainder still in Byzantine hands was the despotate of Mistra, the Ducas despotate of Epirus and the young sister empire of the Comnenes at Trebizond. The mainland was the share of French over-lords, and the entire archipelago went to the Doge.

Greeks propelled a harmonious and unbroken underground river of Platonic thought, sluggish at times, at others leaping forth in cascades and spreading in great serene lakes which irrigated and complemented the Christian dogma it had done so much to form; incidentally affecting at times, out of archaizing allegiance, the iconographic décor; but, more importantly, carrying the figures themselves yet further into transcendence and incorporeality. If Justinian had hoped to halt the speculative thought of the pre-Christian world by closing the philosophical schools in Athens, he closed them in vain. Psellos the Hellenist, during one of these recurring revivals, indicated the spiritual mood when he spoke of 'stealing from intelligence the incorporeal quality of things and realizing the light within the body of the Sun'. The ambience is silent and still and stratospheric in its distance from everyday human passions.

The renaissance that followed the Fourth Crusade, of which I spoke a few pages back, was a reaction from this supernal exaltation. Hard times had come, most of the Empire was divided among infidels and the alien and reciprocally schismatic Franks. The walls now girded a pillaged and half-ruined city full of weeds and rubble and waste land and cornfields . . . the Roman Empire, founded thirteen centuries earlier, had just one and a half more to go. The changed temper—a compound of vigour and melancholy—which had prompted the mosaics of St. Saviour in Chora took general form in the iconography of the Macedonian school. It was a feeling that spread in widening rings all over Greek lands and into the southern marches of the Slav world from the peak of Mount Athos. The move towards purely mortal distress was epitomized by a fixation on the human sorrows of Our Lord and the Panayia. This modification of religious paintings, so glaringly at variance with all that had gone before, had, however, long been latent in the Greek world in Asia. The sorrowful aspect of Christianity, the Passion and the Sufferings of the Virgin, all that which was to run riot in the Western Church, had been simmering in the East since divines like George of Nicodemia in the ninth century had enlarged on the Passion of the Virgin, which, five centuries later, St. Bernard was to spread across the whole of Western Christendom.

Far from the religious radiance of the Metropolis a gloomier, wilder, tougher, more uncouth form of picture had covered the tufa walls of the Cappadocian rock monasteries—anyone who has seen that harsh light and those desolate and fierce volcanic cones in which they are warrened can understand this well.* There must have been something in the air propitious to their emergence now. These new trends, meeting the old on Athonite monastery walls, produced the beautiful Macedonian school. Painting gained in fluidity and human feeling—in the pathetic, indeed—but lost much of the inner luminosity which is the great glory of Byzantine art.† It must be made quite clear, however, that it never sinks (though perhaps it meant to) to the dolorous realism that later swamped the West. The divine Protagonist and the Blessed Virgin, even when she is fainting at the Cross's foot, have the hieratic dignity of figures from Greek tragedy; and the ritual character of an ancient chorus pervades the bowed heads of mourning women. There is no element here that presaged the stagey rictus and pictorial syncope, the dark wayside fetishism of Italy and Spain or the amazing northern excruciations of Grünewald; no hint of the religious trend which rears the black sil-

---

* See *A Time to Keep Silence*, Patrick Leigh Fermor (John Murray, 1957).

† I warmly recommend to the reader *The Birth of Western Painting* by Robert Byron and David Talbot Rice. He will follow and perhaps disagree with the complex arguments elucidating how the same trends blossomed exactly simultaneously in Florence where, possibly short-circuiting Constantinople and Athos, Byzantine painting had already been at work; and in Sienna in the pictures of Giotto and Duccio, and thus of Cimabue and Lorenzetti and Barna da Siena and the best of the *trecento*. He will not only be able to compare the photographs but read a magnificent appreciation of the prominence and eclipse of Byzantine art; and also, incidentally, enjoy some of the most spirited, uncircumspect and powerful English prose written this century. It has the quality of a high mettled horse. He will smile at the brio with which Robert Byron deals with obstacles and opposition. Instead of evading or dismantling them he points the target out, as it were with a sabre, and then, with dazzling bravura, clears it in a magnificent leap or gallops over it roughshod, slashes and kicks it to matchwood and rides on.

houette of Golgotha and the panoply of the lance, reed, sponge, whip, hammer, nails, pincers and thorns between the eye of mankind and the splendour of God.

* * * *

Suddenly, on the steep and rocky flank of a detached cone of the Taygetus, seventy miles north of the point on the Mani coast where these last rambling pages began and five miles from the first page of the book, on the very eve of the Empire's collapse, all the luminosity, all the splendour and radiance of Eastern art suddenly emerged with a changed and newborn vigour that seems, to-day, a challenging salute of the condemned. Houdini-like, the painting of Mistra had elbowed itself loose alike from the hindering bonds of the ancient iconological formulae and from Macedonian hypochondria. Retaining all that was most precious in both, it put forth new and bold juxtapositions and interlocks of colour and, as though by magic, humanized gods, angels, saints and mortals without draining them of a flicker of their spirituality. They not only exalt the beholder, which is an almost unfailing attribute of Byzantine painting; they touch and move him as well. It is a miracle of delicate balance, and it is almost a solution to the question these pages have been asking. How long could it have continued? It is exactly contemporary with the *trecento* and early *quattrocento* in Tuscany and Umbria which, all too soon, without the disaster of alien conquest, were to be water-logged by Latin materialism. Perhaps it was too frail and rare a thing to endure. Certainly its setting and its incubation were unique; for all these Mistra frescoes were painted within a few decades of the Empire's fall. The town was to survive the Capital by three strange years. With the exception of the minute far-away Empire of Trebizond, which went out sadly and ingloriously after yet another couple of years, it was the last lonely star of the great constellation of Greece. Only the south-east corner of the Peloponnese—the triangle contained by the fortresses of Mistra and Monemvasia and the Mani—comprised this isolated Byzantine despotate. A few miles away, at the wreck of old Sparta, Frankish feudalism began; and further north, as the time grew short, the armies of Amurath and Bajazet the Thunderbolt, pigtailed and shaven-pated under their pumpkin turbans, were ravaging and subjugating Greece. Brass-crescented horsetail banners, the baleful green flags and the kettledrums and all the martial and barbarous clangour of the Mongolian steppes were just out of sight and earshot. From the great crenellated palaces of the Palaeologues and the Cantacuzenes, dominating the belfries and the cypresses and the bubbling domes and cupolas of the steep honeycomb town, fluttered as though they would flutter for ever, the silken banners charged with the linked B's of Byzantium and the two-headed Imperial eagle.

In this airy casket of a city, surrounded by the elaborate and fastidious array of an imperial household and a court of nobles and prelates and aulic dignitaries and men of letters, a succession of purple-born princes reigned: strange and stately figures in their fur-trimmed robes and melon-crowned caps-of-maintenance. The libraries filled with books, poets measured out their stanzas, and on the scaffolding of one newly-risen church after another painters mixed their gypsum and cinnabar and egg-yolk and powdered crocus and zinc and plotted the fall of drapery and described the circumference of haloes. It was the last age of Byzantine mysticism, and, most important of all, Mistra, right up to its eclipse, was the seat of the last Greek Neoplatonist revival, presided over by the Great Gemistus Plethon, one of the most redoubtable scholars of Europe. He it was who argued the niceties of dogma with the Western Cardinals at the Council of Florence; and, long after Mistra had died, Sigismondo Malatesta, to add the lustre of scholarship to his usurped principality, translated his bones to a splendid sarcophagus on the walls of his temple at Rimini. In courtyards murmurous with philosophic argument and debate and syllogism, Gemistus contrived the same Platonist system and semi-pagan cosmogony that he presided over at the court of Lorenzo the Magnificent.

Far from the twilit, miasmal, gong-tormented Bosphorus and the vapours of the Golden Horn, this was the world, rock-perched in the heart of the crystalline air above the loops of the Eurotas and the olive woods of Lacedaemon, which fostered the genesis of these paintings. Mistra is an extinct star now; but, embedded in that upheaval of mineral,—battered and cracked and weather-fretted on the walls of the churches of the Periblepton, the Metropolis, the Brontochion and the Pantanassa,—one can see a miraculous surviving glow of the radiance that gave life to this last comet as it shot glittering and sinking across the sunset sky of Byzantium.

* * * *

Almost anything, in the boundaries and possibilities of Byzantine art, would be a step back after this. Cretan painting is more a step aside than a regression. Those bonds of tradition which Mistra had shaken loose are there, but they have changed; where they induced a droop in the Macedonian school, they are worn in the Cretan with a swagger. The muscular and etiolated faces assume an unearthly frown of defiance, sometimes a scowl; and in their robes the flow of multiple folds and pleats in contrasting colours, as though of shot material—one of the great features of all Eastern painting—take on something more violent; they become taut radiations of expanding zigzags from the bent elbow or knee which has confined them. Goat-skin becomes shaggier, caves in the mountain-side look as though torn open with a blade and the jutting Sinais and the stepped and toppling crags, sundered by ravines with all the fierceness of the actual Cretan ranges, are in a state of faction: they are an insurrection of colossal geometric ghosts. As in the island itself, dramatic tension is stretched between those soaring commotions of rock—golden or peach-coloured, or vitreous or ice blue or hard as steel or ashen and aghast—on taut invisible threads. The figures, like the Cretans themselves, are illuminated and intensely masculine, a manic-depressive compound of brooding melancholy and exaltation; and the inner light, which the Macedonians lost in a measure, shoots from the sinister shadows undimmed. But in spite of their energy, there is nothing uncouth or brutal in these painted saints as there was among the Cappadocians; and, for all their vigour, they are instinct with Byzantine introversion. They are far removed from materialism, and the tension, the violence and the tragedy are all in the world of spirits. The detail is subtle and delicate: the cartographic wrinkles and circling contour-lines on the saints' faces, the line of nose and nostril, the sweep of those hoary eyebrows over each of which beetles an outlined irascible and thought-indicating bulge; the dark and, by contrast, etiolating triangles that project point downwards from the lower lids, the bristling curl of the white locks round foreheads that catch the light like polished teak, the prescribed complexity of their beards cataracting in effulgent arcs or erupting like silver quills from swarthy physiognomies—all of this, on close inspection, proves to be built up of complementary planes of brick red and apple green applied with delicate impressionism to the black phantom of the saint or paladin beneath. The emergence of this dark background under a luminous and fragmentary carapace of skilfully superimposed light and colour (a technique explained in precise detail by Dionysios of Phourna for those wishing to paint *Krétika*) is the earmark of the Cretan mode. I am tempted to relate this very strange technique, especially in ikons of Our Lord, with reasons that are not purely plastic. It calls irresistibly to mind a characteristic passage of St. Dionysios the Areopagite: 'The Divine Dark', writes this other Dionysios, 'is the inaccessible Light in which God is said to dwell, and in this Dark, invisible because of its surpassing radiance and unapproachable because of the excess of the streams of supernatural light, everyone must enter who is deemed worthy to see or know God.' *

The Cretan school is like a wonderful reprieve after the final catastrophe, for, owing to its mountainous inaccessibility and the division of spoils at the Fourth Crusade, which allotted it to the Venetians—or rather to Boniface of Monferrat, who sold it to the Doge at once—Crete was Venetian still. It became a place of

* *Letter to Dorotheus the Deacon*. This way of mystical thought became endemic in the West. See especially the contemplation *In Caligine* of Jiacopone da Todi (*Lauda LX*), and, of course, the *Cloud of Unknowing*.

refuge for the Greek world, a centre of Hellenism and a workshop of literary and artistic energy. We have seen* that the Cretans had established strong roots in Venice; in Crete itself they more than held their own, large quantities of Venetian families settled in Crete and many of their great names are now scattered among the villages and sheepfolds. This strange gunshot marriage of lagoon and crag seems to have continued (at any rate on the intellectual level), with the inevitable insurrections, in a protracted honeymoon. The island was graced with a positive pleiad of painters, poets and playwrights. Cultures interwove and the educated Greeks and the long-established Venetians were largely bilingual. It is thus remarkable how little Venetian influence can be detected when the Cretan school first came into prominence, just as it is remarkable that there are scarcely a dozen Italian words in the ten thousand lines of the great Cretan epic poem, the *Erotokritos* (1604), in spite of the author's name, which was Vincentios Cornaros. Towards the end Venetian influences crept in and, decadence though it may be, even though the peculiar Byzantine radiation grew tamer in the conventions of chiaroscuro, there is something both captivating and splendid about the flame reds and the hints of Titian and Veronese in the folds of satin and velvet and the red-gold glint of the scaly breastplates of warrior-saints.

After the island fell in 1669, the movement succumbed to the usual Ottoman blight; little remained, and, dispersed abroad, it died in the eighteenth century. But it was during its virile zenith in the fifteenth and sixteenth centuries that it affected Greece. Its finest monument in fresco—one of the few that remain—is in Mount Athos. Others survive, half-way to the sky, in the Meteora† in Thessaly. But Cretan ikons, glowing on slabs of olive, walnut, hard pine, poplar and plane, travelled all over the archipelago and the mainland and to Venice, where dark Cretan madonnas had long adorned palazzi; and to Russia. Alongside the Macedonian school, and often painted by non-Cretan hands, the Cretan

---

* See page 29 *n*.

† See my 'Monasteries of the Air', *The Cornhill Magazine*, No. 986.

technique was the strongest strain in the iconography of occupied Greece. These fierce saints and holy heroes and haggard Christs and Panayias formed a kind of pictorial resistance movement against apathy. It is lucky such a definite and vigorous style was there to fend off the inevitable catalepsy. One by one the sources of inspiration—Asia Minor, Cyprus, the Mainland, Constantinople, Mistra, Trebizond, the Archipelago and finally Crete—had been trampled out. When at last the stagnation of endless reproduction set in, their function became indeed that of Celestial guerrillas; at war not with a theological foe but against the occupying stranger.

There is another development or deviation which is of great sociological and historical interest, but of little relevance to the present theme: the Italianization of painting in the Ionian islands. For this western archipelago remained in Venetian hands from the crusades until the French Revolution (when after a short French interregnum, they were British for half a century) and though the inhabitants remained staunchly Orthodox—indeed, some noble families of Italian origin, and thus Catholic, like the Capodistrias of Corfu and the Romas of Zante, ended up themselves as Orthodox—the influence of Venice and the Italian studios and universities, especially Padua, was strong. To such an extent was Italian the cultural language of the bilingual élite that the Zantiot poet Ugo Foscolo wrote exclusively in Italian; so it was too, until he was well on in years, with one of Greece's greatest modern poets, his fellow-islander, Solomos.

The Ionian islands were the only part of the Greek family which entirely escaped the dead hand of the Turks. Cut off for six centuries by only a few miles of sea from the tragic doings of the mainland, they were part of Europe. Crescents and minarets rose on the Epirote shore, while, across the narrow channel, the Ionians, in Elizabethan ruffs, then powdered wigs and finally stove-pipe hats and cutaways, participated in a quiet and provincial fashion in the Renaissance and the ripening afternoon of the seventeenth and eighteenth centuries and in the early Romantic movement of the nineteenth. It is a proof of the vitality of Hellenism that the comparative mildness of the Doge's suzerainty and the absence of the mainland's ruthless challenge should have left their intrinsic Greekness so unimpaired. Without the age-old identification of Greek with Orthodoxy, perhaps they would have become Uniates at least, like the Orthodox of the Ukraine or the Banat and, finally, the Maniots of Cargese. But they often took part in hostilities against the Turks (notably at Lepanto), under the Lion of St. Mark; and after the fall of Candia, Cretans flocked as thickly into the Ionian as they did into the Mani; and the islands were for centuries a refuge for the klephts and armatoles of the mainland. Despite the Venetian fleshpots, their sympathy and their participation in the struggle of their fellow-countrymen was entire. The first head of the resurrected Greek State—Count Capodistria—was an Ionian and the Seven Islands became a great national hearth of Greek poetry. There might have been advantages to the Ionians later on, in remaining part of the British Empire; but towards the end of our occupation the ideological outcry for reunion to the Greek State became loud and determined. Wisely, and with lasting benefit to all, Enosis was conceded.

In spite of the unwavering Hellenism of the Seven Islands, Venice inevitably left strong superficial traces culturally, socially, architecturally, and to a very slight extent, linguistically, but most considerably in the arts. It certainly influenced ikon-painting. The first detectable symptoms of deviation from the Byzantine canon is a mild softening-up that might be traced to Tiepolo. This trend was hit by Cretan influence from two sides: from Venice, where it was already established, and from Crete itself before, and especially after, the Fall. The results of this are lively and original. But slowly, with passing of time, the figures echoed in their provincial and less deft way, the metropolitan prototypes of Venice and the rest of Italy; and many of the ikons among the gilt and brass of baroque and rococo iconostases became oval or circular, which is very rare in the rest of Orthodoxy. The treatment of sacred subjects drifted further and further from the abstraction of Byzantium until the ambience is the tired, diffused and muted light of a minor Italian studio when the Counter-

Reformation had spent itself. The umbered faces are all too human and unillumined and unenigmatic in their verisimilitude of smooth cheek and appealing eye and droop of lip and fold of mantle. The supernal light is filtered through the dishcloth of chiaroscuro, the cosmetics of morbidezza are busy. I demanded, some pages back, a more comprehensible notation: I am killed with kindness here; for, in these ikons, the purpose of the concession is lost. This elegant subsidence to earth is not what I was after, which was some kind of iconographic change to enable the ethical and moral part of religion to keep pace with the tribal and magical part until the expulsion of the Turks. But this late Ionian painting is part of the general western European deflation in religious art, a slow draining away of the supernatural from pigment and stone and clay. Some of them—framed in a leafy swirl of baroque gilding—are very fine indeed: but they are no longer, —except geographically—Greek.* They are part of the painting of the West, and, as such, worthy of a much more dignified place in any conspectus of European art than they have yet received, except in an admirable study by Procopiou. But they have defected completely from the line we have been following and have no relevance to it. They have, of course, apart from their merits, the great charm of historical oddity. The beautiful eighteenth-century ikon—if it can be called that; it is closer to an enlarged predella—of the Procession of St. Dionysius in the Cathedral of Zante (happily saved from the 1953 earthquake; I saw it next day in the burning wreckage of that lovely vanished town), in which the saint's catafalque is escorted by a crocodile of tricorned *nobili huomini*, might be the work of a remote septinsular cousin of Longhi or Guardi. We have floated a long, long way from St. Sophia and Ravenna and the old basilicas of Rome and Holy Luke and Torcello and Athos and Daphni and Salonika and Palermo and Cefalu and Monreale and the Chora and SS. Sergius and Bacchus and Nea Moni in Chios and Kastoria and Nerezi and Mistra and the Meteora and the Cappadocian rock monasteries; and almost as far from the ikon-painting in progress in the klepht-

* My mind flies to the Zantiot painters Doxaras and Katouni.

haunted and bullet-echoing crags of Acroceraunia and Epirus and Acarnania just over the water. . . .

    ★   ★   ★   ★

The inscrutability of ikons has done nothing to choke off devotion; indeed, the oldest and most indistinct invite the steadiest fervour of rural iconodules. This is especially true if they have thaumaturgic acts to their credit—feats of healing, the repulsion of barbarians and infidels from a city wall or timely intervention in battle, like the vision of Pan at Marathon, or of the Gemini at Lake Regillus. Some of them have miraculous origins: they were dropped from heaven or dug out of the earth after their location had been revealed in a dream. Our Lady of Tinos, who is responsible for many miraculous cures at her yearly feast, had such a beginning: she was exhumed on the very day that the standard of revolt against the Turks was raised in 1821, which surrounds her island with a patriotic as well as religious and thaumaturgic aura. Several ikons have specific healing properties, a function they share with certain holy remains, like those of St. Gerasimos on the slopes of Mt. Ainos in Cephalonia, whose reliquary, borne yearly over the prone ranks of ailing pilgrims, cures madness. Ikons have been known to fly many homing miles through the air to resettle in the chapels whence profane hands have reft them. There is a category known as *acheiropoietoi*—'not made with hands'. One of these, Our Lady of Edessa (where iconoclast troops were later to stone a wonder-working Christ), led the Emperor Heraclius all the way to Ctesiphon to rescue the True Cross from Chosroes in the battle which is immortalized on the walls of Arezzo.

Attributions to the brush of St. Luke are much less frequent than in Italy. There are only three, I think, which, in the Orthodox world, are incontradictably held to be the apostle's work. I have seen two of these Lukes, one in the monastery of Megaspelion which juts from the high rock face of an Achaean gorge, the other in the monastery of Kykko in western Cyprus. It was difficult to discern more, in either case, than the uneven convexities of what appeared to be black wax jutting from a buckled and almost all-obscuring plastron of silvergilt. The third is our Lady of Soumela, an ancient lodestar for oriental pilgrimage in the huge monastery towering above the valley of the Of, inland from Trebizond.* When the Greeks (who had lived there without interruption almost since the occasion when Xenophon's army espied the sea from a neighbouring height) were uprooted at the exchange of populations in 1922, she came too; and after four decades of obscurity in Athens, she was re-enshrined with great state in a part of western Macedonia where a population of her former Laz-speaking votaries had been resettled.

Black holy objects, in the world at large, seem to invite special veneration; I think of these ikons, and of the vanished smoke-blackened Virgin, from which the old Byzantine Church of the Kapnikarea in Athens derives its name; and of the Virgin of Guadalupe in Mexico, the Black Christ of Lucca and a small dark Virgin among the canefields near the pitch-lake in Trinidad, all of them heavy with mana.

The obverse of this addiction to black images seems to be popular indifference to white ones, whether of alabaster or marble. Perhaps their very clarity and scrutability is antiseptic to the germ of magic. They are un-mythopoetic, and the most beautiful in the Christian world, those of Michelangelo, must be content with the praise of the educated. Is this because their very perfection, and the lack of mystery surrounding their origin, over-humanizes them? At all events, piety and superstition seek darker loves. Perhaps the gods of ancient Greece, had they been snow-white as we see them in museums, would have suffered a like fate. But they were coloured all over, and their votaries were innumerable. It is easy to forget that the Parthenon and Delphi and Olympia were painted ox-blood and deep blue and ochre, and that the hosts of polychrome, black-eyed and staring statuary bristled with gold ornaments. The insides of the temples were obscure and mysterious and black smoke darkened the giant chryselephantine statues. They were curtained in purple and dripping with honey and wine

---

* It was vividly described to me by the late Professor Dawkins, who visited it in the early years of the century.

and glistening with oil and blood, while the reek of carrion and burning meat filled the batlike gloom. Not only the gods of Olympus but the sinister chthonian demons haunted those precincts. I feel, too, that the archaic statues, because they were a further remove from the real, must have been magnets for a more fervid cult than their classical offspring.

It is perhaps odd that none of the great religious paintings of the Renaissance, none of the swirling baroque statues of the Counter-Reformation, with their welter of stone clouds and sunbursts, their crocodile tears and their brassy clamour, became cult objects on the same footing as their uncouth predecessors. Overstatement defeats them. Perhaps, after all, anthropomorphosis is a deterrent. There is, of course, an exception at the other end of Europe that represents a whole class of saints in facsimile: the amazing Virgen de la Macarena in Seville, borne out shaking among fanfares above the vast crowd from her church at midnight on a camelia-covered float sprouting into hundreds of candles under a canopy: a sad, pale and beautiful infanta of painted wood, with rings on her upheld fingers, a green and cloth of gold cloak sweeping six yards behind, a vast diadem on her head and an aureole of radiating gold spikes and the fortunes of half a dozen grandees round her neck in pearls and diamonds. Gasps and cries fill the air at her emergence and an outbreak of cheers and clapping, while the stifling swarm, like an English crowd at a glimpse of royalty or a film star, thrust yet tighter and climb on each other's backs with cries of '¡O la guapa! ¡La linda! ¡la hermosa!'

Greek iconography, of all Christian art that includes the outward forms of sacred beings, seems to me to have set itself the highest and most difficult task. This does not mean, I hasten to say, that I am trying to compare the Michelangelo frescoes of the Vatican unfavourably with the worst eighteenth-century daub on a plank in a wayside chapel in Aetolia, or indeed (and only then with due allowance made for chronology) with any but the noblest in the achievement of the East. It is not a matter of technical skill or intrinsic beauty or the workings of plastic genius. What I do mean is this: in the foredoomed task of indicating the unfathomable mystery of Godhead in visible terms, the Greek ikon-painters chose the hardest way. They sought ingress to the spirit, not through the easy channels of passion, but through the intellect. Religion and philosophy were as inextricably plaited as they had been in pre-Christian times and this was due to the same philosophical temper which had saved Judaic Christianity (a brief and local thing) and made it Greek, then universal. Skilled in the handling of abstractions, knowing that the representation of Christ as God was as impossible a task as uttering the ineffable, they tried to indicate the immediately assimilable incarnation of Christ in such a way that it gave wings to the mind and the spirit and sent them soaring through and beyond the symbol to its essence, the Transcendent God, with whom, as they themselves had defined, He was consubstantial. If they failed in this aspiration it was failure on a vertiginously exalted height.

With wonderful exceptions in every case, the West, even in Romanesque and early medieval times, even in spite of the strange Eastern intimations in the *trecento*, especially during the Renaissance and above all and in spite of every opposite intention in the Counter-Reformation, the West has painted and sculpted Christ as man. The intellectual heights that beckoned the Byzantines remained unscaled and religion was propagated in art through the emotions. It is spiritually and theologically much less ambitious, but it is, quite obviously, more practical and reasonable; and in the long run it succeeded. It can drive one nearly insane to speculate what would have happened if the Crusaders had not scotched Byzantium and the Turks killed it; if, in fact, it had participated in or led the Renaissance, as even in its last throes it led and made possible the approach; instead of expiring at its outset. What course, for instance, would painting have taken, how would Mistra have been followed up? It is hopeless, because, without these events, one can play with the appalling thought that the Renaissance might never have happened. But, assuming for a moment a miraculous turning in the Empire's fortunes when all that made the Renaissance was already under way and all the stimuli were working, one cannot but see a Golden Age of unmatched wonder: palaces and cathedrals out-soaring the already existing splendours of the most beautiful city in the world, the City which, before they looted and smashed it, struck the Crusaders dumb; one dreams of serene and exquisite cities springing up again round the Acropolis and at Salonika, Patras, Nauplia, Volo, Yanina, Larissa, Kavalla, Serres Komotini and Didymotikon; one guesses at the evolution of architecture, sculpture, poetry, thought and painting into new and unimaginable forms which would bear the same relationship to the Italian Renaissance that Greece bore to Rome. . . . A wry smile must halt these thoughts.

It must indeed. This sudden shining mist of impossible surmise is one that floats again and again before the eyes both of Greeks and of strangers who look for more in these seas and islands and mountains than the dispersed and beautiful skeleton of the ancient world. It leaves a deposit, however, of hope and conviction (which I profoundly share and which are not weakened by their present Utopian air) that when the hindering contingencies at last disappear and Greek tribal obsessions, by the solution of their causes, lose their urgency and disencumber the dominating position in Greek thought which history has forced them to usurp; when the dogmatism of further East (against which almost all politicians and all the Church contend) loses its intermittent glow, and the materialism of the West (with which only Greek poets are at war)* loses its beguiling glitter and fades into proportion: when—I was about to say, when political harmony is achieved, but this is perhaps no more possible than it was in ancient Greece and Byzantium; when all this comes about, I think that the restless, dispersed and unharnessable but indestructible Greek genius, released at last, will produce something which will astonish and enrich the world again beyond all our imagination.

Let us brush this enticing mist from our eyes for the moment

* In this context, I would like to recommend most strongly Mr. Philip Sherrard's remarkable book, *The Marble Threshing Floor* (Vallentine Mitchell), on Greece's five greatest poets since the War of Independence: Solomos, Palamas, Sikelianos, Cavafy and Seferis.

and focus them once more on the Greek pneumato-iconographic (if I may be allowed so hideous a word) hypothetical dilemma. When Greek religious art took shape it was an elaborate and beautiful cypher implicit with transcendental meaning for the most civilized race in the world, the only one outside the Far East that was accustomed to dealing in religious abstractions. Outside events drastically reduced these powers and redirected Greek energy, perforce, into the single grim channel of survival; and as the Dark Ages of Greece advanced deeper into darkness, the aloof and luminous faces of heaven, though they were no less cherished or venerated, became an allegory to which the key was lost. The practical West, which knew neither the exalted spiritual and intellectual heights of the East nor the obliterating ordeal which followed it, had, in their rational and materialist Roman way, been wiser: by appealing iconographically to a laity free of exaltation, through passion and fallibility and the easily apprehensible fellow-feelings of motherhood and pain; by, in fact, the pathetic. However alien the whole may seem to Northern and Judaistic Christianity, simple Latin formulae maintained a firm ideological grasp on the imagination by their very scrutability. They saved the religious pulse of countless simple millions from sclerosis and to a large measure kept religion free from confusion and extraneous principles. Would a modification of Eastern iconography, a simpler, an earthier and more 'pathetic' medium, have had the paradoxical result of saving the spiritual content of Orthodox Christianity? Aesthetically the mind shies from the thought; but perhaps it would. Such outward modifications, quite consciously applied from above, have successfully redirected the character of religions; one thinks at once of the plastic changes that marked the end of the iconoclast disputes at Byzantium, of the Tridentine Decrees that generated the baroque imagery of the Counter-Reformation and of the total abolition that accompanied the Reformation in the North. What form this pragmatic alliance of Greek abstraction and Western naturalism could have taken is hard to determine; the frescoes of Mistra with their more accessible humanism were the result of a unique coincidence of pressures and stimuli. It was an even more delicate and fleeting thing than the primitives of Italy, far too frail to withstand the Ottoman blizzard; and who could expect four centuries of Grecos? This too, the culmination of Byzantine art, was a freak, the explosive fusion of three contradictory civilizations with perhaps the most eccentric genius on record; and he died without offspring.

The old significances took wing and religious symbolism, gaining talismanic power of its own, assumed new connotations. The Cross and all its sacred pictorial accompaniment were no longer an indication of the Logos and the divine mysteries, but, quite simply, the opponents of the Crescent: family totems that lent celestial sanction to those humbler and more direct implements of rescue, the yataghan, the scimitar and the long-barrelled gun. In this new function Greek iconography—which had been alive and developing, with periods of coma, since the mosaic and sculpture of the scattered declining kingdoms left by the conquests of Alexander and the dusky wide-eyed paintings in Fayoum— seized up: and in the dark period before the first glimmer of freedom, its life ebbed imperceptibly away. It survived for the remainder of its span only as heraldry—a recondite, archaizing and beautiful skill held captive by an untransgressible code (obsolete of its true function in England since the Battle of Tewkesbury, when, for the last time, symbol and essence and purpose were exactly congruent)—may still be said to survive. Gleaming smokily in the concavity of churches and presiding as familiar lares in every house, from Trebizond to Corfu and from Macedonia to Cyprus, ikons were the arms-parlant, the shields, devices, helmets, crowns, crests, supporters and the stiff swirl of mantelling of the King and Queen, the warriors and the magicians, of a lost Arthurian Byzantine Olympus to which they would come back again one day.

*   *   *   *

These ramifying tendrils of digression have obscured, like a tangle of ivy, the walls of the desolate little church of Layia from which they sprang. The reader may think (and he is right) that they have slowed up our progress along the east flank of the Mani. We will shake loose and get a move on.

What really held us up at the time were, of course, not these leisurely historico-religious broodings at all, but astonishment at the battered and cobwebby frescoes on these very walls. They ran round the church like a sequence of comic strips. The rectangular cartouches contained what can only be called religious cartoons. So uncouth were they that it was hard to believe one's eyes. There was no traceable kinship either with the last rustic descendant of the ancient iconography, examples of which are common enough, or with any of the primitive religious paintings which followed its demise. Most of these illustrate local saints usually martyred by the Turks, and often quite recently, for trying to convert them, e.g. the only Koutzovlach saint, Nicholas of Karditza who was burnt at the stake in the Pindus Mountains; the kilted St. George of Yanina, painted as he swung from the gallows where the Turks hanged him in 1838, and St. Gideon of Tyrnavos, slowly dismembered, slain, and flung down a privy by Veli the Pasha of Thessaly and second son of the terrible Vizier, Ali Pasha, in 1818.* They are mostly in northern and central Greece. But there were none of the give-away contemporary details here. The usual scenes in the life of Christ were depicted, the Nativity, Epiphany, Baptism, Transfiguration, the Marriage at Cana with rows of spherical wine jars, the raising of Lazarus with the invariable tombside figure burying his nose in his robe against the possible reek of corruption, the Entry into Jerusalem under arching palm fronds, the stages of the Passion, the Ascension and the cloven flames of Pentecost. They looked very old and quite free of any known influence and so gangling and awkward and comic, and at the same time so uninhibited by any kind of rule that one would, at a glance, have dated them in England as

* The fragments of St. Gideon, when retrieved, immediately cohered in an outburst of the odour of sanctity and they have been credited since with many miracles. It must be remembered that Thessaly and Epirus, and all of Greece to the north, were in Turkish hands until the First Balkan War in 1912.

coeval with the Saxon paintings of Chaldron or Worth. It was with the same shock of surprise as that prompted by the date of the Nyklian tower at Pyrgos, and another sharp reminder of the Mani's isolation from the outside world, that I spotted at last a figured oblong with the year they were painted. It was 1851.

Very often in old frescoes the painted eyes of the saints have been scratched or picked out with sharp instruments, leaving ragged white holes in the plaster that make a painful impression. There is usually an old villager at one's elbow to tell one that it is the sacrilegious work of Turks, and probably it often is. (On the lake-islands of Yanina, the saintly ranks are riddled with fanatic bullet-holes.) It is one of the commonplaces of Greek travel, as common as the 'miraculous' way in which an ikon's eyes, painted, as they nearly always are, gazing straight ahead, 'follow you all over the church'. Some of these mutilations were visible on these walls, and before discovering the date I pointed to an empty socket and asked Vasilio (knowing, as I thought, the answer) what had happened. She laughed and said nothing, so I asked her again.

'É!' she said, 'people in former times—perhaps even to-day —used to dig out the plaster and sprinkle it on the food or wine of people they wanted to fall in love with them. Girls mostly . . .'

'It wasn't done by the Turks?'

'The Turks? Why?'

She had never heard of it! Was this another indication of the Mani's impregnability? Or are the Turks elsewhere less guilty in this particular matter than it is thought?* It is a tradition I would find it hard to relinquish.

* Another odd peculiarity in Greek churches: though men are allowed behind the three-doored iconostasis, it is, at any rate usually, out of bounds for women. I could never understand what this discrimination and suggestion of defilement was based on. Shortly after the war an old priest was showing three people—a woman and two men, of which I was one—some frescoes in a church between Kozani and Kastoria. The best, he said, were in the sanctuary. I pointed to our companion and asked if she could come. He scratched his beard in puzzlement and whispered a question. I didn't at first understand. At last I grasped that exceptions could sometimes be made; they depended, rather

embarrassingly, on feminine physiology and the phases of the moon, a gloomy veto that must go back to the fifteenth chapter of Leviticus.

Rare mentions in ancient literature put this matter in a wholly different light. In fact the philosopher and physicist Democritus, echoed by Pliny and Columella, held that if maidens, at the appropriate times, ran three times round a field that was about to be harvested, the standing crops—whose early growth may perhaps have been fostered by sprinkling with ashes mixed with the urine of centaurs—were guaranteed against the onslaught of noxious insects. The contrast between Hebrew jurisconsults and kind Demeter needs no underlining.

CHAPTER 16

An Amphibian Matriarchy
and a Maniot Poet

THE wine that washed down this late and long-drawn-out second breakfast seemed to attach wings to our heels. We flew along the side of the rocky coast at mercurial speed, in spite of the sun's ascent.

There is a lot to be said for starting the day like this. In dashing households in many mountain villages the day begins with a minute cup of Turkish coffee, a doorstep of black bread, a handful of olives, hunks of rank and excellent goat's cheese, and a glass— or several glasses—of fiery distilled spirits. In Epirus, northern Thessaly and Macedonia, slugs of bracing *tsipouro* often usher in the day and in Crete, where the practice is more widespread, down, each one at a single swashbuckling gulp, go several glasses of *tsikoudia*, the Cretan raki distilled from the stalks, skins and pips after the grape-treading, sometimes deliciously flavoured with crushed mulberries. Each shot drops to its destination with the smoothness of a tracer-bullet and the somnolent organism is roused with the same shock as that of an oyster under the lemon, ummoning startled gasps from the novice and making his eyes leap from their sockets. 'One more,' says the flask-wielding host, 'just to kill the microbe. *Dia na skotosome to mikrovio.*' And so the gnawing worm of death's sister, sleep, is scotched anew each morning and up one starts ready to tackle whatever the day may bring with the optimism, the vigour and the dauntlessness of a giant. There is a great deal of ritual drinking-terminology and singing and inter-weaving of toasts in Greece, and it is in Crete that they reach their most elaborate flowering. Often it is an antiphony of challenge and response. 'May we become as rich as the Sultan Amurath!—*Sta Mourátia mas!*' they cry in some villages on Mount Kedros, and 'May the All-Holy One scour the rust from our guns.' It is only there that one hears, with great astonishment, on the morning after a long dionysiac vigil, an exact echo of a certain well-known English phrase: 'Of the dog that has bitten you,' they say, 'throw in some of the fur.' '*Skýli pou se dángose, vále ap' to malí tou.*' And then comes the soft *glou-glou* of pouring fur. . . .

There is a tendency to drink in unison after a concentric clink of glasses, a solitary drinker usually giving a ritual tap to the glasses standing nearest. How often have I heard this clinking explained: how the fifth sense of hearing, not only taste, sight, smell and touch, must be requited! Then, purely for fun, there is drinking *kalogerístika*—monkishly: grasping the little tumblers in the palm of their hands the drinkers muffle the impact of glass on glass by only touching knuckles ('so that the abbot won't hear us'). Not that there is any need of secrecy in Greek monasteries. Many of them are famous not only for their vineyards and their lavish hospitality, but for the jovial and Friar Tuck-ish capacities of the brethren. There is a rare and charming Cretan custom of drinking 'like little frogs'—*ta vatrachákia*, it is called or, in the deeper dialect, *t'aphordakákia*. Two drinkers hold their glasses ightly by the upper rim furthest from them, and swing them gently together so that the bottom edges intershock, bounce away and strike again with a series of light impacts that mimic a soft and far-away croaking. It is repeated thrice. '*Vrekekekex!*' murmurs one. '*Koax!*' the other; and at the third time both murmur a final '*Koax!*' in unison. Wine glasses are never filled more than half, on the principle that one drinks more that way; it goes down in one gulp and needs restocking at once.

Some of the old 'black' and amber-coloured wines of Crete are followed next day by an aftermath which is only to be allayed by a glass or two of the same fur and the delicious frothing egg-and-lemon soup which is the pan-Hellenic nostrum for hangovers.

Retsina, however, tipped into the little tumblers from carafes, or better still, from chipped blue enamel mugs which are replenished again and again from vast barrels, seems to possess the secret of inducing high spirits and rash and uninhibited conduct with no sad retribution, as though a plenary absolution accompanied every gulp. This, for those lucky enough to like it as I do, places retsina high on the list of the manifold charms of Greece. Nobody seems to know when the Greeks first treated their wine with resin. Certainly it was known in Byzantine days. Some place its origin much further back, basing their assumption on the pine-cone, which, in old sculptures, sometimes tops the vinewreathed thyrsus of Dionysius. It is assumed that the taste began fortuitously with the custom of caulking the leaks in barrels and wine skins with lumps of resin. The vine- and pine-clad slopes of Attica are its true habitat, but many other regions are famous. Perhaps the two most celebrated sources, both for drinking on the spot and for export to regions and islands less generously blessed, are the ancient town of Megara, half-way between Athens and Corinth, and Karystos in Euboea. Bad retsina can be excruciatingly nasty; the best—and Athenian tavernas, except for a few which remain unswervingly reliable, show an alarming tendency to degenerate in this matter—is incomparably good. It should never, to my mind, be drunk outside Greece, for one of its secrets is drinking it with unstinted abundance. It seems to have an alliance with the air in the promotion of well-being. Many people think that it bestows the gift of bodily health as well; a belief I accept at once without further scrutiny. A year after the war I told Mitso, a boatman in Poros I hadn't seen since 1938, that he looked browner, haler and younger than ever.

'It's the air,' he said, pausing over his oars, 'and not only that. What with the brine outside and the resin in, it pickles us. If I died now and you were to bury me, I wouldn't start stinking for ten years or more.'

Such themes occur often in his conversation. When I saw him a month ago on the way to Hydra, he said: 'Why not stay in

Poros? There's nothing but bare rock on Hydra. Why, they say they even have to bring earth from the mainland when they want to bury anyone. . . .'

* * * *

The hill-side over which we sped, charioted by Bacchus, was utterly bare. Scarcely a thistle, not a trace of thorn or cistus, no withered stalk of asphodel, not even those onion-like bulbs of the bitter sea-squill which punctuate the sternest terrains with dark green explosions, jutted through the rubble; nothing, indeed, all day, but the turmoils of prickly pear running amok along the empty village lanes. We passed an isolated house which had fallen into ruin, and Vasilio told a macabre tale that admirably corresponded to the insanity of the landscape. Not long ago, she said, a boy from a nearby village, married for a year but incensed and goaded by his mother about some hanky-panky in the payment of the dowry, burst into this very house and murdered his father-in-law. He was promptly arrested, whereupon the bride, abandoning her newly-born child, sought out her husband's father, killed him with an axe, decapitated the corpse and flung the head down a steep slope. Vasilio described the bounces with loops of her forefinger. The bride was arrested too, and the upshot was still *sub judice*. Far-away mountains are rich in these fierce eclogues.

* * * *

What a powerful link god-relationship is! *Koumbariá!* A *Koumbaros** is anyone who has stood sponsor, as best man or god-father, at a wedding or a christening. The link is considered as

---

* The word is originally the same as *compadre* in Italian and Spanish. In Crete, where the godbrother network is very strong (I know, because I am deeply involved in it through many font-side ceremonies during the war), the word *synteknos* is used for the baptismal tie. The relationship is sometimes used as a joke, in addressing total strangers—'*Yassou, Koumbare*'. It strikes a note of friendly collusion.

close as blood-relationship, and it links the families concerned with an indissoluble tie.

Thus, when we descended the steps and passed through the arched doorway of one of the few houses of Kypriano, a minute un-towered hamlet that only a few yards of pebble separated from the sea, our pretensions to hospitality were backed by the fact that Vasilio's family and the newcomers who suddenly surrounded us in the dark living-room were bound in this manner. Tall figures unlashed our stuff from the mule and soon, after farewells, I watched Vasilio zigzag up the slope, whacking the great mule in the direction of a village further inland to which she was taking the two sacks of corn.

The *koumbára* was a widow, a tall grey-eyed woman of amazing distinction and the remnants of great beauty. Eight of her nine sons, ranging from the ages of five to twenty-four (one was away on his military service in Macedonia), lived with her under the same roof. Lying half asleep in a late siesta, I watched their random comings and goings. The youngest was huddled on the steps with his head in his fists listening raptly to his immediate senior reading aloud to him from an Epirote tale, *The Brave Katzandónis, Veli Ghega and Ali Pasha of Yanina*, one of many blood and thunder pamphlets, the equivalent of Robin Hood, which, with *Karaghiozi*, *Nasr-ed-Din-Hodja* and the *Arabian Nights*, are the staple reading among children in the country. Every so often, with a sound of bare feet on the earthern floor, another son would appear from the sunlight lugging a sack of newly threshed corn or with a fish, fresh-caught and hanging Tobias-like from his fist, and ask for food. Their mother would then lay aside her distaff and spindle, sticks would crackle as small fry were poured into the pan, a ladle full of lentils was doled into a tin plate and a titanic wedge of dark bread was sawn from a loaf like a millstone. Taking the tight clump of thorn from the neck of the bulbous jar—it is placed there as a barrier against thirsty flies—she would fill a tumbler, throw the water out into the sunlight in a deft and glittering arc, wipe it with her apron and fill it up again. Putting the bright cylinder by his plate, she would say 'Eat, my child,' and pick up her spinning things again. The entire family was so good-looking and of so patrician a bearing that they resembled a rustic aristocratic matriarch surrounded by a brood of dukes. From my somnolent vantage point, sheltered on the ledge running down one side of the room, it was a great pleasure to watch them, their mother especially. Every gesture was performed with a deftness and ease and lack of fuss that amounted to very high style indeed and her conversation with her sons had a bohemian note of affectionate banter and irony. It was punctuated with laughter on either side, a not unusual relationship between women, especially widows, with a number of high-spirited sons.

The house was a large, empty barrel-vaulted room half sunk below ground level. It was blessedly shadowy and cool after the clanging afternoon. One could see the glare through a deep-walled window sub-divided into smaller squares by thick iron bars and through a blazing half-circle at the far end under an archway at the top of a flight of shallow steps. The healing penumbra, the glaucous and stone-walled emptiness transformed the room into an empty underwater cavern, a haunt for tritons. It was only empty in the Western sense; free, that is, of the immovable archipelago of furniture with which European rooms are encumbered; except for the invariable great loom as unwieldy and rooted as a fourposter bed. Otherwise tables, chairs and stools are tidied away when not in use. The floor space is a blank agora in which any newcomer looks queerly isolated and momentous, the protagonist of a few seconds' drama until he subsides on the stone ledge. For the household gear is centrifugal; it gathers round the walls and piles up in corners, under the twinkling ikon lamp, the photographs of King, Queen, Plastiras or Venizelos or the faded tuppence-coloured posters of Petrobey and his klephts or fireman-helmeted Kolokotrones or scimitar-wielding Athanasios Diakos and his kilted pallikars at grips with turbaned and blaspheming Turks. These pictures are absorbing. Often they depict cavalry charges in the Balkan wars or a ferocious evzone actually burying his teeth in a kalpacked and moccasined Bulgar green with panslavism and wickedness and fright. They have recently been joined by a crude and magnificently uninhibited crop of reconstructions of the glories of 1940 in Albania: evzones again, this time bayoneting bersaglieri, who are always (as indeed they were) on the run. Hoisted on hill-tops by sword-wielding officers, the blue and white Greek flag is blown taut by the wind of war and the whole battlefield—Koritza, Tepeléni, Argyrokastro or Premeti—is plumed, as though by an irregular bed of crimson tulips, with exploding shells. Among them on the wall, touchingly preserved under glass but dark with dust nevertheless, one can often see the white petals of old marriage crowns intertwined, and, pinned across calligraphic citations, faded medal ribbons from one or other of Greece's tragically frequent wars. Here, too, are vast cloudy enlargements, retouched with sepia, of daguerreotype ancestors: coiffed women and bearded men with yataghan-stuffed belts and guns across their knees, and more recent emigré relations: plump figures in straw boaters, high stiff collars, bright tiepins and macassared hair and moustaches, signed by photographers in Chicago, Detroit, Alexandria, Khartoum, Odessa or Dar-es-Salaam.

The walls of this dim chamber, except for the twinkle of a solitary ikon-lamp, were almost bare of pictures. But the edge of the floor, which was trodden as hard as marble, was a forest of paraphernalia. A cooking-oven and a bread-oven tunnelled subsidiary caves into the walls, three great grooved amphorae and a congeries of smaller jars crowded together. Oars, a small mast dislodged from its socket, fishing rods and bamboo poles stood in sheaves. There were great extinct acetylene flares fitted for a boat's prow, and glass-bottomed metal cylinders, both of them for *gri-gri* fishing; loops of net, cork- and gourd-floats, rolls of twine, patched sail cloth and unshipped rudders; various baskets and maze-like osier fish traps and a couple of rusty anchors. This maritime apparatus mingled with mule saddles and harness, sieves and sacks of corn just threshed and winnowed. There was chopped wood and thorn-faggots for kindling. A ploughshare, spades, sickles and adzes were assembled like an arsenal of burglars' tools for extorting a livelihood from the iron-hard Mani. Long tridents and fish spears for sea quarry, two double-barrelled guns for quadrupeds and avifauna and a rifle for bipeds lent against or hung from the walls. Ropes of onions and garlic and of dried tomatoes, threaded and strung for making that dark russet sauce called *belté*, dangled from the beams. Various sons, two dogs and a number of cats and hens in ones and twos pecking jerkily indoors after dropped wheat grains and now and then an enormous lop-eared nanny-goat, wandered in and out. Husks of chaff floated in the shadowy air and the warm and dusty smell of the wheat and the tang of brine told of a hard, amphibious life. The water's edge was only a few yards away and the faintest splash was captured and magnified by this concavity as though every so often the slow summer sea were rippling through the house. Through sleepy lids I watched my hostess spinning; her left hand pulling and twisting a thin thread from the hank of wool on the end of the distaff she wore tucked into the top of her apron, the gyrating spindle sinking floorwards from her nimbly flickering right forefinger and thumb and then slowly rising again like a slow-motion yo-yo. She looked a beautiful, sardonic but benign underwater potentate. It was plain that the door was never shut except in winter, for two swallows' nests hung among the beams and vaulting in the dark nether end of the room. A swish and a flutter marked their exits and their entrances and a momentary breeze from their wings would brush one's cheek or forearm.

* * * *

It has been said that the Mani is, poetically, the least fertile area of Greece. One exception to the Maniot sterility in folk poetry—the dirges—has been discussed. But there is also a single exception—a modest one, it is true—to the general lack of formal poetry. It is only formal, really, in the sense that the author's name is known: *The History of the Whole Mani, its Customs, Villages and Produce*, by Nikitas Niphakos. It is written in the 'Political' metre, the usual peasant metre, that of nearly all klephtic ballads. It is so called, not from its contents but because the origin of all Greek fifteen-syllable-line poetry—a decapentesyllabic heptameter with a feminine ending—is attributed to Constantinople, the *Polis* or City. This verse-scheme has been the vehicle of some of the greatest of 'modern' Greek verse—*The Epic of Digenis Arkitas*, for example, in the Middle Ages, the *Erotokritos* in seventeenth-century Crete, and in modern times *The King's Flute* by Palamas; but it is prone in careless hands to degenerate into banality and tedium. The tradition is so instinctive that any Greek, literate or illiterate, seems able to turn it out as faultlessly and easily as breathing. It is as natural and indigenous to modern Greece as the hexameter must have been to the Greece of Homer. No doubt the shift of tonic stress, a process as imperceptible as soil erosion, which occurred in the early centuries of the Christian era, accounts for this important vernacular change.

Little is known about the author of the 385 lines of this poem. Nikitas Niphakos came from the village of Mília not far from Leuktra and the point where our Maniot journey began. He is presumed to have lived approximately from 1750 to 1810. Professor Kouyeas thinks, on good grounds, that he was captured, while still a boy, by a Moslem-Albanian expedition into the Mani; that he escaped and fled to Bucharest, the capital and throne of the Phanariot Greek hospodars of Wallachia, where he probably learnt to read and write. He probably returned to the Mani during the reign of Zanetbey Grigorakis, who reigned from 1782 to 1788. (The praise of this celebrated Bey is laid on so thick that it is fair to assume that Niphakos was one of his clients.) His poem is little known either inside the Mani or out—deservedly perhaps, for it has no great poetical value. But it is of considerable linguistic interest; it is studded with Maniot dialect words, some of them already obsolete. Yet it gives a fascinating picture of Maniot life in the late eighteenth and early nineteenth centuries, a picture, alas, which would corroborate the darkest reports of Western strangers. It is full of regional Maniot prejudice. He cracks up the Lower Mani but, rather oddly, has not much good to say of the Outer where his own village lay. But it is the Deep

Mani that catches it hottest. He seems to have put the poem about, in the first instance, himself. Col. Leake came across a manuscript in Mistra in 1810. There have been others since, all slightly different. When we were in Areopolis, I got permission from the kind gymnasiarch there to consult the great Greek Encyclopedia* in the library of the Lycée, and came across a copy of the poem there, and laboriously copied it out.†

After supper that night we sat about talking on the steps under the archway, half in lamplight, half in moonlight: the submarine *koumbara*, her two guests and her assembled brood of amphibians. They were a delightful, handsome, easy-going lot, full of charm, intelligence and fun. We had been talking about dirges, and the *koumbara* sang us a few fragments she remembered from her childhood. I asked them about Niphakos. They had all heard of him but none had actually read the poem. When I said I had got a copy, they suggested that I should read it out loud. I had copied it in a hurry without paying much attention to the content, so I fished out my notebook and confidently let fly.

'A great mountain stands on the Morea,' it begins, 'in the region of Laconia. The ancient Spartans called it Taygetus, and the Maniots, the Far Away Elijah.‡ . . . Other smaller mountains lie between it and Cape Matapan. To these mountains fled the ancient Spartans, the same men who to-day are known as the Maniots.'

'That's right,' said Petro, the youngest but one of the sons. 'We're ancient Spartans.'

'. . . To save their lives and their freedom they built villages and strong places in the mountains. It was not in their nature to be slaves, but to live as free men. No mules they. The poor lads were true Spartans, free-born and well-skilled in battle. That is

* This invaluable work, of which I at last possess the twenty-two enormous volumes, can be found and consulted in the Greek Lycée or the Demarcheion—Town Hall—of any decent-sized town.

† I have translated the bits which appear later from a version in the oft-mentioned book by Mr. Dimitrakos-Messisklis.

‡ Helios? *Makrynas*—the Far Away One—is the demotic name for the Taygetus as well as for the demon of the Mani. See p. 68.

why they built hamlets and refuges in the mountains, and there they live in freedom to this very day.' So far so good.

'*Kalá ta graphei*,' said another son. 'He writes it well.'

Niphakos goes on to enumerate the villages of the Mani: 'Seven and ten and a hundred are the villages held in freedom by their arms.' Considering the geography of the region, it is an enormous number. All travellers, and notably Lord Carnarvon in the 1830's, have commented on the proliferation of villages and the teeming population in this desolate region. (Many of the villages are almost empty now.) The inhabitants had, quite literally, fled there at one time or another and taken root, for freedom's sake. The poverty of a region so heavily populated was the source of all the Mani's troubles.

There is no further mention of history—two thousand years are skipped with enviable nonchalance—until the tangle of contemporary politics. The bulk of the poem is a harmonious concatenation of the names of the hundred and seventeen villages of the Mani, region by region. Here and there a region or a village is singled out for qualification. 'The Lower Mani, rich in cotton and vallonia acorns'; 'Korogoyianika stands like an unhappy bride'; 'Layia', I was glad to see, is 'beautiful and holy'—largely perhaps because the Greek word for holy (*áyia*) is such a splendid rhyme. Likewise, Skoutari 'shines among the other hamlets like the moon' (*fengari*). Again, Korea is as cold as the north wind (*vorea*). 'The Outer Mani produces plenty of silkworms and oil and acorns.' 'It has terrible gorges and wild ravines, wonderful hamlets and powerful villages.' 'Androuvitza, with all its birds, lies in the foothills of Far Away Elijah.' 'On the cape is Kelepha with its castle; but it is a desert and has nothing else.' 'And so I come to Arachova the far-renowned, hidden away in a witch-haunted valley; and then to the paths of the wolves, the land of sheep- and goat-rustlers and of night walkers. I will name the villages of the eaters of stolen goat's meat, the hole-dwellers and mule-thieves and the murderers of flocks.' He does so. But further on lies 'Kastanitza, well known in many a battle and feared by the Turks, drunk though the villagers be.' The captaincies and the captains thereof are catalogued like a genealogical passage out of the Pentateuch.

At last we come to the great Zanetbey, 'hero and wonder, father to orphans and firm pillar of his fatherland. He should be the first leader and bear the princely rank through all the confines of the Mani, even in all Laconia. He is great and hospitable and a mighty warrior. He does things that no one else in the Mani can do. I tell of things I have seen, not lies. A bell rings in his palace for the banquet in the evening and whoso hears it may go and eat at his table and come away filled. He loves strangers and the poor . . . but the evil he chases away and pounds to powder, like salt. So young and old obey him, and all the captains too. All except one, the lord Koumoundouros, who ravages his regions like a hawk and treads down the poor and steals their goods and eats their food and makes all the region sigh. He longs to hold sway over all the Mani, to take its silk away and seize its oil.' When he took troops and ships to attack Androuvitza, the effect was Biblical: 'The brave youths answered him, dreadful captains went out before him. They met at Skardamoula, there they answered him, there they pounced on him like lions. One man repelled a hundred, and a hundred drove back a thousand. They stripped their enemies bare and sowed them to the winds. He (Koumoundouros) fled across the country in sore fright with his troops. On the shore he left the black Seraskier* and his army trembled until they were safe in the ships. And from his great fear he filled his breeches full.' This passage was a great success. 'That's what the Lower and Outer Mani are like in arms. They devour their foes and would lose themselves for their friends.'

A long plea for civil peace comes next. Let murders, piracies and robberies cease, let no more houses and churches be destroyed. All the disorder springs from carelessness and illiteracy. Disorder provokes battles, robberies, murder, destruction and upheaval. If only there were a few schools! If only the priests would lead and teach their flocks! If only the lowly would order themselves humbly before the great! 'I indeed', this passage concludes, 'am

* The Turkish commander-in-chief.

deep in bitterness. I depart in sorrow, and I leave your [my?] homeland overshadowed with evening.' I paused.

'Yes, but what about the Deep Mani?' everyone cried.

'We're just coming to it. Here we are.' I cleared my throat. '*The Deep Mani.*'

'With bitter sorrow in my soul and misgiving in my heart I enter . . . the land of Evil Council.' This sounded unpromising, but it continued harmlessly enough with a list of the twenty and six villages and hamlets of the Deep Mani. (Oddly, and perhaps just as well, there was no mention of Kypriano, the village where we were sitting.) Tzimova (Areopolis) is the first on the list, 'and there rules the captain, one Mavromichalis'. The poet speaks of 'Mina and Kitta the many-towered, and Nomia too . . . Vatheia and Alika . . . The Deep Mani it is called. It is all the same and quails and Arabian figs* are their only fare. Of woods, trees or bushes there is not even one. There is nowhere to stand in the shade on the burnt hills. There is not a water-spring in the whole Deep Mani. Crops? Nothing but chickpeas and dried oats. The women sow them and the women reap and women scatter the sheaves on the threshing floor. On their unshod feet they grind them on the threshing floor and winnow them with their bare hands. Half-naked they load the grain on their backs, picking out the thick chaff lest it should harm the rest. And from the boiling heat and the burning of the sun their tongues hang out like the tongues of heatstruck dogs.'

'*Po, po, po,*'† interjected the *koumbara* deprecatingly here.

'Their hands and feet are horny and cracked, as tough as leather and hard as a tortoise's shell. They grind away lamenting all night at the quern, pounding the grain at the handmill and singing dirges. Out they go betimes with their baskets, running to gather the droppings in the hollows and the places where the beasts go to drink at noon and to scatter their dung. Thither run the women and gather it up for fuel to cook their breadflaps on. There you see them, whiter than *kourounes* and more slovenly than pigs, for they knead the cattle droppings with their hands and spread

---

* Prickly pear.   † The modern Greek '*Tk, tk, tk!*'

dung-cakes in the sun to dry ("*Po, po, po!*") and then take them home to cook the food of the widows and orphans.'

I was beginning to regret embarking on this poetical reading. I looked up in some trepidation, and was relieved to find them all smiling with amusement and interest.

'The hornwearer!' said one of the sons, and 'What do you expect? He was only an Outer Maniot,' another; and a third, 'Read on, Michali.'

'The men,' I began.

'Now for the men!' one muttered.

'The men are for ever stalking forth in search of plunder, seeking how they can outwit their neighbours. Hither and thither they go seeking whom they may rob, everyone lying in wait to slay someone. One stands on guard in his tower lest another should capture it, one hunts one, another another. Neighbour looks on neighbour, godbrother on godbrother, true brother on true brother as if each were Charon himself. One claims death in vengeance, another is the debtor. . . . One lies in wait for the brother, another for the son, another for the father, another for the grandfather and another for the greatgrandsire himself . . . yet another for cousin or nephew or indeed, any other kinsman. And when they find them, to Hades they send them straightway and they are held accursed till they are avenged. They neither change their clothes nor wash nor barber their chins till they have their vengeance. You can see them there all bearded and smothered in filth, armed to the teeth and wilder than vampires: old men of eighty and even more, all bristling with arms. Savage is their frown and hideous their glance; their eyes are red and their nails as long as the talons of savage beasts. Only when someone dies a natural death who should have been slain do they weep, someone from whom they might have wrung vengeance and consolation. When children are born they distribute pancakes to bring him luck, and everybody gathers at his door and fires off his gun. The widows and married girls gather . . . and cry: "Welcome! May he live and learn how to handle arms and wipe out all his foes! . . ."'

'That's correct,' the *koumbara* said.

'When strangers stray into their regions by chance they turn them into godbrothers and bid them to table. But when the stranger rises to leave, they hold him back, talking in soft and cozening voices. "Godbrother," they say, "we have only your welfare at heart, please don't misunderstand us. Quick! Off with that jacket with its hanging sleeves,* your waistcoat and sash and those baggy trousers too in case an enemy should steal them. Should an enemy strip you bare, should others rob you, great shame and ill-renown would fall on us! That is why, dearest godbrother, it is best to tell you outright that we would be happier if you left your fez and your shirt with us as well. And off with those slippers, they will be no use to you. Now, at last you are safe from all harm." Thus they strip the wretched stranger down to the bone and send him pitilessly on his way.'

This passage was accompanied by a crescendo of laughter, concluding in a happy outburst and murmurs which were half amusement and half censure laced with admiration.

I think the sheer impossibility of such a crime against the laws of hospitality—nowhere more binding than in the Mani as the reader will have gathered and as all the memoirs prove—placed it in the realm of pure clowning and robbed it of its sting, harming neither satirist nor satirized.

There is a tradition that Niphakos was beaten up somewhere in the Deep Mani, probably in Kitta, *dia gynaikodoulies*, for 'woman-business'—improper suggestions or worse. His gall seems unstaunchable. 'Woe betide, if ever, for her sins,' he goes on, 'a sailing ship chances on these shores, be she French, Spanish, English, Turk or Muscovite, be she large or small—everyone wants his share, my son. They dice for shares on the backgammon board without another thought in their heads. They have neither shame before man nor fear of God; they have neither compassion for the poor nor pity for strangers. Such are their rawness and beastlike madness that they bear no likeness to humankind. They

* The embroidered Greek loose-sleeved jacket known as the *fermelé*, in Crete the *yeléka* or *zopáni*.

sully the earth they tread upon, the devil himself is their only companion. These are the men who have given the rest of the Mani a bad name. Men and women, old and young, none of them even smell like human beings. Even to eat with them were a pollution and a curse on the soul. No one should as much as bid them good-day, but fly from them as from a serpent.'

A parliamentary cry of 'Oh!' went up.

'Only the men of Tzimóva are any good—and even they are merchants on the outside, but really secret corsairs. May the winds blow them all away!' He winds up with a repetitious lamentation about the internal discord of the Mani, the savage customs, the illiteracy and the general declension from the great old days of the Spartans. 'Ah! Ah! Would I could shed a river of tears to submerge my fatherland! Once it was alive and famous, now it is dead and befouled. My country, covered once with glory and renowned through all the kingdoms of the world, what has become of you? Where are all your lances and your bows?'

In view of the Maniot passion for arms, it is a singularly inappropriate and ill-conceived peroration.

It was bedtime, the night was warm and still except for the drilling of crickets and the intermittent note of the little owl. The moon shone almost as bright as day, and we were led by three of the sons, carrying pillows and blankets and a water-pitcher, to a straw-padded threshing floor on a ledge of rocks just above the house. The beautiful *koumbara* was still spinning on the descending steps, the moonlight sending her shadow and a long loop of silver across the dark floor indoors.

'Light sleep and sweet dreams,' she said, 'but remember where you are. Better put your clothes under the pillow.'

'Don't worry, *mamá*,' cried one of the sons, 'I'll get their coats and shirts, whatever happens.'

'I've got my eye on their shoes,' another said. 'Never fear.'

We climbed up the rocks past an enormous clump of cactus. The pewter-coloured blades, that seem moonlit even at noonday, were shining now like a sheaf of platinum. A small figure—the youngest of the sons—stepped from its shadow with a stage moan, his eyes eerily ablaze with a most peculiar light. We all jumped, as we were intended to. The still, fiery eyes were hauntingly strange and enigmatic. Suddenly he seemed to pluck them from their sockets and then to place one in each of our hands. They were enormous glow-worms which he had somehow stuck on his eyelids. He skipped off downhill. A strange conceit.

CHAPTER 17

Up the Laconian Gulf:
Animals and Winds

APHRODITE, CYTHERA, was painted smartly across
the poop of the fast and racy looking caique we boarded
next morning. Indeed, everything was as bright as a pin.
There was silver paint on the cleats and, along the bows, touches
of grass green, ox-blood and gilding in the swirl of carved wooden
foliage from which the bowsprit sprang. The mast was painted
in the blue and white Greek colours in a bold barber's pole spiral
for a third of its height. A tin framed picture of St. Catherine was
nailed to it and on a folded sailor's jacket a sleek and well-fed
tortoiseshell cat stretched sleepily at the pother of embarkation.
The entire glittering craft, presided over by a jolly whiskered
Cerigiot captain who abetted our embarkation with cheerful cries
of 'aidé!' and a hauling hand stretched overboard and avuncular
pats on the back, was as full of livestock as Noah's ark. There
were the usual trusses of chicken, three Maniot pigs and a whole
flock of goats. There was even a donkey with its foal. As
though this were not enough, just as we raised anchor, a cicada,
rashly flying a few yards out to sea, alighted on the gigantic
white whisker of an old man who lay sleeping with his mouth
open in a stertorous recurring semibreve. After a few seconds on
this flimsy perch it struck up. The din, so close to the sleeper's
ear, must have sounded like an alarm clock. He broke off in
mid-snore and leapt up beating his head while the insect went
whirring inland to safety.

* * * *

I shall fill the leisure of our journey up the gulf with a digression on cats and divers kindred themes.

Caiques often have pet cats on board and I have twice seen an important sailing held up—not that this takes much; anything suffices to postpone or expedite without warning the departure of these Bohemian barques—until the ship's cat was hunted up among the rubbish and fishbones on the quay. A story told me by my old friend Tanty Rodocanaki* suggests that their presence is sometimes to be ascribed to more utilitarian reasons than pure cat-fancying. It seems that once upon a time a sea captain, distressed by the quantity of rats that infested his caique, summoned a priest and asked him to perform the special service for casting them out. The appropriate chants were intoned and the priest censed and aspersed the ship from stem to stern. Pocketing the usual fee, he assured the captain that he would have no more trouble with vermin: the rite had never failed yet. 'But there's just one point,' he said. 'What's that, Father?' The priest stooped his bearded head to the seaman's ear and whispered: 'Get a cat.' Since then the phrase 'getting a cat' means, in maritime circles, making surety doubly sure.

Dogs are much less frequent members of a crew but you see them now and then. Once, during a hard winter storm between Samos and Chios, I heard barking through the thick mist. It grew louder till the mist cleared for a few seconds to reveal another caique dangerously near and lurching unsteadily among the great waves. A brown dog, with his forepaws on the bulwarks, was barking desperately into the storm. The mist soon obscured the other craft but I could hear the dog's hallucinating protest for long seconds after it had vanished, growing fainter as the wind drowned it. Perhaps cats are better sailors.

Eastern European cats bear little resemblance to the ribboned pussies of the West. They are a completely different shape. The division runs roughly north and south through the Istrian peninsula. East of this line, their ears grow to the size, proportionately with their bodies, of bats; their bodies, their necks and

---

* Alas, he died last year, a sad loss to his friends everywhere.

their tails are longer. They are more alert, intelligent and enterprising, above all, wilder and distinctly more raffish. They are to be seen at their most disreputable in Constantinople, where the city pullulates with them. After dark these noble but sordid streets seem to move and writhe in the lamplight, an illusion induced by the criss-crossing itineraries of thousands of cats, sometimes alone, sometimes in little troops, all of them setting out on thousands of dark and questionable errands. Many of them have the air of broken-down musketeers with fractured noses, tattered ears and the equivalent of eye patches, their moth-eaten tails carried swaggeringly like long rapiers in worn-out scabbards. The Turkish attitude to dogs is one of contempt and hatred. It is well-known how they rounded up the myriads of dogs that once ran riot there and marooned them without food on an island in the Sea of Marmara until they had all eaten each other or starved to death. Their attitude to cats is different. They never kill them, nor do the Greeks, though both races expose unwanted kittens to die or to fend for themselves and survive as freebooters. So outlaw cats abound. I have heard this Turkish —or rather Moslem—forbearance attributed to a whim of Mohammed. The prophet was about to set off on a journey; rising, he found that a cat was asleep in a fold of his robe and, rather than wake it, he called for scissors, cut the cloth all round it and set off with a round hole in his cloak, leaving the cat still asleep.* The Greek attitude to dogs—some of the noisiest and

---

* I have heard, on equally uncertain authority, that the Turks have a superstition about storks and never shoot them. They are now jealously preserved in Greece, but apparently it was not always so. Many thousands of storks spend the spring and summer in Greece, but none of them nest south of a line running south of Epirus and Thessaly from the Ambracian Gulf to the Gulf of Volo. This was roughly the Greek-Turkish frontier until the first Balkan War in 1912, when the Greeks captured and retained all of northern Greece which is now the storks' chief habitat. It must have been about then that the laws protecting them came in. Storks have proverbially long memories, but (if this story is true) I hope they will let bygones be bygones and return to their old haunts in Roumeli and the Peloponnese; old prints show that they were common in Turkish-occupied Athens at the beginning of the last century. They are unknown there

often most frightening barkers in the world—is, like much of the Mediterranean, roughly affectionate, sometimes thoughtless and inconsiderate, seldom cruel. In some parts they have the quaint custom of calling them by enemies' names in order to be able to speak sharply to them. I have often heard Cretans shout: 'Come here, Achmet! Mustapha, be quiet! Boris—outside!' During the war they were called Mussolini, Benito, Ciano (a favourite bête noire of the Greeks), Hitler and Goebbels. Then it became Stalin, Gromyko, and Molotov. (Now, alas, perhaps Andoni or Selouin.) Cardinal Manning enjoyed scolding his butler, who was called Newman, on exactly the same principle.

The cats of Athens, like the citizens, are very intelligent. Just after the war I used to eat almost every night in an open-air taverna in the Plaka. One end of the garden was separated by a high wall from an outdoor cinema, and at the same moment every night, a huge black and white tom-cat stalked over the tiles to sit with his back towards us on this wall, intent and immobile except for the slow rhythmic sway of his hanging tail. After exactly five minutes he would saunter away again over the roofs. The waiter's verdict on this procedure was obviously correct: 'He comes for the Mickey Mouse every night,' he explained. 'You could set your watch by him.'

In far-away islands each community develops with the centuries on slightly different lines; just as each island or isolated region puts forth various botanical species which are to be found nowhere else in the world. Crete, for instance, has over a hundred, and the small island of Hydra where I am writing these pages, two: the blue campanula tayloria which lodges in wall-crevices and the strange brown and butter-coloured Rodokanaki fritillary which grows high up the watershed. It must surely

now. Their nests and their graceful flight ennoble the humblest village. A strange example of traditional fear among migrating birds comes into Alan Moorhead's *Gallipoli*. A vast column of duck and other birds flew over the Dardanelles at a moment of total deadlock in 1916. Exasperated by inaction, the two entrenched armies opened upon them with all they had. It was a massacre and the birds avoided the baleful straits for many years after.

be the same with island cats, interbred for generations in steep un-cat-like habitats with only an occasional outside strain that comes to flower after the brief visit of some caique-dwelling tom. Certainly the two small animals crossing the middle distance as I write these words have little in common with any other kittens I have seen. It is not their markings—white with tabby patches like a sudden drift of mackerel sky on the face or flank—nor is it the engaging absurdity of the enormous bat-like ears, the wide kohl-rimmed eyes, the lean elegance and the bold carriage of their tails. They were found mewing desperately, their eyes just opened, and brought here to the walled and terraced seclusion of Niko Ghika's house. Growing up without seeing or being corrupted by other cats they are Garden of Eden animals free of original sin and there is something peculiar and prelapsarian in their conduct. Stroking or fussing is uncongenial to them; they take no notice or walk away. But should one go for a walk they follow, but at a distance, as though their presence were fortuitous. The other day I found them both nibbling a cactus. The same evening I brought them the delicious remains of a red mullet wrapped in a newspaper. They sniffed the remains for a second, then went back to a slice of melon peel they had discovered somewhere; the fish remained untouched. They are as lithe as jaguars and their behaviour swings between almost lunatic activity and the loose-limbed stretching contortions of an odalisque, rolling over and over with all legs outstretched and suddenly falling asleep on their backs with their mouths open and their forearms wide apart and hanging like the flappers of capsized turtles.

Beyond the skimming gulls, the steep mountains of the coast followed each other southward with scarcely a village. I asked the captain if it was true about the seals at Egg Island, off Cythera. 'Absolutely true,' he said, '*tous vlépei kanéis na kánoun vengéra—na seirianízoun kai na perásoun tín óra tous*'—'you see them hobnobbing and strolling about and passing the time of day'. This reminded me of a phrase I heard years ago when I asked Katsimbalis, before going there, what the Sporades were like. 'Wonderful islands!' was the answer. 'Skiathos! Skopelos! Skyros! The lobsters in Skopelos are the best in the world, and the biggest! They're all over the place. Why, you see them walking up and down the streets and sitting down at tables—reading newspapers, playing tric-trac, ordering coffees and smoking narghilehs. . . .' It was practically true. The first thing I met on landing in Skopelos was a young deacon carrying an enormous lobster under each arm, their slowly swivelling antennae covering so wide a span that they quite barred the narrow lane. But I have been unlucky with strange animals in Greece. Most of my contacts have been at one remove. I have never seen a wolf in Greece, though I arrived in Grevena years ago just after a party of Gipsies, trudging across the snow to play at a wedding, had been eaten to a man, little remaining except their boots and a hand clutching the neck of a fiddle with which its owner had obviously been laying about him as a weapon of defence. I once saw a wild boar on the Albanian border, one or two deer in Pindus, a bear never, though a few years ago, just after the civil war, an old Vlach shepherd in Samarina said to me: 'Last year, when the hard fighting was going on up there,' he pointed to the surrounding peaks, 'the bears all moved down into the valleys and villages. You met them everywhere. They couldn't stand the noise, and I don't blame them.' I think, but am not quite sure, that I have once caught a distant glimpse of an *agrimi*, the mad, shy, fierce, the all-but-invisible and nearly extinct ibex of the White Mountains in Crete. I have seen a landslide caused by its leap and I am deeply ashamed to say I have eaten a bit of one in the last tiny hamlet in the Samaria gorge. It was dark and gamey and incredibly good. A turtle I have seen only once, from the deck of a ship, floating languidly and then sculling steeply down into the blue-green depths between Bari and Corfu almost exactly at that point in the dotted line down the middle of the Adriatic where the *filioque* drops out of the Creed. I have once or twice seen the top half of their shells sliced from their base and, turned upside down, transformed into a cradle. One had a fisherman's daughter asleep in it and very comfortable and decorative it looked. I have never seen a shark. They are extremely rare but they are, unfortunately, occasional visitors, following ships through the Suez Canal and straying into Greek waters. There was a terrible tragedy a few years ago—again, off Corfu—when a beautiful girl fell a victim to one, vanishing for ever on the eve of her marriage. But these monsters cannot be entirely due to the digging of the Canal. Solomos, the great Zantiot poet, wrote a moving elegy on the similar death of a soldier from the British garrison in those same Ionian isles. Fortunately, in spite of local scares, it no more stops people bathing than an occasional train accident stops travel. One never hears much about tunny in Greek waters; they seem to proliferate further west in the Mediterranean though their relation, the palamida, is not uncommon. In ancient times a special watchman, a *thonoskopos*, would keep vigil for tunny shoals on likely headlands and when his warning cry came the young men would run down to the boats with tridents and harpoons.

This journey seems vowed to zoological incident, for soon the delighted cry of '*Delphinia!*' went up: a school of dolphins was gambolling half a mile further out to sea. They seemed to have spotted us at the same moment, for in a second half a dozen were tearing their way towards us, all surfacing in the same parabola and plunging together as though they were in some invisible harness. Soon they were careering alongside and round the bows and under the bowsprit, glittering mussel-blue on top, fading at the sides through gun-metal dune-like markings to pure white, streamlined and gleaming from their elegant beaks to the clean-cut flukes of their tails. They were beautiful abstractions of speed, energy, power and ecstasy leaping out of the water and plunging and spiralling and vanishing like swift shadows, each soon to materialize again and sail into the air in another great loop so fast that they seemed to draw the sea after them and shake it off in mid-air, to plunge forward again tearing two great frothing bow-waves with their beaks; diving down again, falling behind and criss-crossing under the keel and deviating and returning.

Sometimes they flung themselves out of the sea with the insane abandon, in reverse, of a suicide from a skyscraper; up, up, until they hung poised in mid-air shaking in a muscular convulsion from beak to tail as though resolved to abandon their element for ever. But gravity, as though hauling on an oblique fishing-line, dragged them forward and down again into their rifled and bubbling green tunnels. The headlong speed through the water filled the air with a noise of rending and searing. Each leap into the air called forth a chorus of gasps, each plunge a sigh.

These creatures bring a blessing with them. No day in which they have played a part is like other days. I first saw them at dusk, many years ago, on the way to Mount Athos. A whole troop appeared alongside the steamer, racing her and keeping us company for three-quarters of an hour. Slowly it grew darker and as night fell the phosphorescent water turned them into fishes of pale fire. White-hot flames whirled from them. When they leapt from the water they shook off a million fiery diamonds, and when they plunged, it was a fall of comets spinning down fathom after fathom—league upon league of dark sky, it seemed —in whirling incandescent vortices, always to rise again; till at last, streaming down all together as though the heavens were falling and each trailing a ribbon of blazing and feathery wake they became a far-away constellation on the sea's floor. They suddenly turned and vanished, dying away along the abyss like ghosts. Again, four years ago, when I was sailing in a yacht with six friends through the Outer Cyclades in the late afternoon of a long and dreamlike day, there was another visitation. The music from the deck floated over the water and the first champagne cork had fired its sighting-shot over the side. The steep flank of Sikinos, tinkling with goat bells and aflutter with birds, rose up to starboard, and, close to port, the sheer cliffs of nereid-haunted Pholegandros. Islands enclosed the still sea like a lake at the end of the world. A few bars of unlikely mid-summer cloud lay across the west. All at once the sun's rim appeared blood red under the lowest bar, hemming the clouds with gold wire and sending a Japanese flag of widening sunbeams alternating with expanding spokes of deeper sky into the air for miles and spreading rose petals and sulphur green across this silk lake. Then, some distance off, a dolphin sailed into the air, summoned from the depths, perhaps, by the strains of *Water Music*, then another and yet another, until a small company were flying and diving and chasing each other and hovering in mid-air in static semicircles, gambolling and curvetting and almost playing leapfrog, trying to stand on tip-toe, pirouetting and jumping over the sinking sun. All we could hear was an occasional splash, and so smooth was the water that one could see spreading rings when they swooped below the surface. The sea became a meadow and these antics like the last game of children on a lawn before going to bed. Leaning spellbound over the bulwarks and in the rigging we watched them in silence. All at once, on a sudden decision, they vanished; just as they vanish from the side of the *Aphrodite* in this chapter, off the stern and shadowless rocks of the Mani.

'*Kala einai ta delphinia*,' the captain said when they had gone. 'They're good.'

Mythology and folklore are full of tales about dolphins. They all revolve round their benevolence, their love and solicitude for man. It is well-known how Taras, saved from drowning by a dolphin, lived to found the city of Tarentum: the manner of his rescue is immortalized on Tarentine coins. Between Corinth and Syracuse, Arion the lyre-player was rescued from death at the hands of predatory sailors by a troop of dolphins that had gathered round the ship to listen to his playing. There are heart-rending tales of dolphins falling in love with mortals and attempting to join them on land, dying by cruel misadventure and changing, in their death throes, through all the colours of the rainbow.* Their passion for music was queerly illustrated a few years ago. A friend of mine, Dr. Andrea Embirikos, the psychiatrist and poet and a member of the well-known ship-owning dynasty, was rowing peacefully in a boat one afternoon off the coast of his native Andros, listening to a concert on the small portable wireless he had placed on the bench in the stern. After a

* See Norman Douglas, *Siren Lands*, and Lord Kinross's *Europa Minor*.

few bars, half a dozen dolphins appeared from nowhere and began to swim quietly round the boat. Soon, however, carried away by the crescendo they grew more boisterous and leapt out of the water, banging the side of the boat and even attempting to join him on board. The boat rocked dangerously and Andreas hastily picked up the wireless lest it should be knocked overboard and put it under his arm—it was one of those sets that switch off automatically when the lid is closed. Almost at once the dolphins disappeared and all was calm. A few minutes later he opened the set again and an identical scene took place. Finally he was forced to row to land and finish the concert among the rocks, under the reproachful gaze—at a safe distance now—of his would-be companions.*

I was told, for what it is worth, another queer tale, the same year, of a sailor who fell overboard between Crete and Santorin. He was a bad swimmer, and when he was tired out and about to sink to the bottom he felt something large and smooth thrusting between his exhausted and water-treading legs: his knees were being separated by the back of a surfacing dolphin bent on saving him. Soon he was being carried along at a gentle pace by the kind mammal and after a while, afraid of losing his seat, he wrapped his arms round his saviour's neck. But in a few seconds his mount became as stiff as a plank, and rolled over with its white belly in the air, unsaddling the sailor, who had unwittingly blocked the dolphin's blow-hole with his forehead and killed it stone dead by suffocation. But the man's feet touched bottom and he was saved. . . .

Similar tales abound. . . .

Could they have any connection with one of the most notable mentions of the species and one of the strangest scenes in mythology? Once, when Dionysus had hired a ship to carry him incognito from Icaria to Naxos, the crew, a band of conspiring Tyrrhene pirates of the same feather as Arion's malefactors, altered course to Asia to sell the god as a slave. The god changed himself into a lion and the mast and the oars into serpents and

* This happened in Batsí Bay, off the western shore of the island.

entwined the ship with a sudden network of ivy and filled the air with the sound of flutes. Mad with terror, the pirates leapt overboard and, changed into dolphins by the god, swam bewildered away. . . . Could this account for their obsession with music and their age-old courtship of mankind to which, before their metamorphosis, they belonged? Their kindness to mankind might be a protracted atonement for their past harshness and impiety. . . . I don't think so. They seem too transparently good to have been villains in a previous life. . . .

The captain was pleased, because they bring luck to a ship. He leant contentedly on the blue and white striped tiller flicking his tasselled chaplet of amber beads over and over between his index and middle fingers.

'They are strange fish,' he said. 'Some sailors know how to summon them. If they see them swimming in the distance, they shout "*Vasili!*" in a special way they have. The fish stop dead, standing upright in the water, looking round to see who has called. When the sailor shouts "*Vasili*" a second time, they join him like lightning. They all have the same name.'

So they are all called Basil. Is there a link missing, a lost anterior fable that connects them with *basileus*, or King, from which the word derives?

'I've never seen it done,' the captain admitted, 'but I've often heard of it. They have a special way of shouting. . . .'

* * * *

The watershed of the Taygetus climbed steadily, and its retreat inland indicated that the Mani was growing wider. It rose in a sierra as desolating as a dirge. Lolling satrap-like among the corn-sacks, we watched the dry ravines succeed each other above the restless jungle of goats' horns. The captain gave an occasional shift to the tiller and shouted an order and then continued humming to himself.

* * * *

Most of these orders and many maritime terms in Greece are

274

of Italian origin, in the same way that so many English sea terms, though to a lesser degree, are Dutch. They are a legacy from the Venetian maritime empire. The same nautical *lingua franca* holds good, irrespective of nationality, from the Pillars of Hercules to the Red Sea and along the southern Euxine coast as far as the Caucasus. The Greek *Laska!* is *Lascia!*—'pay out rope', or 'let

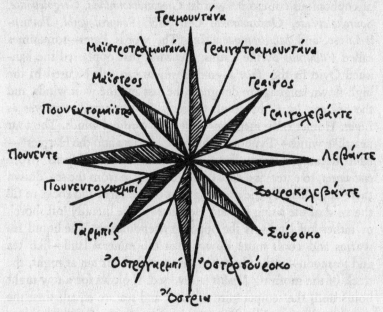

loose'. *Founda!* is 'let the anchor drop to the bottom!' *Vira!* is 'haul in', with the suggestion of twisting a winch. *Karina* is keel, *bastouni* bowsprit, *albouro* mast; and so on. Time has distorted many of them. I can never hear these orders without a momentary glimpse of a many-oared galleon slave-propelled under a crimson gonfalon charged with the gold lion of St. Mark.

The winds have nearly all changed their names and they too whisper a garbled echo of the long-dissolved Venetian power. The north wind is the *Tramountana*, though the ancient Boreas, one of the very few of the winds that Odysseus kept tied in a bag, still survives as well. *Ostria*, the south, in the Latin Auster, though the ancient *Notos* is still sometimes used. *Levante* is the east wind and *Pounente* the west. N.E. is *Grego*, the Greek wind, S.E. the African *Souróko*, S.W. the Arabian *Garbís*, and N.W. the *Mäistro*, or Mistral. The heart of this wind-rose seems to be somewhere off Sicily, the heart of the Mediterranean in fact. The subdivisions—N.N.E., E.N.E., E.S.E., S.S.E., and so on—are a string of euphonious composite words: *Gregotramountána, Gregolevánte, Sourokolevánte, Ostrosoúroko, Ostrogarbí, Pounentogarbí, Pounentomäistro,* and *Mäistrotramountána.* The words *Euros*—sometimes called *Vulturnus* by the Latins, the wind that oppressed the banished Ovid in the *Tristia*—and *Zephyros* can still be used in the high-flown language to designate the east and the west winds, and the ancient *Lips,* the south-westerly Libyan wind, survives as *Livas.* Homer only mentioned the four cardinal winds. The four beastlike winds—Typhon, Echidna, Chimaera and the Harpies*— have decamped from the Greek air for good. *Mpátis* (from *embainein,* to enter) is a cool breeze coming in from the sea, drawn there at midday by the growing heat of the earth and rocks to fill the void of the rising hot air. *Apógeios*—quite literally 'off shore', or rather 'off land'—is the opposite phenomenon. The liquid sea warms and cools more slowly than the mineral land—like tea and teaspoon—and so between sunset and about ten at night, the track of the morning *Mpátis* is reversed. It blows for a few night hours until the temperature of earth and sea are equal; then the vagrant airs are still. The ancient Etesian winds which blow through the summer months can be a blessing or a curse: they cool the archipelago but drive caiques off their course or lock them in harbour. They are a *Mpátis* on a giant scale, a wind that rushes south across the Mediterranean to fill the airless ovens of the Egyptian and African deserts; which repay them, now and then, with a long dragon's breath of sirocco. This wind is now called the *Meltém* which philologists derive from the Venetian *bel tempo* because it only blows in summer. When the *Meltémi* blows hard the inhabitants of the island of Spetzai called it *Trapez-*

---

* The harpies have settled in the two desert islets of the Strophades. I shall have much to say of these bird-winds in another book. See the *Æneid,* bk. III.

ókairos—'table weather'—because one gust of it will capsize all the café tables along the harbour. Except that it was too late in the year, this could have been the 'tempestuous wind called *Euroclydon*' that gave St. Paul's ship such a rough time south of Crete, when the last chapters of The Acts turn into an Odyssey. But 'neither sun nor stars in many days appeared', so it was winter. *Euroclydon* is called *Euraquilo* in the Vulgate, a north-easter. It was *Notos*, the south wind (*Auster* in St. Jerome's text), which till then had been blowing so softly. How well I remember, during the war, gazing from caves on Mount Ida to 'the island called Clauda' under which they ran so close (it is Klauda or Kauda in the Greek testament, Gavdos in modern Greek). The only Western traveller to describe this islet in recent times is an old friend and brother-in-arms from those peculiar years.* Anyone who has tried to land on that coast from a small boat will appreciate the apostle's difficulties. The Levanter, the strong east wind that blows across the Adriatic, had a deep influence on ancient Greek history. Rather than confront the fierce weather that lay further up the long gulf, Greek emigrants avoided the Adriatic coasts. Following the prevailing wind, they were scattered like grain over southern Italy, Sicily, the coasts of Provence and even southern Spain, and flourishing Greek colonies sprang up there while the coasts north of Epirus and Illyria, so much nearer home, remained practically unknown.

Caique sailors are for ever peering at the surface of the sea like joiners studying the grain of a piece of wood to see what ripples or markings the wind makes and murmuring '*garbis*', '*maïstro*', or '*sourokolevánte*', and predicting *bonatza*, fair weather, or, with gravely shaking heads, *phourtoúna*, a storm. (In Crete, foul weather is called *cheimonas*—winter—even if the season is midsummer.) The air in Greece is not merely a negative void between solids; the sea itself, the houses and rocks and trees, on which it presses like a jelly mould, are embedded in it; it is alive and positive and volatile and one is as aware of its contact as if it could have pierced hearts scrawled on it with diamond rings or be grasped in

* See *The Stronghold*, by Xan Fielding (Secker and Warburg).

handfuls, tapped for electricity, bottled, used for blasting, set fire to, sliced into sparkling cubes and rhomboids with a pair of shears, be timed with a stop watch, strung with pearls, plucked like a lute string or tolled like a bell, swum in, be set with rungs and climbed like a rope ladder or have saints assumed through it in flaming chariots; as though it could be harangued into faction, or eavesdropped, pounded down with pestle and mortar for cocaine, drunk from a ballet shoe, or spun, woven and worn on solemn feasts; or cut into discs for lenses, minted for currency or blown, with infinite care, into globes. On top of this, all the nautical wind-talk and scrutiny of the elements fills it with innumerable unseen coilings and influences and cross currents and comings and goings. It is no wonder that the Greek word for wind—*anemos*—should have produced the Latin word *anima*, for soul; that *pneuma** and *spiritus* should mean spirit and breath and wind in both languages. Perhaps it is not strange that the age-old Greek war-cry—the equivalent of *St. George!*, *Montjoy-Saint Denys!*, and *Santiago!*—should be the single word *Aera!* which means both wind and air.

There is, in fact, more in the air than meets the eye. The element is further complicated by the presence of *ta aërika*, the spirits of the air. They have cropped up earlier on in these pages. They are less of a problem to present-day sailors than they used to be a few decades ago. But there is a subdivision of the species of daemons, or genii, of the air which has an immediate relevance to sailors. They are known as *ta telonia*: the customs offices and, by extension, officers. Popular fancy has created a whole hierarchy of hovering excisemen through which the soul has to pass on its way to Paradise or to Hades. Soaring souls are examined by invisible *douaniers* who scrutinize their psychic luggage for unatoned sins, both deadly and venial. Tradition has degraded them from their severe but benign status to the rank of evil harm-wreaking spirits whom the corpses—or their flying spirits—can placate with a coin that may, alternatively, have been placed

---

* The *Spiritual Exercises* of St. Ignatius Loyala can be exactly paraphrased as *Pneumatic Drill*.

in their mouths either to placate Charon or to block, with their metal barrier, the ingress to other evil spirits. Shooting stars, comets and other celestial portents are considered manifestations of *ta telonia*. These affect—or used to affect—all mortals; but the customs-phenomenon most dangerously and specifically aimed at sailors is St. Elmo's Fire. This sinister light flickering and shuddering about the mast and the yards of a caique foretells with certainty the onslaught of these baleful air-denizens. Exorcism and incantation used to be effective antidotes, but the surest way of all—like the remedy against the Lamia of the Sea when she appears in the form of a waterspout—is to stick a black-handled knife into the mast, if possible after it has been used for cutting an onion. The reek aroints the air. In ancient times, two such airy manifestations were considered propitious; they were the Gemini, protectors of seamen. A single flame, however, betokened their sister Helen whose fatal beauty wrecked towns and ships and lives.

Seamen peer into the sky at night not only to steer by the stars but to prognosticate the future from the tilt of the crescent or decrescent moon. '*Orthio to phengári*,' they say, '*xaploménos o kapetánios*': if the moon is upright, the captain can lie down. If the incomplete moon is lying on its back, the captain stands to the helm; it foretells *phourtoúna*: '*Xaploméno to phengári*', in fact, '*orthios o kapetánios*'. They are great ones for steering by their fingers —holding up a hand at arm's length to measure off one, two, or three fingers' breadth from a cape or a rock and moving the rudder accordingly. I once heard an old ocean-going sailor describing, only half in fun, between puffs at his narghileh, how to sail from the Piraeus to London entirely in such terms. 'When you get to Cape Malea,' he said, 'aim three fingers to port of Matapan, a finger to starboard south of Sicily, two to port at Cape Spaptiventi in Sardinia, one to starboard at Gibraltar, three at Cape St. Vincent, two at Finisterre, two more at Ushant . . . why a baby could do it : . . Then four to port at Margate, follow the Thames upstream, drop anchor at Tower Bridge, then go ashore and order a beef-steak. *Na!* . . .'

We rounded a small cape. A valley full of scarcely believable green trees appeared and a mile or so up the mountain, a towered village. A busy little port sheltered half a dozen caiques. 'We've arrived,' the captain said. 'Kotronas,' he announced and then, pointing uphill at the towers, 'Phlomochori.' Alongside the mole a few minutes later we heard his voice cry *founda!* and down went the anchor with a clatter and a splash.

CHAPTER 18

Short Summer Nights

THE Deep Mani had stopped. This cove, half an hour on foot south of Kotronas, was dominated by a huge fig tree. The cliffs closed to a steep stream-bed thick with oleanders. Two more fig trees grew like polished silver candelabra from a small rocky island composed of a dozen massive and wavy strata snapped off and tilted to an oblique angle, which lay in the position of a star between the crescent horns of the bay about a furlong from the shore. We had swum there half an hour ago and clambered up its steep wall, treading the hot and sweet-smelling herbs on its overgrown summit; then dived in again to swim into a sea-cave whose filtered light turned us a deep green. The water, sliding in and out of it, plopped with a hollow and lulling resonance a few yards away. All of this, with the golden sand and the polished pebbles I could feel against my shoulder blades, belonged to a more familiar Greece. Like one of the seals off Cythera, I was lying half in and half out of the sea, my ears full of water noises and the rise and fall of a million cicadas, letting the sun's horses and chariot wheels ride over me roughshod; leaving my eyelids just ajar so that the lashes split the sunlight into dozens of straight, wire-thin and mile-long rainbows that lengthened and expanded into more dazzling sheaves with every millimetre I lowered them. I had only to close them completely for orange, magenta, grass-green and violet suns to glow against the dark shutter and change into luminous latchkeys and sieves and reef-knots and bowler hats and lopsided harps and tulips and tuning forks against magnificently clashing backgrounds of electric blue and burnt sienna and mushroom and daffodil coloured velvet. Equally, I had only to open them suddenly and gaze accusingly and painfully at the real sun for it to turn jet black and oscillate and put forth petals like a marguerite and revolve at high speed, exactly as it does in Ghika's pictures; then shut them again and watch the contents of a junk-shop collide, expand, shrink and change shape and turn inside-out again in the secret *camera obscura* behind my eyelid and fall asleep with feelings of supreme voluptuousness and idle omnipotence.

Plying my forefinger like a strigil to wipe the salty sweat off my face, I felt it rasp against three days' unmown stubble. Greeks loathe shaving themselves and peasants only really go in for it once a week, on Saturday, when the barber shops are suddenly crammed. I am only too prone, when wandering about like this, to let it rip as well, growing steadily more raffish and ragged in appearance, burnt black by the sun, as caked with salt as a smoke stack and reeking every night more asphyxiatingly of garlic,

> comme un encensoir oublié
> qui fume à travers la nuit,

till conscience suddenly goads me into an empty barber's shop on an off day—any of six, in fact. There is no doubt about it: unless you are used to it, this hispid state looks hideous. Perhaps this permanent pard-like stubble and the prevalence of moustaches among Greek peasants has something to do with foreigners' disappointment at the un-Praxitelean aspect of modern Greeks. There are, as a matter of fact, quite a lot knocking about with regular classical features, fair hair and blue eyes; even, rather sur-prisingly to me, suggestions of that melting of the forehead into the bridge of the nose which I suspect was as much of a convention as the imaginary lateral roll of muscle or fat over the tips of the pelvis. These statues were composite sublimations and, superb as they are, as much an idealization as, *mutatis mutandis*, a fashion plate. The sculptures that can be set down as portraits are, as a rule, perfectly normal and contemporary in aspect; some, as in the case of Socrates, agreeably ugly. But the whole approach, the arbitrary singling out of one century from its provenance and sequel, the failure to regard history as a continuum, is wrong, and to this faulty attitude, on a wider scale, most Western misconceptions about Greece are due. What of the archaic smile—and scowl? The dark-rimmed, incendiary, omniscient blankness of Minoan eyes, Hellenistic softness and complacency, the almond-shaped eyes of Fayoum, the disembodied, staring aloofness of ikons, the dark, hunted, or menacing look of Christ Pantocrator at Daphni, the arrogant, waxen Phanariots of Liotard, the whiskered and fiery-eyed klephts of the broadsheets, the sailors and *mangas* of Tsarouchi? They are all there.

The ancient, like the modern Greeks, were always—as are the English and, with a few usually rather tedious exceptions, most other peoples—a composite race. The process was afoot long before the Periclean age, and it continued afterwards. No one knows exactly where the first Greeks arrived from; Sir John Myers, at the end of his several volumes of *Who Were the Greeks?*, is inconclusive, as, through lack of data, he is bound to be. It is pathetic and idiotic to attempt to stem this traffic in 450 B.C. and to damn the modern Greeks by comparison. It is about as sensible as a Greek in London expecting to be surrounded by ancient Britons or Elizabethans, or deploring a busload of our contemporaries because not one of the passengers is like a druid or a Saxon swineherd out of *Ivanhoe*, or Sir Philip Sidney. What are we? Saxon wall paintings, Bayeux tapestry figures, medieval illuminations and recumbent effigies on tombs, Holbeins, Hilliards, Van Dycks, Lelys, Gainsboroughs, Leightons, Rossettis, Sargents, Laszlos?—Bacons or Annigonis? The answer, I suppose, is all of them. The most striking and revealing thing about Greek faces—especially Greek peasant faces—is the eyes. The whole of Greek history seems to be coiled up behind them. They are a mixture of experience, a rather sad wisdom, and innocence. They are at the same time melancholy and deep-gazing, alert and ready for thrusting from their sockets with anger or for kindling with amusement, collusion, or laughter; above all, they are filled with a wide, phenomenal, uncircumspect candour. Many of the ugliest faces are illuminated by them and they make beautiful ones inexpressibly moving. If the Greek landscape had eyes they would be exactly these and I have often toyed with the vision of such an eye, a solitary one several acres in extent, gazing cyclopically and compellingly from under a thick half-mile of curved black eyebrow from the barren side of a mountain or from the sky.

After a time I opened one of my own and saw that the shadows had begun to broaden on the eastern corrugations of the little island and fell to thinking of the innumerable islets scattered round the coasts of Greece: some bearing the ruins of a fort or a shrine, some scattered with un-shepherded flocks during the summer months, some with a fisherman's hut or two, others with a prison or a hermit or a lonely *skite* with a couple of shaggy monks half mad with isolation; some utterly deserted. Last of all I thought of Gavdopoula, a satellite islet of St. Paul's Gavdos of a few pages back, and began to laugh. Joan, half asleep a few yards away in the same beachcombing attitude, wondered what I was laughing at, so I told her a story I had heard from my Cretan guide during the war.

The tiny island was acquired long ago by a Sphakian family called Seiradanis. This region of Crete—Sphakia— was one of the few places, like the Mani, to remain independent of the Turks, thanks to the wild nature of the country and the bravery of the Sphakians. The Seiradanis family, before and since, played a prominent rôle in this struggle, but, in the 1821 war, one of them turned traitor, and, like Ephialtes and Ganelon, sold the pass. The result was invasion and slaughter and the Turks rewarded their ally with the gift of this minute island, seven leagues south of Crete; it has remained in the family ever since and they sometimes pasture their flocks there. Shortly after the last war began, one branch of the family was seriously perturbed by the almost permanent drunkenness of their grandfather; so they marooned him on Gavdopoula near a spring with a plentiful stock of food, hoping to sober him up and change his ways. When they came with a little caique to pick him up, a reformed character they hoped, at the end of two months, they were astounded and horrified to find the old greybeard spreadeagled under a shady rock beaming happily and unregenerately, and still, exactly as they had left him, dead drunk. The first thing he had seen when they had sailed away (he told them between hiccups) had been a black dot on the horizon which floated toward him across the Libyan sea growing steadily larger. When it was close to the land it turned out to be an enormous barrel which soon came to rest on the shingle. It was half-full of Italian wine, probably from some ship recently sunk off Cyrenaica. In a moment he was rolling it up the beach. He managed to site it with the bung strategically placed over a basin-like hollow in a rock. Every half-hour or so he would fill the hollow and lap up the wine like a goat, as he said. 'So—hic—you see, lads,' he concluded, waving a horny forefinger, 'God and the All-hic-Holy Virgin were on my side.' It was incontrovertible. Back they sailed and the old man finished his life happily and unhindered in the tavernas of Sphakia. . . .

We left this Argonautish bay with reluctance. It resembled most convincingly a brief anchorage on any of the great mythological voyages, where a shipload of heroes might have landed and sacrificed to Poseidon and banqueted and wrestled and run races, perhaps buried a dead shipmate and marked the place with an oar stuck in the shore and sailed away. As Seferis says in his poem:* 'The water left on their hands the memory of a great happiness.' This country, even after years of familiarity, often calls forth these sudden feelings of naïve and Marvellian gratitude: What wondrous life is this I lead?

Cypresses and poplars fluttered beside the climbing path above the oleanders of the torrent bed. All this random green seemed frivolous, reckless, and miraculous after the harsh regions to which our eyes had become attuned; but beyond it the stern biblical rocks soared through the evening air. In the middle of them half a mile away a goatherd, with his flock scattered about him like cave-paintings, waved his crook in salutation. How large and distinct he looked! Almost as disturbing as the gigantic Eye of my imagination. This rocky world has the property of

* *The Argonauts:* George Seferis, translated by Rex Warner.

making all look momentous, for all is isolated, nothing congregates, everything becomes archetypal and, as it were, symbolic of its own essence, so that the landscape is very sparsely and, probably because of this, over-significantly furnished with arch-trees, archthistles, archcactuses, archgoatherds and archgoats. The portrayal of this momentousness and solitude is one of the triumphs of Byzantine mosaic and ikon-painting. Animate and inanimate objects, on ikon and church wall and mountain-side, have the same spiritual effect, the same mystical and animistic aura of immanence. No wonder that Greeks of all centuries have populated these hills with a magical fauna and a *dramatis personae* and a pantheon.

This light, of which I have talked so much, has many odd foibles and conjuring tricks. One of these is the lens-like function of the air. All the vapours that roam the Italian atmosphere and muffle the outlines of things are absent here. A huge magnifying glass burns up the veils of distance, making objects leagues away leap forward clearly as though they were within arm's length. The eye shoots forth a telescopic braille-reading finger to discern the exact detail and texture of a church, a wood or a chasm ten miles off. Things in the distance co-exist on equal terms with those hard by; they have a proprietary and complementary share in the patterns that immediately surround one. A distant cordillera completes a curve begun by the vein along the back of a plane-tree leaf, a far-off belfry has the same intensity as a goat's horn a few yards away, a peninsula leans forward to strike the stem of a dried-up thistle at right angles. Mountain ranges that should melt with the heat-haze and recession, lean forward and impend till one is at a loss to say whether a hill is a small nearby spur or a far-away Sinai. Perpendiculars only exist in walls and towers and tree trunks—unless the trees are olives, in which case they unite and revolve like dancers or contortionists—and the only horizontal is the horizon. The sea stands bolt upright and the sun's track across it is not a highway that retreats with the curve of the globe's surface, but, till sunset flattens it and lays it on its back again, a blazing pagoda. At this late afternoon hour, the hard-hearted mountains turn golden and lavender, the valleys become ground porphyry and powdered serpentine. Where the weathered limestone has fallen away in a landslide, the virgin rock glows bright orange as though infernal forges were at work within. The light also performs several simultaneous and contradictory acts; it chisels and sharpens everything so that the most fluid curve can be broken up at once, by a shift of focus, into an infinity of angles; it acts like an X-ray, giving mineral and tree and masonry an air of transparence; and it sprinkles the smoothest and most vitreous surface with a thin layer of pollen like the damask on a moth's wing. The stones and walls, as well as staying warm to the touch long after the light has left, are absorbent to the light; they glow as if lit from inside with a wick that burns down very slowly as darkness deepens. The strangest phenomenon of all occurs with the shadows. What little there is at noon is grey and dead, and when the colours revive in the afternoon, they are a cool clear blue and archways are curving waterfalls. But in the late evening they outglare the solids that fling them, falling across white walls or grey stone courtyards or the dust of a pathway with an intensity like a magnesium flare, standing from the surfaces that register them in electric-blue and orange and sulphur-green shapes as separately as though they were in high relief or deep intaglio. The motionless trench dug by a tree-shadow or the shifting and instantaneous bird-shaped cavity that crosses a terrace looks far more real than the tree trunk or the swooping bird which they echo; both of these the light, by comparison, has immaterialized. It is probably because of all this that a strong mystical and sentimental significance pervades the actual surface of the earth, the rocks and the stones, of Greek mountains. The adjective *theobadiston*, 'trodden by the feet of gods (or God)' in ancient Greek and in the Byzantine liturgy, comes to mind. In an old ballad which describes a quarrel between two great mountains, free Olympus is held to be good because it is *Klephtopatiméno*, 'trodden by klephts', as opposed to the *Tourkopatiméno*, the Turk-trampled, the shameful flank of wretched Ossa.

These characteristics have a strange effect on the Greek

landscape. Nature becomes supernatural; the frontier between physical and metaphysical is confounded.

All the evening phenomena were at work as we climbed through the groves and the first houses of Phlomochori. The shadows cast by the rising moon, shining like a silver fish beyond the network of olive leaves, were crossing swords with those of the sun: so faintly that they might have been made of flimsy material which could be snipped off with scissors and rolled up. A number of hawk-like birds were hovering and wheeling in the air above the village. It was a cloud of gregarious red-footed falcons, great ruin-haunters and birds of prey that thrive on such small quarry as the high-flying insects that abound in the evening. The high watershed soon blocked out the sun and the moon's shadows and her glimmering light were uncontested among the olive trees and the gathering towers. The warm dust underfoot was succeeded by cobbles and there was a sound of running water. Cigarette-ends glowed in doorways and under the trees and each orange constellation of cigarettes sent out a murmured chorus of greeting.

* * * *

These summer nights are short. Going to bed before midnight is unthinkable and talk, wine, moonlight and the warm air are often in league to defer it one, two or three hours more. It seems only a moment after falling asleep out of doors that dawn touches one gently on the shoulder, and, completely refreshed, up one gets, or creeps into the shade or indoors for another luxurious couple of hours. The afternoon is the time for real sleep: into the abyss one goes to emerge when the colours begin to revive and the world to breathe again about five o'clock, ready once more for the rigours and pleasures of the late afternoon, the evening, and the night.

This night was no exception. There was no inn, but our adoption as guests by a villager for dinner and accommodation occurred as though the hamlet had been long forewarned. There was much affectionate talk under the trees after dinner of British soldiers who had taken refuge here and been fed and hidden by the villagers when the Germans overran Greece. Did we know Sandy, Len, Jack, Sid, Peter, Stanley and Ron, *Herbertos* and a tall Australian from Adelaide—'*o Lophtis*'? The tall one? And Spike —*Spaïk, o Neozelandos*—and Yanni from inside London, the one who was so badly wounded in the arm? 'Po, po, po! He was a good boy,' an old woman croaked. 'We hid him in our olive grove for two months, and I used to take him eggs and cheese and potatoes. How his arm must have hurt—it had swallowed three bullets, but he was always laughing. We got a doctor for him. He used to call me "*Ma*".' There was a pleased reminiscent cackle. 'They took him off to England by submarine in the end.'

'Not to England,' said the priest gently, 'to Egypt.'

'It's the same thing. To London. He went with the good, poor lad. I wonder how he is in London and if he found his mother and father all right. He had one married sister—she was married to a rich man, an important baker—and one was still free.'

Oddly enough, we did know one of these names. A couple of men from further north in the Mani asked us if we knew an officer who had come in secret to organize rescue parties—*O Markos*, Captain Marko the Skotzezos, who was captured by the enemy?* Indeed we did, and were able to give recent news. Our shares shot up and we basked in pride of friendship as a fresh supply of wine appeared. There had been one more such encounter, but a sadder one, while we were in the Deep Mani. On the way back from the temple of Kiparisso an old man asked us if we had any news of an Englishman called David—a tall chap, who walked across the hills like this—he took a few giant strides —making notes about all the Frankish castles of Greece? Always writing? He had come that way a year or two before the war. It was easy to recognize David Wallace. Here our news was not good. He and all his brothers except one had been killed in the war, David fighting the Germans with a party of guerrillas in Epirus, where he had been parachuted. We told him he had been buried in the churchyard of the little cathedral of Paramythia,

* It was Mark Ogilvie-Grant.

289

where a street had been named after him. The old man crossed himself sadly. '*Krima sto pallikari!* May the earth rest light on him. . . .'

This was the last night in the rustic Mani. To-morrow we were leaving for Gytheion, at the head of the Laconian gulf. A hint of valedictory sadness hung in the moonlight overhead as I lay, agreeably drugged with wine and padded by half a dozen blankets from the thick layer of newly threshed grain which was spread from parapet to parapet of the flat rooftop. Ruined towers stood all round. A nightingale, a little way downhill among the trees by the stream, made everything seem yet more liquid and fleeting and sad. A nibble on one side of the moon showed that its course was more than half run, but it was still too bright for all but a few undistinguished stars to twinkle dimly in the corners of the sky; they hide themselves, just as Sappho says, when the moon at its full shines over the whole earth. In a few days all the famous constellations and a myriad other stars would be back: steady patterns across which the showers of summer comets fall in long and erratic arcs. How familiar some of them become, in their slow marches across the heavens, from constant sleeping out! One lies there gazing like an astrologer. The fixed North Star, both Bears, the large W of Cassiopeia and the tilted lozenge of Orion with his three-star belt; Greekest and subtlest of all— again, perhaps, because of Sappho—the Pleiades, that fugitive and misty little group that resolves itself into a far-away badminton racket warped by the dew through being forgotten overnight on a vicarage lawn.

The brief night over, it was only a question of standing up. Except for shoes, dressing was done. A small boy playing a flute in a doorway, as much as the sun, had performed the act of rousing. The sun was well over the Laconian peninsula the other side of the gulf, the gulf itself shone pale and new, and the Mani stretched to north and south below us in an imponderable imbrication of stage-wings lightening slightly with each successive cape. The cypresses and poplars and olive trees sent long backward-seeming shadows sloping up the hillside towards us. After coffee and farewells we climbed down through the oleanders along the bed of the brook, swam in the cool waters of the cove, to the island and back, and walked along the coast to Kotronas. We had left our bags here in a kapheneion, the day before. In an hour or two, a steamer would call and carry us up the gulf to Gytheion.

CHAPTER 19

Castles and the Sea

IT was lucky that Kotronas was such an agreeable haven, for the weekly boat was hours late. They often are. There was another giant fig tree for shade, from one of whose lower branches someone had hung a big *synagrida*, the fish that kindled the envy of Poor Prodromos, the Villonesque beggar poet of Byzantium, friend, it is said, of the Emperor Alexis Comnene, when, peeping through the window, he saw one stuffed with spices and covered with sauce on the table of a rich abbot. . . .

The waterfront was given over to net-making. One had to walk with care. Strips of filmy russet netting three feet broad were draped a hundred yards along the ground, the fishermen sitting on the ground at one end, stretching the net wide with their big toes and skilfully crocheting mesh after mesh with darting shuttles. A row of fishermen sitting along a low wall were busy baiting their lines for trolling. One had lost a hand through dynamiting, as usual. A basket on his knee was filled with a coil of twine, the rim set with corks stuck full as a pincushion with fish hooks. He looped the slack round his stump, tied a short length of nylon thread to the brown twine with his other hand, pulled it tight with his teeth, baited the hook with a chunk of fish and paid it out onto another loose coil, all at high speed, smoking ceaselessly and only stopping for a second to throw me a cigarette when he saw me fumbling my pockets in vain.

It looked as though no ship could ever come. The horizon sundered the identical light blues of sea and sky with a dark blue ruler-stroke and the smooth surface of the water was dulled here and there with a faint wind like breath on a looking glass. Across these misty patches occasionally ran a smooth narrow line caused by a current or perhaps a faint contrary breeze, as though traced by the erratic rub of a fingertip. A large, full-bottomed schooner weighed anchor heading south for Matapan and Kalamata. There was not enough wind to hoist sail. Trailing a dinghy, she swung swiftly out of profile till the two bare masts converged, leaving a long scar across the polished and the arrowy water: then, turning the first stage-wing of the promontory, she profiled again and dwindled against the espalier valleys towards Matapan, as though being thrust up the perpendicular screen of sea on the point of her lengthening wake. The fierce and bandit-like kapheneion keeper gave us a large red rose apiece to console us for the delay.

But, within half an hour, we were off; sending out, as the steamer left the little gulf of Kolokythia, one of those siren blasts that sound so strange inland when they reach the ear along a maze of canyons.

This coasting steamer, sailing to and from the Piraeus and calling at all the small ports of the south-eastern Peloponnese once a week, seemed very sophisticated to our bucolic eyes. The panelled Edwardian saloon, the brasswork and the curtains, the striped canvas chairs, the elaborate *ouzo* glasses and the saucers full of fat Kalamata olives and the slices of Cretan cheese and salami brought by a stylish steward (white-jacketed but, like me, unshaven) were symptoms of almost Capuan luxury.

When we emerged from our early luncheon the coast of the Mani had changed completely. The mountains had receded inland and the Lower Mani, with the forty-four villages of which Niphakos speaks, stretched in a flat green plain rimmed with low trees and pronged with cypresses and poplars; plentifully stocked, according to the poet, with cotton, and with those vallonia oaks whose acorns are sold for dyeing and tanning. How mild and beautiful it looked! But after a few flat green coast miles, up inland soared the Taygetus again to great heights, dipping at the head of the gulf where more distant ranges showed beyond the Helot-haunted lowlands of eastern Laconia. To the east the rocky spine of the Laconian peninsula, as immaterial at its distant points as a soundwave, oscillated south to Cape Malea.

A pass winds through the north Maniot reaches of the Taygetus from Gytheion to Areopolis. It is the Deep Mani's only road-link with the rest of Greece and some distance along it, at a strategic point, stands the wreck of the Frankish fortress of Passava, hidden now in the curling blue waves of the range. It was built, like most of the other feudal castles in Greece, in the thirteenth century, when the Peloponnese, now styled the Principality of Achaea, was split up into subsidiary baronies. Some antiquaries derive its present vernacular name from *Passe-Avant*, others from *Pas Avant*, which has a hint of the battle of Verdun.

I have always instinctively hated Frankish ruins in the Greek world. This needs a little explanation; for a long time it needed it—as I am by no means immune to the romantic spell of Gothic ruins anywhere else—even to myself. In the damp forests and fields of western Europe, rearing their machicolations or their broken clerestories in Normandy, by the Rhine or in an English shire—in the heart of their native lettuce, in fact—they fill me with an almost Huysmansesque addiction. I derive nothing but pleasure, too, from crusading relics in Saracen countries; the eyries of Knights Templar in Syria, scowling holds like Krak des Chevaliers and the battered coats of arms on the city wall at Acre evoke reactions of which Sir Walter Scott and Heredia would both have approved.

Similarly, old Turkish houses in Greece, the domes of an abandoned mosque, a broken minaret and the cupolas of a madrasseh seem quite all right.* They tell a calamitous tale of mistakes and

---

* Palm trees, however (of which there are fortunately only a few), look desperately wrong. West of the Bosphorus, they should stick to Torquay and the Côte d'Azur. It is odd that an antipodean tree, the Eucalyptus, unknown before the voyages of Captain Cook, should look so beautiful and appropriate along many a Peloponnesian road. I think they unconsciously suggest the dream vegetation in the imaginary classical landscapes of Poussin and Claude—both of them, it is true, quite unlike Greece. Norman Douglas launches a splendid attack on these trees which falls, in my case, on deaf ears. One is illogical and eclectic in these matters. A British Army barracks or a

of the clashing of irreconcilables and fierce conquest and large-scale tragedy; but there is an authentic splendour about the crusades in the Holy Land; and though one may bitterly deplore, as I do most fervently, that the Turks ever set foot in Europe, it would be as absurd to blame them for the destruction of the Byzantine Empire as it would be to arraign the laws of hydrostatics for damage by flood. But one can and may blame the wicked Fourth Crusade for making that destruction inevitable and bringing about the wreck of eastern Europe for centuries. We need not go into it all again. Western feudalism was utterly foreign to the Greek world and when it vanished, it left, beyond these ruined castles, not a trace. It is sad that those vanished tournaments and courts of love, the distant echo of horns and Burgundian hounds along the ravines of Achaea, the sound of lutes and plainsong and all the transplanted flowering of Western chivalry—much indeed that in the West I love—should touch me, in this instance, so little. I must admit that in Cyprus, something of the spell of Cœur de Lion and the Lusignan dynasty breaks through in those Gothic cathedrals turned to mosques, in the Abbey of Bellapais and in the castle of St. Hilarion, which hangs in the air like an illuminated detail from the *Très Riches Heures du Duc de Berri.*

Monemvasia, too, has a derelict lunar grandness and it cannot be denied that the castle of Karytaena, high on its Arcadian rock above the winding Alphaeus, is hard to beat for chivalric splendour. The largest, the most formidable and the most intact of the Frankish holds are usually Venetian and built much later, at points on the mainland or on the islands that the Republic retained by treaty with the Turks and by force for centuries after the Frankish hegemony had vanished. (Some princely families, however, still retained a forlorn claim to their lost fiefs *in partibus*; the Duc de Nevers in the early seventeenth century, who—yet another!—claimed the Byzantine throne, actually planned to

London pillar-box in Cyprus looks detestable while our architectural legacy in the Ionian islands is full of charm. Of course, it is more beautiful and it tells a story with a happy ending.

regain his putative empire in collusion with the free Maniots.*)
The fringes of the Greek world are dotted with enormous
Venetian bastilles, each one a vast brooding complex of slanting
curtain walls, miles of moat, donjons, flèches, demilunes, glacis,
bastions, barbicans, redoubts, counterscarps, sally-ports and draw-
bridges, all of well-nigh impregnable thickness. Slabs bearing the
Lion and Latin inscriptions adorn them, commemorating some
governor or general or gonfalonier called Zorzi, Mocenigo,
Morosini or Bragadino. Many—at Corfu, Levkas, Coroni,
Methoni, Nauplia, and Herakleion (which withstood the great
Candia siege), at Nicosia and the titanic affair at Famagusta
—are astounding, awe-inspiring and immensely depressing. A
Greek writer has described the great stormbeaten and cormorant-
haunted castle at Coroni as 'the architecture of hatred'. And so
it is. But these latterday strong points, gloomy though they are,
are many of them untainted by the guilt that hangs over the
others. They acted as barriers against barbarism, not, like their
Frankish forerunners, stepping stones to it. Occasionally a castle
turns out to be Greco-Turkish, like those of Seven Towers at
Constantinople and Salonika and the one that looms above
Navarino. This, like Nauplia, was used till quite recently as a
prison. I was astonished to see, some time after the present
journey, that the inner courtyard was divided up in a warren
of narrow yards bounded by high walls. I learnt that as it was
the nearest prison to the Mani it used to be full of Maniot convicts inside for killing people in vendettas. As many of these
feuding rivals found themselves in the same courtyard at all hours

* His claim to the Byzantine throne was through his descent from Androni-
cus II Palaeologue, who married Yolanda, sister and sole heir of John the Just,
Marquis of Monferrat. The marquisate passed to her second son, the Despot
Theodore Porphyrogennetos, and continued in the male line of Monferrat-
Palaeologue for six generations and then devolved upon an only daughter of
Boniface de Monferrat who married Federigo Gonzaga, Duke of Nevers, a
scion of the great Mantuan house, who begat Duke Charles II, the claimant in
question. He planned, with the help of the other powers, to raise the entire
Balkan peninsula in revolt. The help never came and the ambitious scheme
faded away.

—Greek prisons are very easy-going—the crop of internal murders reached such a pitch that this honeycomb of little open-air pens had to be built, to keep them apart.

But it is a cruel fact that the early Frankish castles seem more alien and baleful than the later Venetian or Turkish fortresses. They encircle the Grecian mountain-tops like so many crowns of thorns.

It is hard to allot fairly the guilt for the ecclesiastical rivalry that split the East from the West. Certainly both sides were to blame for not contriving to avoid schism over trivialities and for letting the *odium theologicum* bite so deep. I have found that Catholics are the more generous of the two in acknowledging a share in the responsibility to-day; quite rightly, Sir Steven Runciman would say;* but for the military blackguardism that made the break irreconcilable and finally ruined half Europe, the West are utterly and inexcusably to blame. 'We may hate the infidel,' Petrarch said, 'but we must doubly hate the schismatics of the East'; sectarian imbecility can go no further. There is only one figure in the West who came out of it well and then it was too late: Aeneas Sylvius, the great Pius II Piccolomini. He alone seemed to grasp the magnitude of the disaster and ten years after Constantinople had fallen he attempted to call the sovereigns of Europe to a last crusade, one that would have redeemed the monstrous Fourth for ever—and which he planned to accompany himself to deliver the City and the Empire from the Turks. But it was too late. The sovereigns failed to send their promised armies and he died at Ancona (as we see in the last of Pinturicchio's frescoes of his life in the library at Siena), in sight of his half-assembled fleet.

So I did not mind missing the shards of Passava.

* * * *

Rich in digressions and vallonia acorns, the plain and the pale blue ranges glided by, their relationship flowing and changing fast as we advanced up the wide gulf. Skoutari and Kalyvia and

* *The Eastern Schism*, by Steven Runciman (Oxford).

its peninsula had drifted south, and Ayeranos and the hump of Mavrovouni. The green world continued.

Gytheion, to which a small island was tethered by a long narrow mole, trembled towards us through the afternoon haze. It was sunk in afternoon catalepsy. Nothing moved among the shipping and the cranes along the waterfront or among the inert tiers of houses that climbed the hill-side. Beyond the ship's awning the sun beat down like a curse and I could feel the heat of the quay through the soles of my shoes as though I were treading across a flat-iron. Every shutter was down. 'Not a cat stirring,' a fellow passenger said as we crossed the Sahara-like waterfront. 'The only people about at such a time would be adulterers heading for an afternoon assignation. But perhaps not in Gytheion. It's not Athens, after all! . . .'

*   *   *   *

I woke up a couple of hours later. Sounds coming through the closed shutters indicated that the spell-bound town outside was stirring into life. Two rogue-wirelesses were in full blast and very strange they seemed after the unpolluted Mani. There was the exhaust of a motor or two, voices, a ship's siren, the clip-clop of horses and donkeys and the occasional clash of those portable brass scales that fruit-sellers and grocers hold up like statues representing Justice. All the sounds, in fact, of an important provincial town that is also a port, the chief of the south-eastern Peloponnese, the seat of a bishopric, of law courts, several schools, a naval centre in a small way and a thriving market. The rumour of awakening activity, however, penetrated the darkened cube of my room in the Actaeon Hotel at one remove. At the end of my bed, just to be discerned through the carefully contrived gloom, hung an oleograph, completely faded and kippered with age, of Othello recounting his travels to Desdemona and the Doge. This picture, usually on the walls of kapheneia and tavernas, is inexplicably widespread in Greece. Another wall was adorned with a picture in cheerfully contrasted colours which is also one of an unexpectedly popular type: a Swiss meadow with cows grazing in front of a chalet and a dizzy range of snow-capped Alps. It is, I suppose, the equivalent of the bay of Naples in a Belfast boarding house.

Lying in a bed again, vaguely shrouded like a corpse on the brink of resurrection, seemed an incomparable, almost a guilty luxury. The penumbra was pierced by a thin blade of afternoon light falling from the junction of the two shutters. It was all the brighter by contrast with the tomb-like shadows. I lay smoking in a sybaritic trance watching the clouds of cigarette smoke slowly cauliflowering across the room to turn, when they struck this dazzling stratum of air, into a paper-thin cross section of madly whirling grey and pale blue marble. The soft murmur of the town was suddenly drowned by the furious jay-like voices of two women below my window, arguing across a narrow lane about something that I couldn't catch. It didn't matter. The point was the inventive richness of the language, the splendour of the vocabulary, the unstaunchable flow of imagination and invective. I often have the impression, listening to a Greek argument, that I can actually see the words spin from their mouths like the long balloons in comic strips; however debased and colloquial the theme, the noble shapes of the Greek letters, complete with their hard and soft breathings, the flicker of accents with the change of enclitic and proclitic and the hovering boomerangs of perispomena sail through the air and, if a piece of high flown language or a fragment of the liturgy should be embedded in the demotic flux, which it often is, iota subscripts dangle. Some letters catch the eye more than others: the perverse triple loop of Xi, the twin concavity of Omega, the bisected almond of Theta, Phi like a circle transfixed by a spear, Psi's curly trident and Gamma's two-pronged fork. As the argument kindles and voices wax louder, the lettering matriculates from italics to capitals and out like dangerous missiles whizz triangles and T-squares and gibbets and acute angles, pairs of Stonehenge megaliths with lintel stones, and half-open springs. At its climax it is as though these complex shapes were flying from the speaker's mouth like flung furniture and household goods, from the upper window of a house on fire. Then suddenly the conflagration subsides as abruptly as it started, the dialectic geometry fades from the air and silence ensues; as it did now. The soft murmur of the town took over again, wooing me down into its midst. It was time for a clean shirt and a shave.

CHAPTER 20

Lacedaemonian Port

THE timing, manner and mood of a private assault on a
new town are a serious matter. If the town should be one
of the world's wonders, it is crucial. To arrive at Constantinople by air, for instance, and reach the city by the airport bus is
to be swallowed up by the saddest and most squalid of Balkan
slums. It must be attacked from the sea and the haggish but
indestructible splendour, crackling with all the atmospherics of
its long history, allowed to loom slowly across the shining
Propontis. Care should be taken with such cities, for the vital
rendezvous of anticipation and truth can never be repeated. The
maidenhead in question is flawed for a lifetime. Lesser towns
should be broken into and entered by night; burgled, as it were;
for like this there is the impact of two different towns: one in
which the shapes of lamps and signs and lighted windows burn
golden holes and parallelograms in the huge nocturnal mystery,
drawing the eye indoors and filling it with unrelated fragments
of detail; and another in the morning when all is dark indoors
but the whole town's anatomy, sprawling or soaring or grovel-
ling, is laid open by the sun.

None of these predicaments applied to our private *rapport*
with Gytheion, for the town had been deflowered by earlier
contact.

But the manner of our approach was important, nevertheless.
The necessity to visit Gytheion would drag a hollow groan from
most Athenians. But the broad streets, the din of shops and the
urban bustle filled us with the elation of bumpkins. The town
might have been adorned with towering cathedrals, picture

galleries and acres of museum; fabulous cellars might have been waiting at our beck. Even as it was, to lie in hotel bedrooms contemplating the fissures like forked lightning across the whitewash, to turn on a tap again—even if it gave egress to nothing more than a few Titian red drops and an outraged centipede—inspired us with the awe of a Red Army corporal in the state rooms of Tzarskoe Selo. The same marvelling pleasure persisted along the crowded waterfront. Contrast is all.

Athenians may groan but the antecedents of Gytheion are respectably hoary. There is no mention of it in Homer, but Pausanias sets down a myth attributing its foundation to Herakles and Apollo in celebration of the end of their long quarrel over the theft of the Sybil's tripod at Delphi.

Others say that it was built after the destruction of Las by Castor and Pollux on their return from the Argosy. Phoenicians from Tyre used to put in here to fetch the murex up and the Laconians themselves soon learned and developed the industry; for all these waters, from Gytheion to Cythera, were rich in the purple-producing mollusc; presumably it still proliferates there undisturbed. Later it became the main seaport for Sparta, the scene of many a siege; most notably, on one occasion, when Tolmides with an Athenian fleet of fifty triremes sailed up the gulf and disgorged four thousand hoplites round the walls. Alcibiades once landed here, and Epaminondas captured it from the Spartans in his campaign along the Eurotas valley. The Macedonian Philip V and the Spartan tyrant Nabis contributed warlike pages to its annals. The town was wrested from Nabis by the liberal Roman general, Titus Quintus Flaminius, who was bent on destroying the pirate fleet of Sparta. He did so and annexed the town to the Empire. Rather strangely, he was honoured in Gytheion thereafter almost as a god. The town's history under the Romans was a peaceful and prosperous one: the Free Laconian Federation founded by Augustus was in every way preferable to Spartan tyranny. In Imperial days the Roman addiction to purple expanded from the sober senatorial stripe on the republican toga into a craze. The industry boomed and along with it also the export of porphyry and *rose antique* marble: one can still see incised slabs here and there in the Mani and faded gashes on the hillsides whence it was quarried. This stone was the chief adornment of the palaces of Alexander Severus and Heliogabalus. New temples, dedicated to a widely assorted range of gods, sprang up alongside the old. They were followed by a theatre, forums and villas and aqueducts and baths.

Little is known of the end of this thriving city. It must have suffered the fate of other Free Laconian towns—centralization, standardization, bureaucracy and loss of privilege—in Diocletian's general shake-up of the provincial government of the Empire in the fourth century. Was Gytheion demolished in the great south Peloponnesian earthquakes of A.D. 375? Was it laid waste by Alaric and the Goths in 395 at the same time as Sparta: or wrecked by the Ezerite Slavs that settled later in the Eurotas valley? Nobody seems to know. Invasion and neglect destroyed many ancient and noble cities. They left little behind them but the beautiful names which cover their skeletons or their ashes like so many embroidered and threadbare shrouds; and Time frequently plucked away even these last rags. So it was with Gytheion.

When the heart of the Greek world moved to the Bosphorus, these regions withered into remote and seldom-visited provinces and their ancient radiance grew dim. They flicker in the pages of Imperial chronicles and ecclesiastical records and cast an alien and uncertain glow on the faded feudal vellum of the Franks. They become little more than a crackle of parchment. Gytheion was the centre of that corner of the Morea which was regained by the Byzantines after Pelagonia, becoming part of the Palaeologue and Cantacuzene princedom. The region revives for a while in the transactions of shadowy despots and sabastocrators and dies again with the Turkish capture of Mistra. But, contradictorily, it was the tragedy of Turkish conquest which eventually breathed Gytheion back to life.

The town itself seems to have vanished in the interim for neither under its ancient nor under its later demotic name does

it appear as a specific township during the first centuries of the
Turkish occupation. There must have been nothing there at all,
although the name 'Gytheion' was sometimes used as a term for
the surrounding villages, which built up a fierce and splendid
fame for themselves defending the Maniot marches. Nothing,
that is, except a scattering of overgrown Greek and Roman ruins
among the mulberries and the vallonia oaks and the cornfields
and perhaps a few fishermen's huts by the shore. The town sprang
into being again during the last half of the eighteenth century
with the rising fortunes of the Grigorakis clan, which, especially
in the person of the great Zanetbey, have often found their
way into these pages. When Hassan Pasha treacherously hanged
Zanet's uncle in Tripoli, whither he had gone to treat with them
under a safe conduct, Zanet led the reprisal attack on the Turkish
garrison and population in the castle of Passava. It ended in
massacre. Later he drove the Turks from the lowlands round
Gytheion, turning many miles of the coast to north and south of
the ancient town into a family apanage* which he fortified at
strategic points with many a strong tower. He became rich and
powerful and the acknowledged leader of the north-east Mani,
achieving a position similar to that of the Mavromichalis of
Tzimova. For a long time he refused the Beydom of the Mani;
the last two rulers had been hanged by the Turks. He was forced
to accept the title in the end when two of his sons were taken
and held as hostages at Constantinople. He had long since established himself on the Marathonisi, that little island lying a couple
of furlongs out to sea opposite the centre of Gytheion, from which
the locality had long taken its demotic name.† It has now re-
verted, as is so often the case, to its ancient name, but for many
humble generations the place was known as Marathonisi. He
established his little court in the heavily fortified and cannon-
bristling castle he had built there and devoted his long reign and

---

* This branch of the family (which was originally from Alika in the western
Mani) had been powerfully established for a long time in the region of Skoutari
and Ayerano, past which we had sailed that afternoon.

† It is now joined to the harbour by a mole.

his fortune to the cause of Greek freedom. The Mani became a meeting place, a refuge and an arsenal for the great klephts of the Morea—notably for Zacharia and the elder Androutzos—and Maniot waters were the haunt of irredentist sea captains, the greatest of whom was the fabulous Lambros Katsonis. He was in communication with the Russians and when they abandoned the Greek cause, he broached negotiations with Napoleon. The visit of Napoleon's emissaries, the ex-Maniot Stephanopoli brothers from Corsica, has already been mentioned. He was eventually deposed in favour of a more accommodating bey— Koumoundouros—for equipping the Mani guerrillas with French arms and gunpowder. His castle withstood several fierce sieges, and his battles have passed into legend. His generosity, as we have seen from the poem of Niphakos, was on a grand scale and he was revered for his justice and magnanimity. He died in abject poverty.

When Leake visited Gytheion in the beylik of his successor, it was still not much of a town, no more than a hundred wretched houses of mud-brick round a large church with a belfry in which a single bell was suspended. The best house had a floor of trodden mud. But it was full of activity. The lanes teemed with warlike Maniots with girdles stuffed full of pistols and with whiskers that almost touched their shoulders.

* * * *

It is very different to-day. There is nothing particularly magnificent there but the long waterfront, with its anchored steamers and its shops and its one or two hotels, has a certain decaying Victorian charm. Here and there in this battered matrix the blank façade of a modern building is embedded. It is sad that Greek provincial towns began to expand and prosper at a moment when European architecture was at its most unrewarding nadir. If only they had been built with arcaded streets! How splendidly they would ennoble and dramatize those evening promenades! What a blessed shelter from the deluge of winter and, still more, from the onrush of the meridian glare!

It seemed a long time since I was in that barber's shop in Sparta. When I had emerged from the Gytheion hairdresser—un-Praxitelean perhaps, but half de-bumpkinized, with hair neatly combed and my razored chin sprayed with scent and shining cheeks braced with rubbed-on alcohol—I felt that Gytheion was my oyster. Even the hot African gusts of wind coming up the gulf had no effect. I found Joan and together we set off to explore the early evening town.

The whole place was on the move, for it was the very time when—south of a sociological isobar which runs from north-west Spain and then through San Sebastian to Bordeaux, north of Provence, south of the Alps, up through Vienna and Bratislava; then north of the Hungarian plain and Transylvania, north again to Cracow and across to Kiev and thence, no doubt, far into Asia—it was the time when the citizens of every single town pour into the streets and deambulate slowly for a couple of hours in a dense and complicated ebb and flow. In Greece, unless the mixture is ratified by official courtship or sanctified by wedlock, the sexes remain rigorously separate. It is a chasm that only the dumb crambo of rolled eyes and fluttering eyelashes can bridge. The prominent citizens in neat white suits and their wives in high-heeled shoes had a strangely smart aspect. There were numbers of schoolboys from the Gymnasium with shaven heads, all of them wearing those hideous shiny-peaked caps with gold braid emblems: headgear that makes even the smallest ones look like miniature admirals or S.S. men. The clanging of Leake's single church bell, now reinforced by several more, hinted that it was some feast day or its vigil. The girls were all in their best white summer dresses. It occurred to us again that Maniot girls must surely be some of the most beautiful in Greece. The very young ones all had their ikon-like aspect enhanced by big white bows like votive offerings pinned to their smooth bobbed hair. But it was the older ones, with their thick dark plaits and their immense eyes under thick brows, their beautifully shaped mouths and the smooth golden brown texture of their skin, who, again and again, arrested and held our glance. Large numbers of villagers, laden with market bundles, were scattered about in the slow urban current and the contrast with the townspeople underlined their stern and resolute features. Those frowns, the jutting bridge of the nose, the sweep of brow, cheekbone, nostril and jaw seemed to be depicted with fierce and slashing pen-blows.

We fished ourselves out of the throng and climbed uphill through a steep warren of lanes which swarms the mountain-side and dies out among the cactuses of a menacing limestone spur. From here we could look down on one side over the cascade of old tiled roofs and the labyrinth that lay behind the waterfront; beyond lay the toy ships of the harbour and the single battered tower on the island which is all that remains of the fortress of Zanet. On the other side the Taygetus resumed its sway, concealing in folds and ledges the many villages of Bardounia whose Moslem Albanian settlers used to be the bitterest enemies of the northern Maniots. The back part of the town still has the air and the architecture of the slanting mountain village it once used to be. Not five minutes from the centre of the town, the houses died out in a flat no man's land of scattered cottages and lentisk and calamus reed, the edge of the flat country that runs away eastward to the pebbly, alluvial and now half dried up estuary of the Eurotas. Here, among bamboo fences and the byres of a little farm and a small forest of olive trees, the remains of the old theatre sweep in a broken tufted arc round a paved semicircle. The sun had left the stone, but it was still warm. A goat nibbled the grass growing between the slabs and a donkey, still howdahed with its vast saddle, was tethered to a tree. As we lay along the smooth seats, the invariable spell of peace and happiness that hangs over Greek ruins came dropping all round us out of the sky: a sense of shape, space, proportion, reason and ease. An inscription told of a shadowy foundress. Her blessed influence smoothed our brows, cooled the sirocco, arranged and relaxed our limbs along the marble. In such places life seems to fall to pieces and quietly recomposes itself in the right shape. . . . Through the olive leaves the evening began to glimmer towards night.

*　　*　　*　　*

Where should we go next? We had paused at a kapheneion on the waterfront to ponder the matter. Cythera and Anticythera, stepping-stones on the sea-road to Crete, beckoned us down the shimmering gulf; but we had been there two months ago. Should we advance inland to the heart of the Peloponnese? Cross to the Messenian peninsula? Penetrate the Tzakonian villages of eastern Arcadia and listen once again to their strange Doric dialect? Sail to the Ionian islands or to Epirus or Roumeli or Macedonia? To the Sporades or the Cyclades . . .? We toyed lingeringly with all the golden possibilities and finally shelved our verdict until the next day or the day after that. . . . Meanwhile there were more pressing matters to discuss. We had passed two tavernas in our swift tour of the town. In front of one of them stood an elaborate tabernacle, equipped with four iron shelves of glowing charcoal, before which a yard-long perpendicular cone of *dönnerkebab* was turning, the summit of the spit adorned with a little brass pigeon with outspread wings. It gyrated briskly with the tapering and roasting layers and savoury fumes had courted our nostrils as we passed. In the other taverna, where we explored the cavernous kitchen and lifted the metal lids to haruspicate from the steaming contents of the great cooking pans, lay half a lamb *stiphado*. We were swayed too by the thought that there had also been an old woman in the corner of the kitchen busy cutting the swords off a bundle of those miniature blue swordfish called *sargánes* . . . (These odd and delicious little creatures have curious electric blue and fluorescent spines, as if a filament were threaded through the bone.) Also the retsina, brought from Attica and offered us by the landlord in small thick tumblers, had been excellent.

The wind from the south had died and the air was cool and still. The lights along the waterfront, a long necklace of lamps strung obliquely up the mountain-side along the road that passed the bishopric and the occasional red or green of a neon sign—so hideous at close quarters and so pretty from a distance—gave the little town the air of a flaunting and Babylonian metropolis. It might have been some blazing marine *Haupstadt* full of equestrian statues and pleasure-domes.

Somewhere in these buildings a gramophone scattered tangos into the dusk. The Marathonisi, faded to a dark shape, now lay black against the amber smoulderings of the sunset. The name means Fennel-Island. It is quite bare now but they say that fennel once covered it: a low forest, each tuft springing into the air in a yellow and blue-green Corinthian capital interspersed, perhaps, with the tall thin kind which, when it dries up, makes the whole Maremma reek of curry-powder. The air was suffused with pale blue Venetian light. The lamps on the mole sank plumb lines of reflection into the imperceptibly rocking water: columns of radiance disrupting and rejoining and floating adrift again as though the particles were strung on a thread which loosened or tautened, by turns releasing and marshalling those flashing and fluctuating gold fragments. Then the water grew smooth and motionless and the reflected lights were still. A boat, its dark shape looking faintly ominous, sculled towards the island and broke these flimsy reflections to smithereens. The shards scattered round the boat's track and widened to a flurried rout of gold brackets, their onion-outlined turmoil separated by a band of darkness from the boat's private commotion: an expanse which reflected not the lamps from the mole, but the moon, in a cold flawed circumference of broken silver from which sprang two cool widening tracks of mercury wake, a long silver isosceles. We rose to go. The taverna was calling us. The *stiphado*, the sword-fish. . . . The waiter swept our little heap of drachmae from the table.

'Do you know about the Marathonisi in the old days?' he suddenly asked us. 'Many years ago?'

'Zanetbey used to have his castle there,' I said.

The waiter brushed the Bey and his castle aside. 'All that was recent—my great-great-grandfather was one of his pallikars. I mean long, long ago.'

We said we knew nothing more.

'Ah!' he glowed with the prospect of giving information. 'When Paris, a Trojan prince, stole the beautiful Helen from her husband, the King of Sparta, that,' he pointed to the Marathonisi,

'is where the runaways first dropped anchor. They left the caique
and spent the first night together on the island. Homer wrote
about it. It used to be called Kranae.'

We were dumbfounded. Kranae! I had always wondered where
it was. The whole of Gytheion was suddenly transformed. Everything seemed to vanish except the dark silhouette of the island
where thousands of years ago that momentous and incendiary
honeymoon began among the whispering fennel.

Index

Read more . . .

Patrick Leigh Fermor

ROUMELI: TRAVELS IN NORTHERN GREECE

'A masterpiece . . . softened by warm, human understanding' *Sunday Telegraph*

Roumeli is not to be found on modern maps: it is the name given in olden times to northern Greece, stretching from the Bosphorus to the Adriatic and from Macedonia to the Gulf of Corinth. Patrick Leigh Fermor was so seduced by the strangeness of the name that he immortalized it in this classic account of his travels there.

It is a journey that takes us with him amongst Sarakastan shepherds, the monasteries of Meteora and the villages of Krakora, even tracking down a pair of Byron's slippers at Missolonghi.

'A wandering scholar but with a difference . . . he has become part of the country he describes' *Sunday Times*

'Marvellous . . . we are fortunate to have these unforgettable reports from the fields and the marshes, the peaks and the chasms, the taverns and the waterfronts of Roumeli' *Observer*

Order your copy now by calling Bookpoint on 01235 827716 or visit your local bookshop quoting ISBN 978-0-7195-6692-9
www.johnmurray.co.uk

Read more ...

Patrick Leigh Fermor

A TIME OF GIFTS: ON FOOT TO CONSTANTINOPLE –
FROM THE HOOK OF HOLLAND TO THE MIDDLE DANUBE

The classic memoir of an enchanted journey across pre-war Europe

In 1933, at the age of eighteen, Patrick Leigh Fermor set off from the heart of London on an epic journey – to walk to Constantinople. It was to be a momentous experience, and one that would change the course of his life.

A Time of Gifts is the rich and sparkling account of his adventures as far as Hungary, after which *Between the Woods and the Water* continues the story to the Iron Gates that divide the Carpathian mountains and the Balkans. At once a coming-of-age memoir, an account of a journey, and a dazzling exposition of the English language, Patrick Leigh Fermor is acclaimed for his sweep, intelligence and observation, and the remarkable way in which he captures the moment in time.

'Nothing short of a masterpiece' Jan Morris

'A treasure chest of descriptive writing . . . The resplendent domes, the monasteries, the great rivers, the hospitable burgomasters, the sun on the Bavarian snow, the storks and frogs, the grandeurs, the courtesies, all are revealed with a sweep and verve that are almost majestic' *The Specator*

Order your copy now by calling Bookpoint on 01235 827716 or visit your local bookshop quoting ISBN 978-0-7195-6695-0
www.johnmurray.co.uk

Read more . . .

Patrick Leigh Fermor

BETWEEN THE WOODS AND THE WATER: ON
FOOT TO CONSTANTINOPLE – THE MIDDLE DANUBE TO THE
IRON GATES

**Continuing the classic memoir of an eighteen-year-old's
enchanted epic journey across Europe in 1933**

The journey that Patrick Leigh Fermor began – to cross Europe on
foot with an 'emergency' allowance of a pound a day – proved so rich
in experiences that they have overflowed into more than one volume.

The opening of *Between the Woods and the Water* finds him crossing the
Danube where the first volume – the acclaimed *A Time of Gifts* – left
off. Remote castles, mountain villages, monasteries and towering
ranges that are the haunt of bears, wolves, eagles, gypsies and a
variety of sects are all savoured in the approach to the Iron Gates
dividing the Carpathian mountains from the Balkans. This journey has
captivated generations.

'The finest travelling companion we could ever have . . . His head is
stocked with enough cultural lore and poetic fancy to make every
league an adventure' Christopher Hudson, *Evening Standard*

'A book so good you resent finishing it' Norman Stone

*Order your copy now by calling Bookpoint on 01235 827716 or
visit your local bookshop quoting ISBN 978-0-7195-6696-7
www.johnmurray.co.uk*

Read more . . .

Deborah Devonshire and Patrick Leigh Fermor
Edited by Charlotte Mosley

IN TEARING HASTE: LETTERS BETWEEN
DEBORAH DEVONSHIRE AND PATRICK LEIGH FERMOR

In spring 1956, Deborah, Duchess of Devonshire – youngest of the
six legendary Mitford sisters – invited the writer and war hero
Patrick Leigh Fermor to Lismore Castle, the Devonshires' house in
Ireland. This halcyon visit sparked off a deep friendship and a lifelong
exchange of sporadic but highly entertaining letters which include
glimpses of President Kennedy's inauguration, weekends at
Sandringham, filming with Errol Flynn and life both at Chatsworth
and on the southernmost peninsula of Greece.

'High-level gossip and wit mixed with adventure, history and travel
writing . . . These letters deliver so much delight' *Daily Mail*

'Hugely enjoyable . . . these letters so wonderfully demonstrate an
unfailing appetite for life . . . This marvellous correspondence
celebrates two of the most important things in the world, courage
and friendship' *The Spectator*